USING ECONOMIC INDICATORS TO IMPROVE INVESTMENT ANALYSIS

USING ECONOMIC INDICATORS TO IMPROVE INVESTMENT ANALYSIS

Evelina M. Tainer

John Wiley & Sons, Inc.
New York • Chichester • Brisbane • Toronto • Singapore

Publisher: Karl Weber
Editor: Myles C. Thompson
Managing Editor: Nana Prior
Composition: Publications Development Company

This text is printed on acid-free paper.

This publication is designed to provide accurate and
authoritative information in regard to the subject
matter covered. It is sold with the understanding that
the publisher is not engaged in rendering legal, accounting,
or other professional services. If legal advice or other
expert assistance is required, the services of a competent
professional person should be sought. *From a Declaration
of Principles jointly adopted by a Committee of the
American Bar Association and a Committee of Publishers.*

Library of Congress Cataloging-in-Publication Data:

Tainer, Evelina, 1958–
    Using economic indicators to improve investment analysis / Evelina
Tainer.
        p.   cm.
    Includes bibliographical references and index.
    ISBN 0-471-58049-X
    1. Investment analysis—Statistical methods.   2. Economic
indicators—United States.   I. Title.
    HG4529.T34   1993   93-429
    332.6—dc20

Printed in the United States of America

10 9 8 7 6 5 4 3 2 1

Preface

The ivory tower view that you cannot bring economic theory to the real world simply is untrue. You can easily apply economic principles to your daily life. Consumers and investors can use the information from economic events in their money-making ventures. To promote the best economic policies, policymakers at all levels of government must understand current economic conditions. Unfortunately, economic indicators reported by public and private agencies are sometimes misread. Relevant indicators are overlooked, while less useful ones get too much attention. As a result, people don't always get a clear or correct picture of the current economic environment and what it means for the future. That is why I decided to write this book, which originated several years ago as a pamphlet titled *A Trader's Guide to Economic Indicators*.

Successful trading and speculating, profitable investing, proper policy-making, and effective buying all require a thorough grasp of all the available data. This includes a healthy dose of skepticism for the information in published reports and a constant eye for aberrations in the established trend. This book explains the relevant details of economic indicators regularly reported by public and private agencies. By the end, you'll be able to determine whether such data are reliable at face value or need deeper analysis before you can assess their role in the current economic environment.

The goal of this book is not to transform you into a full-time economist, but to apprise you of the factors and statistical series that economists monitor in assessing the current economic environment. The reported economic series will have the same meaning whether you are making investment decisions for your household or for your firm. However, the strategy that a bond trader will take in following the economic

statistics is likely to be different from the strategy followed by a manufacturing executive or by a consumer in his or her financial investments.
In all cases, the investor (the bond trader, the manufacturer, or the consumer) or the government policymaker must understand the reported
economic indicator to make rational decisions.

I have written this book in plain English—not economic or business
jargon that is understood by only a select few. Economic statistics are described in nontechnical language. Also, I briefly explain some of the
terms familiar to financial market participants so that laypeople will
have a better understanding of the relationship between economic indicators and the financial markets. For instance, while changing interest
rates and foreign exchange rates have an impact on economic activity it
is also true that economic indicators often cause stock prices, interest
rates, and the foreign exchange value of the dollar to change. Consumers
and investors who are not intimately involved with the financial markets
find it difficult to understand that strong economic growth is bad for
the financial markets. (For example, something "good," such as a drop in
the unemployment rate causes interest rates to rise in the bond market.)
I'll explain why.

Many people need to comprehend these basic principles, especially financial market participants, who anticipate fiscal and monetary policy
changes that can ultimately affect interest rates. Market participants
analyze the economic indicators to see if the Federal Reserve System will
ease or tighten credit conditions. If economic indicators are misread or
misinterpreted, then the market reaction will be incorrect. For example,
perceiving a strong economy because nonfarm payroll employment
posted a large gain would lead to rising interest rates. This would actually hurt the economy if activity were anemic and the rise in payrolls
had been caused by one or more special factors, such as auto workers
returning to work after a protracted labor dispute. Policymakers could
also misinterpret the economic figures if they didn't pay attention to occasional quirks in the data. In that case, decisions for policy changes
would be based on incorrect information about the current and future
state of the economy. For instance, a healthy employment scenario might
cause the Federal Reserve to worry about inflationary pressures and induce unwarranted tightening measures.

In addition, all those involved in government should have a healthy
understanding of current economic conditions. This includes government policymakers on the Federal Reserve Board and in Congress, as
well as bureaucrats and agencies at the federal, state, and local levels.

Government policymakers love to quote statistics, but they don't
always have a clear understanding of them. Sometimes, they are

surprised at the reaction of financial market participants at the release of an indicator. At the state and local level, it would be good to understand the interest rate environment when municipalities need to borrow money and bring forth tax-exempt securities.

The interpretation of economic news doesn't end with financial market participants and policymakers. Business students are often forced to study economics, but don't always see a connection between economic theory and the real world. Journalists must understand information before imparting it to the general public, who often must rely on the media to get the information to make economic decisions.

This book is organized so that it can easily serve two functions: (1) to describe the economic indicators and the nuances associated with each of them; and (2) to briefly explain market reactions to those consumers, investors, government officials, students, and journalists who are not directly participating in the financial markets.

Each chapter explains the economic indicator, the market reaction to it (in the fixed income, foreign exchange, and stock markets), and key points to watch for in the particular series. The economic indicators are organized by sectors of the economy such as consumer, investment, and inflation. Thus, a description of retail sales and consumer confidence would be found in Chapter 3, "The Consumer Sector."

If you are a sophisticated financial market participant, the "Market Reaction" section of each chapter may be unnecessary and will appear somewhat simplistic. However, you are likely to find useful information in the section detailing the specific indicator as well as in the "Watch Out For:" section, which points out quirks and potential special factors. For the layperson not intimately involved in the financial markets, the "Market Reaction" section may give insight on the expected direction of interest rates or exchange rates upon the release of an economic indicator.

Chapter 1 links economic indicators to the financial markets. It presents a basic description of cycles in the economy and markets that move within the cycles. The chapter also discusses the bases of market psychology and explains how we are all financial market participants in some way.

Chapter 2 gives an overview of the macroeconomic framework using the standard national income accounting methodology. It concentrates on GDP (gross domestic product) and explains why the Commerce Department decided to shift its focus away from GNP (gross national product). It also provides a framework for analyzing the economy.

Chapter 3 discusses the consumer sector, a major component of the U.S. economy. It includes all the relevant indicators that reflect consumer behavior, which are reported monthly, quarterly, or more frequently. This chapter compares and contrasts indicators of consumer behavior so that you will understand which series are more reliable on a consistent basis.

Chapter 4 discusses the investment sector of the economy. This chapter looks at investment in *physical* capital such as machinery or buildings as opposed to *financial* investments, which include stocks or bonds. Monthly indicators that represent the investment sector are more sparse than for the consumer sector and are often less reliable on a regular basis.

Chapter 5 looks at the foreign sector. Until 1980, the U.S. reliance on trade from foreign countries was considered insignificant (apart from oil imports) and the United States could have been viewed as a closed economy. International trade accounted for a small portion of our GDP relative to other countries. In the early 1980s, the net export balance sank into a tank of red ink from which it has yet to emerge. You will learn how to make sense of the few monthly and quarterly indicators available to understand behavior in the foreign exchange markets as well as in the domestic bond and equity markets.

Chapter 6 looks at government spending. Monthly or quarterly indicators are sparse even though the government accounts for one-fifth of gross domestic product. Nonetheless, you will learn about the federal budget deficit and some hidden indicators.

Chapter 7 considers inflation, its advantages and disadvantages. What is inflation? How do we measure it? Are all measures of inflation equivalent? This chapter tells you that they're not and that it is important to understand the difference between inflation in the goods market and inflation in the services market.

Chapter 8 looks at miscellaneous monthly indicators that don't fit under the sector headings including important measures of production such as the employment situation and the index of industrial production. You will also learn about the leading indicators of economic activity such as the Index of Leading Indicators, and the Philadelphia Fed Survey including how well these series predict economic activity.

Chapter 9, the final chapter, looks at the sources of information available to the public. These include government agencies, which often distribute data free of charge or for a small fee; private institutions that charge (sometimes hefty fees) for their services; and professional economists, who also work for a fee.

Acknowledgments

I would like to take this occasion to thank the people who were instrumental in helping me develop my forecasting and analytical skills as a macroeconomist.

Jim Annable, Chief Economist at First Chicago, taught me how to zero in on the significant details of economic indicators and use my intuition and judgment in forecasting to enhance statistical modeling. The example he set in solving economic problems with creativity taught me much about the application of economic theory not only to the banking industry but also to the real world.

I would also like to thank Gerry Byrne, Senior Vice President at First Chicago Capital Markets, the trading arm of First Chicago. Gerry and his group were some of the primary users of economic indicator forecasts and analysis. Gerry taught me to distinguish between "good" and "bad" economic numbers and made sure I focused on doing good economic analysis rather than on interpreting the positions individual traders took in the economic indicators.

Although I learned about the National Income and Product Accounts (NIPA) from talking to Commerce Department economists as well as my colleagues at First Chicago and other institutions, my greatest single source of information was Charlie Steindel, now a New York economist with the Federal Reserve System. My understanding of the national income accounts improved dramatically under his tutelage. Ida Walters, who served as editor of the publications put out by the Economics Department at First Chicago in the early 1980s, cultivated my writing skills and helped me to see how much more my readers would understand and value the economic analysis if I relayed it in plain English.

Any business economist knows that good contacts in the statistical agencies are worth their weight in gold. During the years, many excellent economists at the various statistical agencies of the Commerce and Labor Departments have been willing to give me their time and expertise in the pursuit of understanding economic indicators. Among them, Phil Rones, a Labor Department economist stands out as my favorite source.

The individuals mentioned here were by no means the only ones who helped increase my understanding of economic matters and economic indicators. I am grateful to my counterparts at other institutions who helped me to better understand economic data and the economy. My heartfelt thanks also go to the traders and marketing staff at First Chicago Capital Markets. This book is a direct result of many of the questions they asked and we pondered together.

While writing this book, I needed data and explanations of many series. Economic and statistical analysts at the government and private agencies were very helpful. In particular, I would like to thank the people at the Bureau of Labor Statistics in Washington, D.C., and Chicago; the Bureau of the Census; the Bureau of Economic Analysis; economists at the Board of Governors; the librarians at the Federal Reserve Bank of Chicago; the Economic Research Division of the Federal Reserve Bank of Philadelphia; the Survey Research Center at the University of Michigan; and the Conference Board.

Last, but certainly not least, I would like to thank the readers of earlier drafts of this manuscript, particularly Dicie Hansen, Schubert Dyche, participants of the Macroeconomics Workshop at the University of Illinois at Chicago, and an anonymous referee. I also appreciate the help from my editors at Publications Development Company and at John Wiley & Sons. Their comments were invaluable. Nonetheless, I take sole responsibility for any remaining errors relating to the economic concepts discussed in this book.

E.M.T.

Contents

CHAPTER 1

Cycles, Markets, and Participants

This chapter covers the concepts typically included in an introductory macroeconomics course. Its intent is to simplify a complex subject, not to be comprehensive. To simplify explanations and to avoid the famous economic apology, "all other factors held constant," the following definitions will, for the most part, focus on one factor at a time. Certainly, the real world doesn't operate like a scientific laboratory, and we would have to disentangle various effects from each other.

Understanding the importance of economic indicators to the U.S. economy requires familiarity with the underlying cycles, markets, and participants in those markets. This chapter briefly describes three kinds of cycles; three distinct markets; and several types of participants, their sentiments and their actions. The key points to each are summarized so that you will have the underpinnings of the economic system.

CYCLES

The Economic Business Cycle

Practically everyone knows about the economic business cycle. The press may not describe it that way, but people often hear the terms *economic expansion* and *recession*. The economic business cycle is measured from peak to peak, or from trough to trough, and has five phases. The business cycle peak is the highest level reached in economic activity—the last month or quarter of economic data before indicators begin to decline. The first drop in a set of economic indicators suggests that the economy has just entered its first phase: downturn, more commonly known as recession. The downturn lasts as long as economic indicators continue to decrease. The second phase of the business cycle is the trough. It is the lowest point in the business cycle and the weakest point in any economic series. The peak and trough of the business cycle are generally viewed as a point in time, such as a specific month (see Table 1.1). The recession can last for several months (or years in the case of the Great Depression). The average length of the ten U.S. recessions since 1945 (including the 1990–1991 recession) was nearly 11 months.

The recovery signals the third phase of the business cycle. A recovery is in progress the first month that a set of economic indicators begin to rise. It means that the recession is over. As a participant in the economy, you are unlikely to notice any improvement in business activity in the first few months of recovery. It is important to remember that the first month of recovery is just as bad as the second-to-last month of recession. You are barely one inch above the ground. The early stages of recovery often continue to feel like recession to the unemployed who can't immediately find jobs and to retailers who have yet to liquidate unwanted inventories. Typically, after the first few months, the economy gathers some steam, and growth is quite robust for about two years.

Economic expansion is the fourth phase of the business cycle. There is no exact point that identifies the end of recovery and the beginning of expansion. A rule of thumb is that the recovery lasts as long as it

Table 1.1   Business Cycles

Peak	Trough	Months of Recession	Months of Previous Expansion
Feb 45	Oct 45	8	79
Nov 48	Oct 49	11	36
July 53	May 54	10	44
July 57	Apr 58	9	37
Apr 60	Feb 61	10	23
Dec 69	Nov 70	11	105
Nov 73	Mar 75	16	36
Jan 80	July 80	6	57
July 81	Nov 82	16	11
July 90	Mar 91	8	92

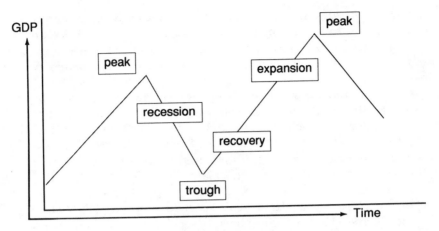

Figure 1.1 This is the classic example of an economic business cycle; real world examples don't usually look this good.

takes to recoup the output lost in the recession. The expansion begins when the economy reaches a new high.

The fifth phase of a business cycle occurs when the economy reaches a new peak; you don't know you are in the fifth phase until the peak has passed and the economy has already headed for a downturn. Figure 1.1 depicts a stylized version of the economic business cycle, whereas Figure 1.2 shows actual U.S. economic activity from 1989 to early 1992. In

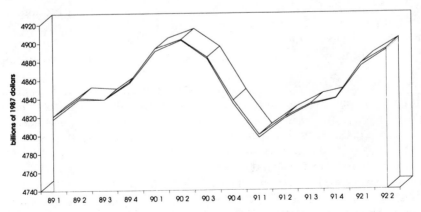

Figure 1.2 This is an example of a recent business cycle with real GDP peaking in the second quarter of 1990 and reaching its trough in the first quarter of 1991. The level of GDP in the second quarter of 1992 is nearly as high as the recent peak. (*Source: Survey of Current Business.* September 1992.)

this figure, gross domestic product (GDP) in the early stages of recovery is at the same level as during the recession. During the 1991–1992 recovery in particular, the growth in GDP was so mild that the average consumer didn't believe economists who claimed that a recovery was at hand.

Aggregate indicators of the economy will post new peaks, but individual series need not. For example, employment as measured by nonfarm payrolls, reached a new high in June 1990 roughly coinciding with the peak of the business cycle as determined by the National Bureau of Economic Research (NBER), even though manufacturing employment reached a cyclical high in January 1989, well before the start of the recession. At that time, factory payrolls were down roughly 8 percent from the all-time peak reached in June 1979. Structural change in the U.S. economy boosted service employment at the expense of manufacturing employment. Thus, while total employment was able to increase, the manufacturing sector never recovered the numbers of workers it had lost during the 1980s.

The National Bureau of Economic Research, which is the official arbiter of business cycles, has several prominent economists on the business cycle dating committee. They analyze many factors before pinpointing the exact date a recession actually has begun or ended. Most recently, the NBER decided that the last business cycle peak was July 1990—meaning that August 1990 was the first month of recession. July 1990 was named as the business cycle peak nearly a year later in April 1991. It wasn't until December 1992 that the NBER business cycle dating committee determined March 1991 as the end of the recession, although many economists (including Federal Reserve Chairman Alan Greenspan) were concluding that the recession ended in the spring of 1991 as early as the summer of that year because several indicators of the economy began to turn around then.

Although the NBER economists analyze several economic sectors and series, many economists use the rule of thumb that a recession requires at least two consecutive quarters of decline in real gross domestic product, the most encompassing measure of production of goods and services. Real (inflation-adjusted) GDP fell in the third and fourth quarters of 1990 and the first quarter of 1991, but it was positive in the second, third, and fourth quarters of 1991 and in 1992 (see Figure 1.2). These data all support the view that the recession ended sometime during the spring of 1991. The recession actually began in the third quarter (August) 1990, yet the Commerce Department had not initially estimated a decline in real GDP during that quarter. That's why the business cycle dating committee must consider more than just one economic series. Moreover, the NBER economists would be foolish to try dating a business cycle prematurely, especially in light of frequent revisions to economic series. They don't want the business cycle dating committee to be viewed as a forecasting mechanism. According to business cycle expert and committee member Geoffrey Moore, the committee wanted to be sure that the economy hit its trough and was not headed for a double dip (recession) before declaring the end of the 1990–1991 recession.[1] Two years after the business cycle peak, the 1992 annual benchmark revisions of the national income and product accounts did reveal that real GDP declined in the third quarter of 1990, confirming evidence suggested by other indicators and the decision made by the NBER economists. Table 1.1 lists the U.S. business cycles since 1945.

The Stock Market Cycle

The stock market also has cycles of peaks and troughs, but rather than discuss expansions or downturns in the stock market, the jargon refers to bull markets and bear markets. The stock market cycle is correlated with the economic business cycle but is actually a leading indicator of it. In fact, Standard and Poor's Index of 500 companies is one of the 11 series that make up the Index of Leading Indicators. This index is more broad-based than the Dow Jones Industrial Average, which only incorporates 30 blue-chip corporations but gets more attention in the press. The stock market is not a perfect leading indicator of the economy. (An astute person once noted that the stock market predicted 10 of the last 8 recessions.)

Although a plunge in the stock market has not always been followed by a recession (the stock market crash of 1987 is the most recent example), an economic downturn has always been preceded by a stock market decline (see Figure 1.3). According to business cycle expert Geoffrey Moore, the stock market responds to economic activity through profits and interest rates. As the business expansion comes to an end, production costs rise, and profits fall. At the same time, interest rates are likely to rise either because of increased loan demand or rising inflationary pressures. Both factors contribute to the drop in stock prices even as business activity continues to expand.[2] On average, changes in the stock market precede changes in the economy by six months, on the upside and the downturn.

This book is not about stock market investment strategies or stock market timing. However, in making investment decisions, it is useful to

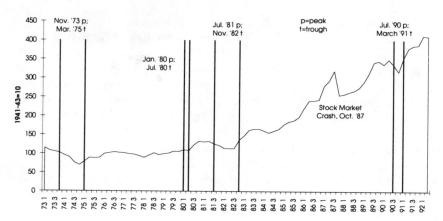

Figure 1.3 Four economic business cycles are depicted here with the corresponding movements in the stock market, represented by Standard & Poor's Index of 500 Companies. (*Source:* Data came from various Commerce Department publications.)

know the current stage of the business and stock market cycles. For example, to follow the adage "buy low and sell high," you would buy stocks of consumer durable goods companies, such as producers of automobiles or furniture, when the stock market was turning around, but the economy was still in recession. The trough of the stock price for any given cyclical business would probably occur when you were wondering if the economy was ever going to grow again. For example, during the 1990–1991 recession, Standard and Poor's Index for stock prices of consumer goods bottomed in October 1990—three months into the recession, and five months before the recession bottomed in March 1991. This series climbed almost continuously through the following year.

The Interest Rate Cycle

Interest rates also follow cycles although there is greater diversity among interest rates than among economic indicators or stocks that don't move exactly in line with their particular cycles. However, according to Geoffrey Moore and other economists who study business cycles, interest rates lag the economic business cycle.[3]

One of the reasons the interest rate cycle seems less distinct than the business and stock cycles is that there is no such thing as "the rate of interest," as described in economics textbooks. Many interest rates exist, and they don't move in tandem. Indeed, long-term interest rates and short-term interest rates move at different times by different magnitudes. Furthermore, Geoffrey Moore suggests that corporate bonds do not move in tandem with Treasury securities; and new issues have a different response rate to the economy than outstanding issues trading in the secondary market.[4]

Short-term rates are likely to decline during a recession as demand for credit softens. At the same time, the Federal Reserve tends to promote a more accommodative monetary stance to ensure economic recovery. The Fed technically can only affect the federal funds rate (the rate that banks charge each other for the use of overnight funds) by adding or subtracting reserves. Other short-term rates such as CD (certificate of deposit) rates, commercial paper rates, and Treasury bill rates normally move in close correlation with the federal funds rate. Studies have found that short-term rates such as Treasury bill rates closely follow the business cycle with either leads or lags of roughly two months.

The picture changes with long-term interest rates, which may edge down slightly as the Fed continues to ease monetary policy, but not nearly as rapidly as short-term rates do. Long-term rates are very sensitive to inflationary pressures. If the participants in the long bond market are worried about inflationary pressures notwithstanding a recessionary environment, the drop in long-term rates may take awhile. (Long bonds have maturities of 20 and 30 years.) As the recession continues, however, long-term rates will also begin to decline. In the past, a drop in long-term rates has always been a key to economic recovery since long-term interest rates determined mortgage rates, which in turn spurred housing activity, the first sector to turn around in the economy. The shift to adjustable rate mortgage loans has modified this relationship somewhat. Figure 1.4 shows how the 3-month Treasury bill peaked in 1989 and then fell consistently throughout the 1990–1991 recession and during the beginning stages of recovery as well. At the same time, the 30-year Treasury bond rate fell slightly in 1989 before the recession, rose slightly during the recession, and remained virtually unchanged until mid-1992 when it finally began to decline in the early stages of an anemic recovery.

Although interest rates have a lagged relationship *to the economy*, these rates have an impact *on economic activity*. Put differently, as the economy grows, demands for loanable funds can put upward pressure

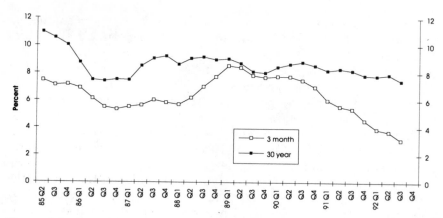

Figure 1.4 A positive spread is typical between long- and short-term rates. Note that the spread narrowed significantly in 1989 before the Fed began its accommodative policy during this business cycle. (*Source:* Data came from Federal Reserve publications.)

on interest rates—the cost of borrowing funds. Conversely, a declining economy will put downward pressure on interest rates—the cost of borrowing money—because fewer people demand loans. But consider the flip side: When interest rates decline, more people are willing to borrow. When interest rates rise, fewer people are willing to borrow money. Thus, the movement in interest rates is not made in a vacuum but has implications of its own. Based on this rationale, Geoffrey Moore looked at the *lead* properties of long-term interest rates.[5] Since he found no consistent time period for a lead relationship, the results were inconclusive.

Although short-term interest rates are roughly coincident indicators of the economy, long-term rates on bonds are lagging indicators. As a consequence, the general rule is that the interest rate cycle lags the business cycle.

Of the three cycles—the economic business cycle, the stock market cycle, and the interest rate cycle—the stock market cycle leads the business cycle, which leads the interest rate cycle. The lead/lag correlation between the business cycle and the interest rate cycle is not as decisive as the relationship between the stock market and the business cycle, largely because short-term rates and long-term rates behave differently over the business cycle.

MARKETS

The financial markets encompass three different markets: the stock market, the fixed-income market, and the foreign exchange market. Just as the different cycles are related to one another, the markets also are correlated. (Regularly, bond traders eye the foreign exchange markets while currency traders watch the long bond market. Who moves whom?) The relationships are not always clear, however, nor are they always consistent over time.

The Stock Market

The stock market, also known as the equity market, is heavily influenced by economic factors. Strong economic activity is the impetus behind healthy growth in corporate profits or earnings. In the long run, corporate earnings drive stock prices. In general, a healthy economy should yield a bull market because company earnings are growing. Conversely, poor economic prospects yield a bear market because earnings are falling. Investors in the stock market are not lovers of inflation. In an expanding economy, accelerated inflation will curtail increases in stock prices even if corporate profits are rising. After all, some of the profit gain is due to rising prices, not increased worker productivity or higher sales.

Declining interest rates are typically associated with growth in interest-sensitive sectors such as housing and capital investment. Thus, falling interest rates are also a boon to the stock market. In addition, the present value of capital increases with low (real) interest rates, and declines with high (real) interest rates. Real interest rates are adjusted for inflation. If the current mortgage rate is 8 percent, and the inflation rate is 3 percent, then the *real* mortgage rate is 5 percent (see box, "Net Present Value").

A weak foreign exchange value of the dollar should be conducive to rising stock prices. A weak or depreciated dollar is associated with healthy export growth and sluggish import growth because, as demand shifts from foreign-produced goods to domestically produced goods, U.S. manufacturers benefit from a depreciated dollar at the expense of foreign manufacturers. A weak dollar will make it more expensive for U.S. consumers and producers to buy foreign goods, and some are likely to shift to domestically produced goods, which are now lower priced. At the same time, consumers in other countries may find that

Net Present Value

Everyone knows that the $1,000 you receive today is worth more than the $1,000 you could receive a year from now even if we assume that prices (inflation) of goods and services will not increase during the period. Today's funds are worth more because essentially you can take the $1,000 and invest it at the (risk-free) rate of interest—currently about 3 percent. At the end of the year, your initial investment of $1,000 will be worth $1,030. If the interest rate were 10 percent instead, you would have $1,100 one year from today. Thus, if anyone offered you the choice between $1,000 today and $1,000 a year from now, you would undoubtedly take the money today, or require the person to give you more than $1,000 a year from now.

Instead of calculating the value of today's $1,000 in a year's time (given some rate of interest), we could also calculate today's value of next year's $1,000. In this case, we are discounting next year's sum of $1,000 to compare it in today's terms. We would use the same interest rate as we did in the first case. Instead of multiplying the principal times the interest rate, however, we would divide the principal by the interest rate. Thus, the value of next year's $1,000 is equal to $1,000/(1.030), which gives a net present value of $970.87. More generally, the present value of a dollar received n years from now is given by $P/(1 + i)^n$. So if we were to receive the funds in 3 years, we would calculate the present value by $1,000/(1 + .03)^3$. The value of $1,000 received three years from now is reduced to $915.14 today.

The higher the interest rate and the longer the time frame, the lower will be the net present value. Using the formula $NPV = P/(1 + i)^n$, we can calculate the net present value of $1,000 for one year (or more) hence, using a range of interest rates. In the following list, note how rapidly the net present value declines as the interest rate rises. The first row gives the net present value of next year's $1,000 with a range of interest rates. The second row gives the net present value of $1,000 earned three years from now with the corresponding range of rates.

Possible Interest Rates and Net Present Value

	3%	5%	7%	10%	15%
NPV ($1,000)	$970.87	$952.38	$934.58	$909.09	$869.57
NPV ($1,000)	$915.14	$863.84	$816.30	$751.32	$657.52

The net present value concept is the premise behind the determination of stock prices. The stock market will decline as interest rates rise because the net present value of the capital representing the stock declines. The higher the interest rate, the lower the net present value of the capital behind the stock. Thus, stock prices will decline as interest rates rise, and conversely, stock prices will rise as interest rates decline.

the U.S. products are cheaper than their own products and thus shift their demand to U.S. goods. This is frosting on the cake. Domestic producers get an increased demand for their goods from American consumers who have shifted away from the more expensive foreign goods; and they also get an increased demand from foreign sales, coming from the weaker exchange value of the dollar.

However, a caveat remains: the assumption that U.S. manufacturers are producing tradable goods. A depreciation in the exchange rate of the dollar will not help all industries, especially those in the service sector. Dry cleaners, barbers, and coffee shop owners have nothing to gain from a depreciation of the dollar. Moreover, manufacturers that use raw materials produced overseas will find that their costs are increasing. If barbers purchase shampoo manufactured overseas and dry cleaners use solvents manufactured abroad, their costs will go up as the dollar depreciates, and this could potentially hurt their profits.

The premise that a weak dollar bodes well for the stock market because it improves the U.S. trade balance (we produce more domestically than we buy from foreign competitors) assumes that higher sales of U.S. goods will offset higher prices paid by producers using foreign raw materials.

The Fixed-Income Market

Like the equity market, the fixed-income market, also known as the debt market or the bond market, is affected by economic factors, but it is divided into long-term, intermediate-term, and short-term securities. The short-term securities market is typically referred to as the money market, whereas the bond market represents intermediate and longer term securities. Different factors have greater significance to each of the markets. Short-term securities, and therefore short-term rates, are most affected by economic activity. If the economy is headed into recession, interest rates are on a declining trend. If the economy is headed into an expansionary phase, interest rates are on a rising trend. This pattern occurs because short-term rates are mainly determined by credit demands. If credit demands are strong, as they would be when capital investment growth is healthy during an expansion, the competition for loanable funds increases. If banks and other financial intermediaries have healthy loan demand, they can demand better credit qualifications from their borrowers and can force weaker companies to pay higher rates, if they lend them funds at all. Conversely, when credit demand is weak (as happens during a recession), producers do not borrow as much money because they now make fewer capital expenditures. This leads to lower interest rates.

Long-term interest rates, which come from securities with a maturity of 20 and 30 years, are primarily impacted by inflation, with other economic factors playing a minor role. Financial participants in the long bond market fear inflation more than anything else because accelerating inflation is the main culprit in reducing the value of bonds (investors were burned badly during the 1970s). Thus, when the inflation rate begins to increase at a faster clip, long bond prices will drop. Since bond prices and yields are inversely related, a drop in prices brings a higher yield. When the rate of inflation begins to moderate, long bond prices will rise. Higher bond prices produces lower yields (see box, "Bond Prices and Yields").

Intermediate securities take into account a time horizon of roughly 2 to 10 years. These rates behave much like long-term rates except that they are not as sensitive as long-term rates to expectations of changes in the economy or inflation. Therefore, the value of your 5-year security would not decline as much as the value of your 20- or 30-year bond in the event of some bad news such as a spurt in inflation. The value of the long bond suffers with inflation because the principal loses purchasing power. A 30-year bond has more time to lose purchasing power than a 5- or 10-year bond: Hence, the smaller sensitivity of the shorter maturity to inflation.

The Foreign Exchange Market

The foreign exchange market is a truly global market; the economic conditions of all countries matter. The four key factors affecting the foreign exchange markets are (1) relative prices, (2) relative interest rates, (3) relative economic growth rates, and (4) the country's current account balance. Although we will discuss each of these separately, it is important to note that they can work against each other as opposing forces. As a result, a country with low inflation might have a weak currency for other reasons, such as low interest rates.

Relative Prices   These prices consider inflation rates of the countries in question. A high rate of inflation is a common scourge for economies across the globe. Those economies with lower and more stable rates of inflation will have a stronger currency. So, the acceleration of U.S. inflation rates will lead to a lower value of the dollar vis-à-vis other currencies. In contrast, declining rates of inflation will lead to a stronger

Bond Prices and Yields

Typically, a new bond will sell at par for $1,000, and it will have a fixed interest, or coupon rate. The interest rate associated with any particular bond is determined by a variety of factors including current economic conditions and the default risk of the corporation issuing the bond. To simplify matters by avoiding default risk, let's look at Treasury bonds.

The U.S. Treasury issues new 10-year bonds, and through the market auction system, the interest rate on the bonds is 8 percent. You decide to buy this 10-year bond, which will yield you two semiannual coupon payments of $40. One of the nice features of U.S. Treasury bonds compared with depositing $1,000 in a bank certificate of deposit is that the bond can be (traded) sold in the secondary market. Therefore, when you decide one month later that you need the $1,000 in cash, you can sell your bond in the secondary market for a small fee. Market psychology has turned bearish, however, and interest rates have increased sharply. The new bonds that the Treasury is bringing to market have an interest rate of 10 percent. You will never be able to sell your 8 percent bond for the $1,000 you paid for it if investors can get new bonds with a higher interest rate. Still, all is not lost. If you really need to sell the bond, you can offer it for $875.35. At the discounted rate, your 8 percent bond is equivalent to a new 10 percent bond. In the meantime, you will have suffered a capital loss of $124.65.

Bond Prices at Given Market Interest Rates

Time to Maturity	4%	6%	8%	10%	12%
1 Year	$1,038.83	1,019.13	1,000.00	981.41	963.33
10 Years	$1,327.03	1,148.77	1,000.00	875.35	770.60
20 Years	$1,547.11	1,231.15	1,000.00	828.41	699.07
30 Years	$1,695.22	1,276.76	1,000.00	810.71	676.77

You may decide not to take the loss. In that case, you will have to hold the bond and wait for a better selling opportunity. A few months later, financial market participants realize that the Fed has successfully wiped out inflation, and market psychology becomes bullish once again. As a result, financial market participants are willing to concede that a 10-year bond of 10 percent is much too high for current conditions. The U.S. Treasury brings new bonds to market with an interest rate of 6 percent. All investors who want to buy new bonds will only earn $60 a year per $1,000 investment.

You are holding a bond that yields $80 a year—a more valuable instrument. If you want to sell your $1,000 bond now, you would sell it for $1,148.77 and earn a premium of $148.77. The premium makes it equivalent to the new 6 percent bonds.

Thus, rising interest rates will make old bonds less valuable and bring down their prices. Falling interest rates will make old bonds more valuable, increasing their prices.

dollar relative to other foreign currencies. Inflation hurts the economy not only because purchasing power is lost but also because inflation is often unstable and unexpected, and distorts investment decisions.

Relative Interest Rates   These rates consider the investment opportunities of various countries in question. The currency of a country with high interest rates will appreciate relative to other currencies. Higher interest rates mean a higher rate of return on investments. This was evident in the early 1980s when high interest rates in the United States relative to other countries led foreign investors to buy U.S. Treasury securities. This demand for Treasury securities led to a demand for dollars, and the value of the dollar soared in the early 1980s before peaking in the first quarter of 1985. The flip side says that low interest rates in the United States, compared with the interest rates in other countries, will depreciate the value of the dollar. A good example is the 19 percent depreciation in the value of the U.S. dollar relative to the German mark from July 1991 to September 1992 when the U.S. economy languished and the Federal Reserve eased several times during the year. By mid-1992, nominal short-term interest rates in Germany were roughly six percentage points higher than comparable U.S. rates. However, high interest rates due solely to high inflation don't yield a high rate of return. As it turns out, the German inflation rate was running at a rate of about 3.5 percent, just a bit higher than the domestic inflation rate of about 3 percent. Thus, the nominal differential in U.S. and German interest rates was roughly similar to the real differential in rates.

Relative Economic Growth Rates   These rates consider relative demands for goods and services. Strong economic growth in a country will actually lead to a weaker exchange rate for that country's currency because strong economic growth is associated with healthy personal income growth. Whenever consumers have more income to spend, they will want to consumer more. Once consumers have increased their demand for goods and services, some of that demand will be satisfied by a greater demand for imported goods, which in turn will lead to a greater demand for a foreign currency (wherever those imports are bought). This causes a decline in the value of the home currency.

  If foreign countries are not growing as rapidly, *their* demand for imports (another country's exports) will not be as strong. Consequently, an offsetting demand for the currency will not arise.

Current Account Balance   A country's account balance also affects the foreign exchange market. The current account includes the balance in trade and services (defined in greater detail in Chapter 5). Running continuous current account deficits weakens a country's currency. For example, a current account deficit in the United States means that we are buying more goods and services from foreign countries than they are buying from us. If we demand more imported goods and services, we are also demanding more foreign currencies. A greater demand for foreign currencies rather than a demand for the U.S. dollar weakens the value of the dollar.

Prices, interest rates, economic growth, and the current account balance are all interrelated making it difficult to understand which of these factors is at play when the value of the dollar is moving in any given time period. The real world doesn't hold all factors constant, as economists would prefer, and this makes the analysis tougher.

The foreign exchange markets are further complicated by political factors that weigh in the currency's valuation. Thus, political instability in any part of the world generally favors the U.S. dollar because the United States is considered a stable country, politically and economically.

MARKET PSYCHOLOGY

Economists always assume that people are rational beings who are motivated by profits, who will require greater return for taking on greater risk, and who will use all available information when making decisions.

If people are rational, the financial market movements will appear rational, and the markets will be efficient. Put differently, an investor will be unlikely to make a risk-free profit in excess of market return on investment or speculation, since the market tends to adjust quickly to any inconsistency in the marketplace. In the long run, that is true.

Looking at the markets on any given day, you may not think that participants are rational because market psychology can lead to peculiar behavior in the markets in the short run. For example, if market participants don't believe inflation really has been wiped out, long-standing fears of inflation might cause *real* (inflation-adjusted) long rates to be 8 percent instead of 4 percent. These anomalies could last for weeks, months, or years. Figure 6.2 in Chapter 6 shows that an 8 percent real rate of interest persisted for more than a year in the mid-1980s. Incidentally, market participants are behaving in a rational fashion if they truly believe that the inflation rate will accelerate. Their attitude only appears irrational "after the fact" when it becomes apparent that inflation rates were actually stable.

Market psychology can depend on any number of factors that cause participants to have a negative or positive view of the market. When market psychology is negative in the bond market, bond market participants are bearish, feeling that bond prices will decline (and bond yields will rise) because of potential inflationary pressures. Consequently, they will view strong economic indicators with a negative tinge: If total durable goods orders decline, indicating a weak economy, but durable goods excluding transportation orders rise, they will cite the latter as an indicator of strength in the economy. (Chapter 4 explains why financial market participants should look at durable goods orders *excluding* transportation.) Negative market psychology causes market participants to look for strong economic data supporting a rise in interest rates.

When market psychology is positive, the fixed income market participants are bullish on the bond and expect bond prices to rise (and bond yields to fall). In this positive mode, financial market participants will view a drop in durable goods favorably even if durable goods excluding transportation (which they should be monitoring instead) should jump sharply. Thus, negative market psychology (a bad mood) looks for and reacts to adverse numbers, whereas positive market psychology (a good mood) looks for and reacts to positive numbers. Money can be made whether the market is in a good or bad mood. All you have to do is correctly anticipate the market and correctly predict the economic news— no small feat, in either case.

Market psychology can shift rapidly. A change in market psychology is difficult to understand. As an avid student of market psychology, I often have been baffled by the turn of events. As an economist, however, I tend to take the long-term view that rational behavior eventually wins out. The key is that you must be in tune with market psychology, especially if you are trading in the short term, even if you don't agree with the market rationale.

EXPECTATIONS

Financial market participants don't necessarily react to the economic numbers that are reported per se. They react to the economic indicators that are *different from market expectations*. Economists for banks and investment houses report their forecasts of most monthly economic indicators to news services and market analysis companies (who then report an average of the economists they have surveyed), in addition to giving the information to their main clients. Market participants pool this information and develop a market consensus of economic forecasts. When the government releases an economic indicator, financial market professionals will not react to the release if the actual figure is in line with the consensus forecast developed in the previous week. The market *will react* if the actual figures are different from the consensus. Potentially, then, financial market participants can react twice to economic indicators—first, when the economists are putting together their forecasts; and second, when the numbers are actually reported. For example, in late August 1992, economists predicted that nonfarm payroll employment would rise by about 150,000 in August. The figures were to be reported on September 4, 1992. Economists also explained that roughly two-thirds of the expected rise would come from a special government program that funded summer jobs for youths. Financial market participants assimilated the information in making their trading decisions—the critical question was whether to expect a Federal Reserve easing move as a result of this news. As it turned out, the Bureau of Labor Statistics reported that nonfarm payroll employment fell by 83,000 in August, even though the federally funded summer youth program added 88,000 to payrolls. This news jolted the markets into rethinking their positions and reassimilating the information. The news justified the belief that the Fed would indeed ease on such a weak employment report. The only question that remained was the extent of the Fed ease: Would it be a 25- or 50-basis-point drop in the federal funds rate? Would the Fed also lower the discount rate? By mid-morning, the Fed ended up lowering the fed funds rate by 25 basis points.

Market participants are also likely to trade on rumors, and these rumors typically make the markets gyrate wildly, especially good rumors. Some rumors have basis in fact; others don't. Rumors concerning an economic indicator on the eve of its official report are common. Usually these rumors are unfounded, but leaks did occur from time to time in the early and middle 1980s. Since the late 1980s, however, the Commerce Department and the Labor Department have gone to great lengths to conceal their figures until the stated release time.

Market participants would regularly claim that GNP (gross national product, now released as gross domestic product) figures would be leaked on the eve of their official release date. Each time a new rumor occurred, I would find myself trying to assess whether it was any good.

I stopped worrying about GNP leaks when Carol Carson, Director of the Bureau of Economic Analysis, informed me that the BEA economists responsible for estimating GNP did not even assemble to discuss the data until 4:00 P.M. (eastern time). Therefore, any rumors that developed during the day could have no basis in fact.

WHO ARE FINANCIAL MARKET PARTICIPANTS?

Financial market participants come in all shapes and sizes: Some have a short investment horizon while others take a long-term perspective; some have a low risk tolerance while others have a high risk tolerance; some investors act as speculators, serving the function of intermediaries between those who borrow and those who lend funds. In addition to individuals in the financial services industry, financial market participants include investors such as home builders and manufacturers, who primarily invest in physical capital. Manufacturers who need funds to expand their facilities can issue bonds or sell equity in the company by issuing shares of stock. Those individuals or companies with excess cash will choose to buy bonds or stocks. Thus, there is a market of buyers and sellers in the financial arena.

Investors who are sellers of funds in the financial market fall into three broad categories: traders, institutional investors, and individual investors. Yet, there is great variety within these three groups. Traders are often speculative in their dealings but even then show varying degrees of risk tolerance. Individual investors typically take a long-term view but, depending on their age, can invest in high-risk growth stocks or lower risk income securities. Financial markets are extensive: they deal in equities (stocks); bonds; money market instruments, such as bankers' acceptances, certificates of deposit, commercial paper; collateralized instruments, such as asset-backed securities; tax-exempt issues; and foreign currencies.

Traders

Traders work in the stock market, the bond market, the money market, the foreign exchange market, and the tax-exempt municipal market. They can trade in the pits of the exchanges such as the Chicago Mercantile Exchange and the Chicago Board of Trade, or in the capital markets divisions of banks and brokerage houses. Depending on where they are working, traders can buy and sell for their own account, their firm's account, or a customer's account. Traders can hold the security or shares of stock in inventory (go long) if they expect the market to increase in value. They will sell securities or shares of stocks they don't own (sell short) when they expect the market to decrease in value. Bond traders will go long (buy bonds) if they expect bond prices to rise when economic indicators point to a sluggish environment. They will go short (sell bonds they don't own) if they expect bond prices to decline when inflationary expectations emerge. A similar process would occur with any money market instrument, tax-exempt instrument, or foreign currency.

Go to any trading room floor in a major bank or brokerage house and you will see each trader glued to not one, but several, screens showing the values of interest rates, foreign exchange rates, precious metal prices, commodity prices, and the stock market. These data allow the trader to move with the market at the blink of an eye. Traders react immediately to economic (and political) data. Indeed, the instant that the Commerce Department releases the news that real GDP grew or contracted during the quarter, or the Labor Department announces that nonfarm payroll employment expanded or contracted, these traders are selling and buying positions. By the time most of the people in this country are still working on their first cup of coffee, the typical trader has earned (or lost) his or her salary many times over.

As traders are buying and selling (bonds, certificates of deposit, bankers' acceptances, foreign currencies, stocks) in reaction to the news, their trading floor economist gives an "instant analysis" of the economic release, based on the complete government report, to the traders and the marketing staff. Was the increase in payrolls large enough to provoke the Federal Reserve into tightening monetary policy or not? Will the rise in payrolls lead to an equally large rise in personal income and therefore promote consumer spending? Will the spending eventually be inflationary? These are questions for economists, but the traders have already asked themselves the same questions—and answered them without the benefit of a detailed analysis. The financial markets have reacted (probably overreacted) in some fashion in the first 10 minutes of the numbers' release before trading floor economists have given their expert analysis.

Institutional Investors

Institutional investors have different risk tolerances and time horizons for investments. For example, corporate treasurers are usually dealing with cash management issues. They might have an extra million dollars that needs to be invested over the weekend, for two weeks, or for a month. They must also determine the instrument in which they want to invest: Treasury securities, federal agency securities, or commercial paper to name just a few. Other institutional investors may be mutual fund managers in charge of the portfolio of money market funds, bond funds, Treasury security funds, tax-exempt funds, and stock funds. Each of these fund managers might be limited in investment choices by the type of fund being managed. Thus, money market fund managers might be interested only in 3- and 6-month securities such as certificates of deposit, commercial paper, or bankers' acceptances. In contrast, bond fund managers interested in 5-, 10-, or 20-year bonds may divide their portfolio by risk—buying some Treasury bonds, some triple A-rated corporate bonds, and possibly even some B-rated corporate bonds.

Pension fund managers are also major institutional investors. Depending on their mandate, they could be buying debt instruments such as bonds and mortgage-backed securities in the short-term or the long-term market, or buying various stocks in the equity market.

When corporate treasurers must make decisions on short-term investments of extra funds (for only a week or a month), then it makes little difference if rates are up a tick, or down a tick. But they also must decide whether they should shorten or lengthen the maturities in their portfolios. Is the yield on the 30-year Treasury bond headed up or down? Should they invest now or wait for the next employment report?

Individual Investors

All individual investors don't act in the same manner either. Risk tolerances and saving propensities vary. An individual's motive to save and invest can be unlike that of everyone else in the market. An individual's demographic characteristics are determining factors in his or her investment style and purpose. Many young individuals just out of college spend a good portion of their income on debt repayment. If they do save, their purpose may be to buy a car or a home within a few years. Whereas a young couple who already own a home may want to save for their children's college education. The time horizon in these two cases is different. In the first case, the new college graduate may want to remain fairly liquid as he or she accumulates a down payment for a car and waits for a good opportunity to purchase a home. In the second case, the young couple may know that it will be 5, 10, or 15 years before their children will use the funds for college. Saving and investing for retirement is an entirely different motive that affords various investment opportunities depending where the person is in the life cycle. For example, a 25-year old might invest the bulk of retirement funds in a growth stock fund whereas a 45-year old may be more inclined to hold some bonds, and a 65-year old may look only for income-producing investments.

The options for small savers have increased dramatically in the past two decades, allowing small savers nearly the same opportunities as wealthy individual investors. Whether individuals are small savers or wealthy investors, however, they are still better off taking a long-term perspective in investment decisions. In the stock market, this is called the buy-and-hold strategy. Don't buy and sell your portfolio daily. Transactions costs can easily offset any small profits.

Why shouldn't the individual investor play the short-term game? Regularly placing short-term speculative bets in the financial markets forces the person to take a special perspective of world events. As an individual, how did you react to the news that a coup took place in the Soviet Union in August 1991? Did you philosophize on the end of communism or empathize with the citizens who may have to fight a war? Most likely, you did both. Financial market participants immediately worried about the foreign exchange value of the U.S. dollar (which typically increases in political uncertainty), the behavior of the stock market (defense-related stocks are likely to increase) and the bond market (possibly reacting to the foreign exchange implications), and the gold market (the former Soviet Union held a lot of gold, will they continue to sell it or stop mining it during a war?). That's not the end of the story. There could be secondary impacts depending how the story unfolds. In this case, the end of the short coup in August 1991 put in reverse all the movements that had occurred: It was like watching a film rewind.

A major difference between an individual investor and the other two groups is their access to data. Traders are hooked into all sorts of information services including news wire services, databases, and computer systems that allow them to do anything from calculating investment alternatives to producing elaborate charts of economic indicators.

Institutional investors may have access to some of these services as well. If not, fund managers and corporate treasurers can access this information by calling their representatives at banks or brokerage houses. In contrast, individual investors are less connected to such resources. They must often rely on their local newspaper or the financial press to get news on economic indicators or explanations of movements in the financial markets that occurred the previous day. This information often is not complete, so that the individual investor makes decisions based on inadequate data.

Individuals have direct and indirect links to the financial markets: As an individual, you may decide to purchase specific stocks, bonds, or even certificates of deposit at the local savings and loan. You may also purchase shares in one or more mutual funds designed to make portfolio decisions for you. In this case, the mutual fund manager determines the quantity of stocks, bonds, and other money market instruments in the particular fund, which is part of a group of institutional investors. Similarly, if you contribute to a 401-K plan through your workplace and these moneys are placed in a mutual fund, you are part of the institutional investor crowd.

Investors in Physical Capital

Financial market interactions involve two types of players: those who need funds for physical investment, and those who provide the funds. Traders and individual and institutional investors are providers (sellers) of funds. Manufacturers of durable and nondurable goods as well as builders of single-family homes, apartment buildings, and commercial and industrial buildings are producing physical investments that must be funded. Thus, they provide the financial markets with the shares of stocks and supply of bonds. While individual and institutional investors may look for high-yielding securities (and might favor a rising rate environment), investors in physical capital prefer a low interest rate environment to finance their borrowing. Often, you will find new bond issues brought to market when companies feel interest rates are bottoming out, or when they find "windows of opportunity" in a high rate environment. On the whole, investors in physical capital benefit from a low interest rate environment.

Governments as Financial Market Participants

State and local governments who borrow to provide roads and other services to their communities bring tax-exempt securities to the marketplace. The federal government borrows to provide goods and services (military expenditures, education, health care) thereby giving the market a spectrum of securities ranging from 3-month Treasury bills to 30-year Treasury bonds. Like corporations, state and local governments may have some flexibility in the timing of their debt issues. The federal government does not have any leeway in timing the financing of the budget deficit. Since the federal and state and local governments are also borrowers of funds, they prefer a low interest rate environment. For the most part, they have little leeway in determining when their issues come to market.

The past few pages suggest that practically every person and institution in this economy is a financial market participant in one way or another. Although I kept the providers of funds separate from the users of funds, a market participant can be both. You can borrow money to build a house at the same time that you have invested funds in the stock market or have bought bonds from your local municipality. Banks lend money to manufacturers and real estate developers, but they also purchase Treasury bonds and tax-exempt municipal bonds.

Key Points

- The economic business cycle, the stock market cycle, and the interest rate cycle are three prime movers in the U.S. economy.
- Economic and political events cause movements in the financial markets.
- The financial markets consist of the equity market, the fixed-income market, and the foreign exchange market.

    An economic or political event is just as likely to cause the three markets to move in different directions as in the same direction.
- Market psychology is everchanging.
- Practically everyone in the economy is a financial market participant directly or indirectly, but investors are not homogeneous; this characteristic allows markets to develop.

CHAPTER 2

Gross Domestic Product

Featured Indicators	Gross Domestic Product
	National Income
	Corporate Profits

Any introductory macroeconomics textbook will tell you that gross domestic product, commonly known as GDP, is a dollar value measure of all goods and services produced in the United States during a given time period. More specifically, gross domestic product measures the value of goods and services used by the factors of production—land, labor, and capital—located in the United States no matter who owns these factors. Production of goods and services is difficult to measure directly, but an accounting system was devised: the National Income and Product Accounts (NIPA). This accounting system measures GDP by the goods and services purchased (the product side) or by income earned from the factors of production (the income side).

Although gross domestic product and national income are quarterly figures, the Bureau of Economic Analysis division of the Commerce Department releases the information monthly in the form of an initial estimate and two subsequent revisions. The initial estimate for any quarter is available roughly four weeks after the end of that quarter. Thus, first-quarter GDP would be first reported at the end of April. Not all data are actual at this point. Economists at the Bureau of Economic Analysis (BEA) must forecast portions of this report. Some entire parts (on the income side) are not even available until the first revision, which is released two months after the end of the quarter. The incomplete data include corporate profits and net factor income, the missing link between gross *domestic* product and gross *national* product. (Net factor income represents the difference between the payments the United States makes to foreigners and those payments made to the United States for the use of labor and property supplied by the foreign country. This is explained in greater detail later in the chapter.) Because the BEA does not have complete actual data when it first releases GDP, revisions can show totally different pictures of the economy over a three-month period from the initial estimate to the final revision. When the annual revisions are considered along with five-year benchmark overhauls, observers can certainly claim that history is rewritten.

THE PRODUCT SIDE

Gross Domestic Product

It is more common to measure GDP by the product side, and one of the oft-repeated identities in macroeconomics is:

$$GDP = C + I + G + (X - M)$$

That is, GDP is the sum of spending on consumer goods and services (C), investment goods (I), government goods and services (G), and exports (X) less imports (M), also known as net exports. Imports are subtracted from GDP because these goods and services are produced abroad, not in the United States. Table 2.1 shows the level of GDP in current dollars and in constant (or real) 1987 dollars. Table 2.2 shows the relative importance of each of the major components in GDP.

Consumption

Overall, personal consumption expenditures account for about two-thirds of gross domestic product. Consumption expenditures are categorized into services, nondurable goods, and durable goods. Consumer spending on services accounts for roughly half of total personal consumption expenditures. Spending on this component is relatively stable over time, but its relative importance has trended upward in recent years, as evidenced in Table 2.2. A more detailed breakdown of this category shows expenditures for housing, household operation, medical care, and transportation. Housing costs represent mortgage and rent

Table 2.1 Gross Domestic Product
(billions of dollars)

	1989	1990	1991	Q1:91	Q2:91	Q3:91	Q4:91	Q1:92	Q2:92
Gross Domestic Product	5250.9	5522.3	5677.6	5585.9	5657.5	5713.0	5753.2	5840.0	5902.3
Personal Consumption Expenditures	3523.1	3748.5	3887.7	3821.7	3871.9	3914.2	3942.9	4022.8	4057.1
Durable goods	459.4	464.3	446.1	439.5	441.4	453.0	450.4	469.4	470.6
Nondurable goods	1149.5	1224.5	1251.5	1245.0	1254.2	1255.3	1251.4	1274.1	1277.5
Services	1914.2	2059.7	2190.1	2137.2	2176.3	2205.9	2241.1	2279.3	2309.0
Gross Private Domestic Investment	832.3	799.5	721.1	705.5	710.2	732.8	736.0	722.3	773.2
Fixed investment	799.0	793.2	731.3	734.0	732.0	732.6	726.8	738.1	765.1
Nonresidential	568.1	577.6	541.0	551.4	545.8	538.4	528.6	530.9	550.3
Structures	193.3	201.1	180.1	190.0	185.2	175.6	169.7	170.1	170.3
Producers durable equipment	374.8	376.5	360.9	361.4	360.6	362.8	358.9	360.8	380.0
Residential	230.9	215.6	190.3	182.6	186.2	194.2	198.2	207.2	214.8
Change in business inventories	33.3	6.3	−10.2	−28.5	−21.8	0.2	9.2	−15.8	8.1
Nonfarm	31.8	3.3	−10.3	−27.4	−27.0	−1.2	14.5	−13.3	6.4
Farm	1.5	3.1	0.0	−1.1	5.2	1.4	−5.3	−2.4	1.7
Net Exports of Goods and Services	−79.7	−68.9	−21.8	−28.8	−15.3	−27.2	−16.0	−8.1	−37.1
Exports	508.0	557.0	598.2	573.2	594.3	602.3	622.9	628.1	625.4
Imports	587.7	625.9	620.0	602.0	609.6	629.5	638.9	636.2	662.5
Government Purchases	975.2	1043.2	1090.6	1087.5	1090.7	1093.2	1090.3	1103.0	1109.1
Federal	401.6	426.4	447.4	451.2	449.9	447.2	440.8	445.0	444.8
National defense	299.9	314.0	323.8	332.4	325.9	321.9	314.7	313.6	311.7
Nondefense	101.7	112.4	123.6	118.8	124.0	125.3	126.1	131.4	133.1
State and local	573.6	616.8	643.2	636.3	640.8	646.0	649.5	658.0	664.3
Final Sales (GDP-Change in Inventories)	5217.6	5516.0	5687.8	5614.4	5679.3	5712.8	5744.0	5855.8	5894.2

Gross Domestic Product
(billions of 1987 dollars)

	1989	1990	1991	Q1:91	Q2:91	Q3:91	Q4:91	Q1:92	Q2:92
Gross Domestic Product	4838.3	4877.6	4821.1	4796.6	4817.1	4831.8	4838.7	4873.7	4892.5
Personal Consumption Expenditures	3223.3	3260.4	3240.8	3223.5	3239.4	3251.2	3249.1	3289.2	3288.5
Durable goods	440.7	439.3	414.7	412.0	411.3	419.4	416.1	432.3	430.0
Nondurable goods	1051.6	1056.5	1042.4	1043.0	1046.3	1044.8	1035.6	1049.6	1045.6
Services	1731.0	1764.6	1783.7	1768.5	1781.8	1787.0	1797.4	1807.3	1812.9
Gross Private Domestic Investment	784.1	739.1	661.1	646.0	649.5	672.0	676.9	668.8	713.7
Fixed investment	754.3	732.9	670.4	671.1	669.9	671.4	669.4	681.4	705.9
Nonresidential	540.1	538.1	500.2	507.0	503.0	498.8	492.1	495.8	514.7
Structures	177.6	179.1	157.6	166.8	162.2	153.0	148.4	149.4	149.1
Producers durable equipment	362.5	359.0	342.6	340.2	340.8	345.8	343.7	346.4	365.6
Residential	214.2	194.8	170.2	164.1	166.9	172.6	177.3	185.6	191.2
Change in business inventories	29.8	6.2	−9.3	−25.1	−20.4	0.6	7.5	−12.6	7.8
Nonfarm	29.9	3.7	−9.6	−24.7	−24.5	−1.0	11.8	−10.7	6.0
Farm	−0.1	2.5	0.3	−0.4	4.1	1.6	−4.2	−1.9	1.8

Table 2.1 (*Continued*)

	1989	1990	1991	Q1:91	Q2:91	Q3:91	Q4:91	Q1:92	Q2:92
Net Exports of Goods and Services	−73.6	−51.8	−21.8	−17.9	−17.4	−31.6	−20.4	−21.4	−43.9
Exports	471.8	510.0	539.4	515.9	536.1	544.2	561.4	565.4	563.4
Imports	545.4	561.8	561.2	533.8	553.5	575.8	581.8	586.8	607.3
Government Purchases	904.5	929.9	941.0	945.0	945.6	940.2	933.1	937.1	934.2
Federal	376.2	383.6	388.3	394.0	393.8	387.2	378.2	375.3	372.7
National defense	281.4	283.3	282.8	291.8	287.6	280.6	271.0	265.6	262.1
Nondefense	94.8	100.3	105.5	102.2	106.2	106.6	107.2	109.7	110.6
State and local	528.3	546.3	552.7	551.0	551.8	553.0	554.9	561.8	561.5
Final Sales (GDP-Change in Inventories)	4808.5	4871.4	4830.4	4821.7	4837.5	4831.2	4831.2	4886.3	4884.7

Source: Bureau of Economic Analysis, U.S. Department of Commerce, *Survey of Current Business*, September 1992.

Table 2.2 Components of GDP and Relative Shares

	% of GDP					
	1979	1987	1988	1989	1990	1991
Personal Consumption Expenditures	64.5	67.2	67.0	66.6	66.8	67.2
Consumer durables	7.6	8.9	9.1	9.1	9.0	8.6
Consumer nondurables	22.7	22.3	21.9	21.7	21.7	21.6
Consumer services	34.1	36.1	36.0	35.8	36.2	37.0
Total Investment	17.6	16.5	16.4	16.2	15.2	13.7
Business fixed investment	11.8	11.0	11.2	11.2	11.0	10.4
Nonresidential structures	4.3	3.8	3.7	3.7	3.7	3.3
Producers durable equipment	7.5	7.2	7.6	7.5	7.4	7.1
Residentail structures	5.5	5.0	4.7	4.4	4.0	3.5
Change in business inventories	0.4	0.6	0.4	0.6	0.1	−0.2
Exports	7.7	8.0	8.9	9.8	10.5	11.2
Imports	8.0	11.2	11.1	11.3	11.5	11.6
Government Expenditures	18.2	19.4	18.8	18.7	19.1	19.5
Federal government spending	7.2	8.5	8.0	7.8	7.9	8.1
Military spending	4.9	6.4	6.1	5.8	5.8	5.9
Nondefense spending	2.3	2.0	1.9	2.0	2.1	2.2
State and local spending	11.0	10.9	10.8	10.9	11.2	11.5

Source: Data are from Commerce Department publications.

payments, and household operations represent payments for utilities such as electricity and gas.

Purchases of nondurable goods contribute a little more than one-third to consumer spending. Although this component grows at a more erratic rate than services from one quarter to the next, it grows at a fairly stable pace from year to year, accelerating during expansions and moderating during recessions. The major components of nondurable goods include food, clothing and shoes, gasoline and oil, and fuel oil and coal expenditures. Spending on both consumer nondurable goods and services is closely linked to income growth, and these factors typically increase and decrease in tandem. Nonetheless, some goods and services are unlikely to be curtailed when income suffers because they are necessities. Table 2.2 shows the change in relative importance for consumer nondurables. The downward shift between 1979 and 1987 is small, but it is a sharp contrast to the upward shift in spending on services and durable goods. The long-term trend could reflect a shift in spending habits from any number of factors including demographics. The downward trend in spending on nondurable goods since 1987 likely reflects the slowdown in income growth as well as the 1990–1991 recession.

Consumer durable goods account for less than one-fifth of consumer spending, but most of its volatility. They are very sensitive to the business cycle—rising rapidly during expansions and falling dramatically during downturns. Like the other two spending components, growth in durable goods spending mirrors growth in income. But, in contrast to services and nondurable goods, spending on durables is also highly sensitive to interest rates. Because purchases of large-ticket items, such as automobiles and furniture, involve large sums of money and are often purchased on credit, the interest rate is an important cost factor. The third and fourth quarters of 1985 provide a dramatic example of the sensitivity of auto sales to interest rates. In late August, auto makers introduced cut-rate financing, which brought the interest rate charged by auto financing companies well below market rates charged by banks and other financial institutions. This reduced the price of the average car loan by $1,000 to $2,000. Domestic auto sales rose sharply at the end of August and throughout September when this program was in effect. After conclusion of the program on October 1, car sales plummeted to three-year lows.

Even though consumer spending on durable goods is a much smaller portion of total consumer spending than spending on nondurable goods or services, it can increase or decrease so sharply that it will cause violent swings in consumer spending patterns on a quarter-to-quarter basis. However, its impact is much smaller from year to year. Other than automobiles and trucks, the durable goods category includes furniture, household appliances such as refrigerators and stoves, and jewelry. Table 2.2 shows an upward shift in the share of durable goods spending since 1979. The higher share of spending on durable goods edged down only marginally in 1990 and 1991 despite the fact that these were recession years.

Investment

Investment spending is a much smaller portion of GDP, less than one-fifth, but it is a highly volatile sector. Investment is categorized into business fixed investment, residential investment, and the change in business inventories. Business fixed investment is made up of nonresidential structures (such as factories, office buildings, and utilities) and producers' durable equipment (such as computers, lathes, and trucks). Spending on business fixed investment is highly sensitive to the business cycle. As the economy expands, corporate profits surge. This leads producers to expand capacity by investing in new equipment or structures. However, when economic activity moderates or declines, producers are faced with excess capacity and low profits, so they cut back their investment spending of factories, commercial buildings, and machine tools. Corporate profits are analogous to consumers' disposable income, but with higher peaks and deeper troughs. Unlike the large portion of personal consumption expenditures that continues to be necessary, a substantially smaller portion of business fixed investment spending is deemed essential during a recession. Consequently, business fixed investment will expand many times more rapidly than GDP during expansions and will decline many times more rapidly than GDP during downturns. Table 2.2 shows that business fixed investment was 11.8 percent of GDP spending in 1979 but fell more than one percentage point by 1991. This is due partly to the recession environment in the early 1990s and partly due to the attempt to absorb the overbuilding of structures that occurred in the 1980s.

Residential investment includes single-family homes and multifamily structures such as townhouses and apartment buildings. Additions and alterations to current structures are also in this category. Whether a consumer buys a dwelling or a real estate developer puts up a skyscraper apartment complex, both purchases are considered "investment." And they are equally sensitive to the business cycle. When the economy is expanding rapidly, consumer (and business) incomes increase at a healthy pace making it easier to purchase a house or an apartment complex. As economic activity weakens, however, and consumer disposable income growth is curtailed, homes become less affordable. Housing's sensitivity to the business cycle is evidenced in Table 2.2, which shows a sharp downward shift in the relative importance of residential investment spending between 1979 and 1991. However, changing demographics also played a key role. The majority of baby boomers had already entered the housing market by the mid-1980s. The cohort following the baby boom generation, known as the baby bust cohort, is smaller. As they began to form new households in the late 1980s, it became evident that they would need less housing than the previous generation. The baby bust cohort will dampen housing market activity through the mid-1990s according to a study by the National Association of Home Builders.

Other factors besides the business cycle affect a consumer's decision to purchase a home and a producer's decision to invest in capital goods. Most notably, interest rates affect investment decisions. Interest rates and investment spending are inversely related: A decline in interest rates lowers the cost of borrowing and in turn increases investment spending. Historically, residential and nonresidential investment spending were considered countercyclical because low interest rates during recessions spurred housing activity. However, investment in structures would slow down when interest rates rose sharply during expansions. During the 1980s, the shift toward a greater availability and acceptance of adjustable rate loans has dampened this effect. Nonetheless, housing activity still leads the economy during the latter stages of recession since low interest rates spur construction.

Tax laws can affect investment decisions as well. For example, the interest deductibility of mortgage payments makes home ownership more desirable when tax rates are high but less favorable when tax rates are low. Similarly, the tax incentives introduced in 1981 offset high real interest rates and made capital spending on equipment and structures more affordable in the early stages of the economic recovery in 1983. According to the American Council for Capital Formation, the investment tax credit was first instituted in 1962, suspended in 1966; reinstated in 1967, and eliminated in 1969. An investment tax credit was then reinstated in 1971 and was increased in 1975 before being eliminated in 1986.

Did You Know? The investment tax credit was eliminated in 1986 because it really did provide powerful incentives for the purchase of equipment. It also changed the behavior of businesses. For example, the investment tax credit was available for building movable partitions in offices rather than walls, leaving workers without privacy. In factories, detachable movable lights were eligible for tax credits, but not permanent ceiling lighting.

Despite the drawbacks of economic distortions induced by the investment tax credit, many economists still favor tax credits to boost the economy, at least as a temporary measure. Says Northwestern University economist Robert Eisner, "If it's temporary, an investment credit gives you a big bang for your buck."[1]

The third major component of investment is inventory investment. Actually, the change in business inventories enters gross domestic product, not the level of inventories. This component makes GDP a measure of production rather than of sales. If production exceeds sales, inventories will increase; if production is less than sales, inventories will decline. Business inventories are divided into farm and nonfarm sectors. Nonfarm inventories are categorized into four sectors: (1) manufacturing, (2) wholesale trade, (3) retail trade, and (4) the ever-reliable "other." Inventory changes can be highly volatile even in the best of times, but especially at turning points in the business cycle. In fact, recessions are exacerbated by inventory cycles.

Generally, producers aim for a desired level of inventories consistent with sales expectations. During an economic expansion, they are likely to increase their inventories as sales increase, and conversely, producers try to keep inventories low during a business downturn, not necessarily replacing stocks as soon as sales pick up. Yet, even with computerized inventory maintenance, it remains difficult to discern the correct level at turning points. As economic conditions deteriorate, producers find they are accumulating stocks of unsold goods, but they keep production levels high because they are unsure of the economic environment. When inventory exceeds the desired level by a wide margin, producers trim production, thus beginning the moderation, or decline, in economic activity. To get rid of excess goods, producers deplete inventories in subsequent periods, thereby accentuating the business cycle.

Inventory cycles continue to parallel the economic business cycle even if and when inventories are lean. In the early 1980s, many economists postulated that the United States was unlikely to undergo another inventory-led recession because easy access to computers and just-in-time inventories were the dawn of a new era in inventory maintenance. "Short" and "mild" were the code words of the 1990–1991 recession for the very reason that inventories were lean. Notwithstanding the bare-bones inventory levels, Table 2.3 shows the inventory cycle quite clearly during this period. When consumers unexpectedly stop spending, retailers unexpectedly are going to end up with full shelves. The pattern of GDP growth and inventory change during the 1990–1991 recession mirrors the 1981–1982 experience despite alleged changing technological trends in inventory management.

Government Spending

Government spending on goods and services accounts for about one-fifth of GDP. Federal government spending is composed of defense and nondefense purchases of goods and services. Federal defense spending is self-explanatory: bombers and aircraft carriers, along with the salaries of military and civilian workers in the armed forces. Nondefense expenditures, besides ranging from paper clips to computers to automobiles, cover the salaries of civilian workers (including the statistical agencies that compile all the economic numbers). Federal government spending tends to be fairly stable from year to year barring a change in fiscal policy. Federal government spending can be volatile on a quarterly basis. For example, Commodity Credit Corporation (CCC) payments to farmers cause shifts in nondefense spending on a quarterly basis. It does not have the effect of increasing total GDP

Table 2.3   GDP Growth Rates Relative to Change in Business Inventories

	81:3p	81:4	82:1	82:2	82:3	82:4t	83:1	83:2
GDP growth*	2.1%	−6.2%	−4.9%	1.6%	−1.8%	0.6%	2.6%	11.3%
CBI ($bil)**	35.7	14.1	−24.4	−1.6	0.7	−44.9	−35.5	9.9

	90:2	90:3p	90:4	91:1t	91:2	91:3	91:4	92:1
GDP growth	1.0%	−1.6%	−3.9%	−3.0%	1.7%	11.2%	6.0%	2.9%
CBI ($bil)	32.8	11.2	−26.8	−25.1	−20.4	0.6	7.5	−12.6

p = peak; t = trough.

* GDP growth is at a seasonally adjusted annualized rate.

** CBI are seasonally adjusted inventory change in billions of 1987 dollars.

Source: Bureau of Economic Analysis, U.S. Department of Commerce, *Survey of Current Business,* July 1992.

growth because CCC payments are typically offset in farm inventories (see box, "Nuances of the Commodity Credit Corporation").

Special factors can also affect quarterly spending patterns. For example, the Persian Gulf conflict reversed the downward trend in military spending for a couple of quarters in 1991. Table 2.2 reveals that government spending increased one percentage point as a share of GDP between 1979 and 1991. This share only incorporates spending on goods and services that measure production; it does not include government spending on transfer payments or entitlements.

State and local government spending is relatively stable. However, spending accelerates somewhat during economic expansions as state and local governments benefit from income and sales tax revenues. Spending activity moderates slightly during cyclical downturns when income and sales tax revenues are hurt by weakening consumer demand and rising unemployment. State and local governments spend most of their funds on salaries of employees, followed by expenditures on structures, such as highway and street construction.

Nuances of the Commodity Credit Corporation

The federal government, through the Department of Agriculture, owns and operates the Commodity Credit Corporation, whose function is to implement farm policy.[2] The goals of the CCC are (1) to stabilize farm income and prices, (2) to assist the maintenance of a balanced and adequate supply of agricultural commodities, and (3) to facilitate the orderly distribution of agricultural commodities. The first goal—the stabilization of farm income and prices—affects the national income and product accounts.

The CCC operates several programs that provide income and price supports to farmers. Farmers can receive nonrecourse loans, direct income support payments, or sell directly to the government at specified support prices. When the CCC makes loans to farmers by accepting certain commodities (wheat, corn, soybeans, sorghum, barley, tobacco, cotton, and sugar) as collateral, they are making "nonrecourse loans." To qualify for these loans, farmers must meet certain criteria. They may redeem their crops at any time during the nine-month loan period by repaying the principal plus accrued interest and storage costs. If a farmer chooses to default, the CCC takes title to the crop as full payment.

Direct income support comes in three packages: (1) Deficiency payments offset unfavorable price relationships; (2) disaster payments recognize that natural disasters can wreak havoc with farm income; and (3) diversion

(Continued)

(Continued)

payments compensate farmers for voluntary conservation. These three methods of income support are mostly aimed at producers of wheat, feed grains, cotton, and rice.

To maintain market prices and farm income, the CCC is authorized to make direct purchases of certain crops. In the mid-1980s, milk, butter, and cheese generally accounted for the largest share of direct purchases.

The functions of the Commodity Credit Corporation affect its treatment in the NIPA. Transactions of the CCC are treated differently from transactions of other government agencies because the CCC is classified as a government enterprise (i.e., corporation). Consequently, operating expenses are netted against revenues in determining the current surplus of the government enterprises component of charges against GDP. Otherwise, operating expenses of typical government agencies are included as government expenditures in GDP.

Another difference between the CCC and other public agencies and private corporations is that the loan transactions of the CCC are included as federal government nondefense expenditures of goods and services. New loans are purchases, whereas repayments are negative purchases. When making a new loan, the CCC essentially is purchasing the crops, which end up in government inventories instead of private sector inventories. A repayment shifts the inventories from the government back to farm inventories, but it is reflected in the GDP figures as a liquidation in CCC inventories and therefore a decline in government spending.

If CCC loans and repayments are small, the quarterly impact on federal nondefense purchases will be negligible. When farm prices change sharply, farmers will either take out sizable loans or will be able to repay their loans in large quantities. In that case, the impact on federal nondefense purchases will be substantial and could give a misleading picture of the economy. Government spending, just like personal consumption expenditures, investment spending and net exports, counts as final sales. CCC inventories are counted in government expenditures as sales because there is no classification for government inventories. This can skew the underlying trend in final sales.

One final comment on CCC transactions. The income side of the accounts must also include CCC loans and repayments so that the product and income side of the accounts balance. Subsidies less current surplus of government enterprises are the key income variable for CCC transactions. To a lesser extent, CCC transactions may be included in other sectors such as transfer payments to foreigners (when CCC donations help foreign countries' emergency relief needs), and net interest paid (due to the loan aspect of the transaction).

Net Exports

The foreign sector grew rapidly in the 1980s increasing its share of gross domestic product. Since 1983, when the strong dollar and the U.S. economic recovery caused imports to surge, the foreign sector has become an integral part of the U.S. economy. Simply put, net exports are total exports of goods and services less total imports of goods and services. Table 2.2 shows that the sum of exports and imports accounted for 22.8 percent of GDP in 1991, up sharply from the 15.7 percent share in 1979. As an example of what that means to the U.S. economy, a 10 percent decline in exports from one year to the next, would reduce the GDP growth by 1 percent; similarly, an increase of 10 percent in imports from one year to the next would reduce the GDP growth by 1 percent.

Just like other sectors of the economy, exports and imports are sensitive to the business cycle. As the economic expansion progresses, imports will grow because U.S. consumers and businesses have more money to spend, and will use some of the extra cash for imported merchandise. These goods can include petroleum from Saudi Arabia, automobiles from Japan, and leather goods from Italy. When the U.S. economy is in recession, the drop-off in total demand for goods and services will include a decline in the demand for foreign goods, so that the decrease in domestic production is mitigated to the extent that consumers had previously bought foreign goods and services. One of the reasons cited by some economists for a mild recession in 1990 was that the drop-off in consumer demand would include a decline in imported goods. Since importers now hold a greater share in the U.S. economy than they did 15 years ago, they would theoretically suffer more now during a U.S. downturn than in previous recessions. When foreign economies are experiencing healthy growth, they will demand more foreign goods and U.S. exports will grow. These goods can include agricultural commodities, airplanes, electrical machinery, and consulting services. Conversely, when economic activity abroad cools off, countries demand fewer foreign goods so U.S. exports will decline.

Both exports and imports are sensitive to exchange rates. As the exchange value of the dollar increases relative to foreign currencies, U.S. exports will decline and imports from abroad will increase. Conversely, if the exchange value of the dollar declines relative to foreign currencies, U.S. exports will increase and imports to the United States will decline because foreign goods are now more expensive.

Did You Know?   In a closed economy with a central government and a single bank, an economy is self-sufficient and not dependent on international trade, interest rates, and tax and spending policies of other countries. However, when countries are open and trade with one another, they also must share one another's problems, points out Chief Market Economist Richard D. C. Trainer of Bank of Tokyo in a weekly newsletter.[3]

To avert major inflationary pressures in 1992, Germany maintained a tight monetary policy. As a result, high interest rates in Germany led to a sharp deterioration in the exchange value of the U.S. dollar during the year. The rapid decline in the dollar, especially in the summer of 1992, prevented the Fed from easing U.S. monetary conditions because of concern that the value of the dollar might fall more sharply and rapidly on interest rate declines.

In the international market, the German Bundesbank was under pressure to reduce its interest rates because of the economic pressures it put on other European countries as well as on the United States.

The early 1980s saw a long period when the exchange value of the dollar was on an increasing trend. Consequently, export growth deteriorated and imports gained ground. The exchange value of the dollar peaked in early 1985 and declined steadily through mid-1987. The plunge in the value of the dollar between 1985 and 1987 set the stage for an export revival, making U.S. goods and services more competitive overseas. During the late 1980s and the early 1990s, the exchange value of the dollar has exhibited mixed behavior.

Throughout the 1980s, net exports were negative. That is, imports outstripped U.S. exports. However, the growth in imports has moderated considerably since 1987, whereas the growth in exports has accelerated because of our weaker dollar. This has allowed the net export position of the U.S. to improve sharply from its trough in 1987. A negative net export balance is a drag on economic growth. However, as the net export balance becomes less negative from quarter to quarter, it adds to GDP growth (see box, "Net Exports and GDP: Not Always a Drag").

Final Sales

Although GDP is an important overall measure of production, economists sometimes prefer to look at sales growth. Final sales are equal to gross domestic product less the change in business inventories. At

Net Exports and GDP: Not Always a Drag

It's easy to see why a negative net export balance is a drag on GDP. The larger the net export deficit that must be added to personal consumption expenditures, investment spending, government purchases, and net exports, the larger is the negative number that must be subtracted from the total. The following example illustrates that the larger deficit in Case 1 causes GDP to be smaller than in Case 2, which has a smaller deficit.

	Case 1	Case 2
C + I + G	$1,000	$1,000
Net exports	−50	−25
GDP	$950	$975

The following step shows how a continuously smaller net export deficit, even though it remains negative, can contribute to GDP growth over a period of a year. For simplicity's sake, the example does not show any change at all in C + I + G over the year.

	O1	O2	O3	O4
C + I + G	5,000	5,000	5,000	5,000
Net exports	−100	−90	−70	−40
GDP	4,900	4,910	4,930	4,960
% change*	NA	0.8%	1.6%	2.5%

*Seasonally adjusted annual rate.

From the first quarter to the second quarter, net exports improved by $10. From the second quarter to the third quarter, net exports improved by $20, allowing the quarterly growth rate in GDP to accelerate from 0.8 percent to 1.6 percent. Finally, net exports improved by $30 in the fourth quarter and GDP accelerated to a 2.5 percent rate of growth.

This process can work in reverse. The net export deficit can go from a smaller to a larger number, deteriorating the growth rate instead of improving it.

turning points of the business cycle or when the direction of the economy is unclear, it is useful to gauge final sales rather than GDP. Final sales measure aggregate demand and are a good indicator of future production. If the growth in final sales exceeds the growth in gross domestic product for an extended period (at least two quarters), it indicates strong demand and signals a pickup in production. Conversely, growth in final sales that is much less than the growth in GDP, indicates soft demand and a rising level of undesired inventories. That combination generally signals moderating production growth.

Real versus Nominal

Production measures physical output. In discussing economic growth, we want to measure real physical output over time. Gross domestic product, as a measure of production, is denominated in dollars. Because we want to compare GDP over time (measure economic growth from one year to the next), we must compare similar things. Consequently, current (nominal) dollar GDP is deflated to a common base. Currently, the base year for real GDP is 1987, which means we denominate the NIPA series in 1987 dollars. The base year typically changes every five years or so. *Real* GDP is simply current dollar gross domestic product adjusted for inflation (see Chapter 7).

Did You Know?   According to the Bureau of Economic Analysis (BEA), the effect of shifting the base of the GDP deflator to a more recent base period typically reduces the rate of growth in real GDP as well as the rate of growth in the fixed weight deflator. Furthermore, the BEA explains that a more recent base period produces lower growth in real GDP than an early base period if there is a tendency for slow-growing quantities to be associated with fast-growing prices, *or* fast-growing quantities to be associated with relatively slow-growing prices.

When changes in technology lower some prices relative to others, buyers will demand more low-priced goods relative to high-priced goods. Computers are an example of such behavior. In the 1991 benchmark revision, the average annual growth rate of producers' durable equipment for the period 1977–1990 was revised down 1.3 percentage points because computers (a low-priced item) increased their share in this category between 1982 and 1987.

What Happened to Gross National Product?

On December 4, 1991, the Commerce Department officially reported GDP for the first time, and virtually ignored GNP. The shift in focus from gross national product to gross domestic product came about for several reasons, one of which is that countries across the globe report GDP rather than GNP, simplifying international comparisons. What is more important, however, is that GDP, not GNP, is closely aligned with other economic indicators such as industrial production, employment, productivity, and investment in structures and equipment. This makes gross domestic product a better measure of current economic activity than gross national product. However, GNP may be preferable for analyzing the sources and disposition of income because the receipts from and payments to the rest of the world may be relevant in the total.

The difference between GNP and GDP is relatively minor. Gross national product covers the goods and services produced by labor and property supplied by U.S. residents *living here or abroad*. Gross domestic product covers the goods and services produced by labor and property *located in the United States*. Table 2.4 shows that receipts of factor income from the rest of the world are added to GDP, while payments of factor income to the rest of the world are subtracted from GDP, to arrive at GNP. Factor income payments to foreigners represent the goods and services produced in the United States using labor and property supplied by foreigners. Conversely, factor income receipts from foreigners represent the goods and services produced abroad using labor and property supplied by U.S. residents. In sum, net factor income measures the difference between these receipts and payments. Thus, the production of Toyota and Honda cars assembled in Kentucky and Ohio is included in domestic product, but not in national product. The profits that accrue to the Japanese manufacturers are also included in gross domestic product, but not in gross national product. The production of Ford and GM cars assembled in Europe is not included in gross domestic product although it is included in gross national product. Profits for Ford and GM coming from abroad are part of GNP, but not GDP. The Bureau of Economic Analysis, the division of Commerce Department responsible for the national income accounts, had always measured GDP, but it was not the conventional yardstick of measurement in the United States as it was in the rest of the world. The Bureau continues to publish GNP as usual, but without the usual fanfare it once received.

Table 2.4   Relationship between Gross Domestic Product
and Gross National Product
(billions of 1987 dollars, seasonally adjusted)

	1990	1991	Q1:91	Q2:91	Q3:91	Q4:91	Q1:92	Q2:92
Gross Domestic Product	4877.5	4821.0	4796.7	4817.1	4831.8	4838.5	4873.7	4892.4
Plus: Receipts of factor income from rest of world	141.1	120.8	136.2	120.9	115.4	110.8	109.7	107.6
Minus: Payments of factor income to the rest of world	122.6	105.4	110.9	106.2	103.6	101.0	92.7	101.0
Gross National Product	4895.9	4836.4	4822.0	4831.8	4843.7	4848.2	4890.7	4899.1

Source: Bureau of Economic Analysis, U.S. Department of Commerce, *Survey of Current Business,* September 1992.

The shift in focus from GNP to GDP is just the first of several changes in the way that the national income and product accounts will be reported in the future. According to Carol Carson, Director of the Bureau of Economic Analysis, the agency intends to introduce comprehensive revisions in the mid-1990s to the System of National Accounts.[4] This system not only will be more internationally focused but also will make definitional changes on the domestic side of the accounts to give a truer picture of U.S. economic activity. For instance, government expenditures will be divided into spending on goods and services, spending on investment, and inventory change. Currently, government expenditures of all types are lumped into the government spending category, which gives a misleading picture of economic activity in the government sector.

Market Reaction   The financial market reaction to GDP is not necessarily what the casual observer would expect. The average consumer in the U.S. economy generally favors strong economic growth coupled with a low unemployment rate because that promotes a rising standard of living. In contrast, participants in the fixed-income markets will react negatively and view healthy GDP growth as signaling either inflation or the Fed's pursuance of a tight monetary policy. A negative reaction means that bond prices will fall and bond yields, or interest rates will rise. When GDP growth is low or negative, it indicates sluggish economic activity or outright recession. In that case, the market reaction will be positive: Bond prices will rise (and interest rates will fall). The fixed-income markets include the money markets, which means that interest rates on short-term securities will also rise on a healthy gain in GDP growth. In the fixed-income markets, the good (economic) news is bad news and bad (economic) news is good news, based on the perception that robust economic growth tends to increase demand for all goods and services. When the demand cannot be satisfied, prices must rise to choke off some of that demand. This perception that healthy economic growth brings inflationary pressure is based on the "demand-pull" theory of inflation. Producers don't have the necessary resources to make enough goods to satisfy consumers, so prices must be bid up, and inflation reigns.

In a period of soft economic growth, or the early stages of recovery, it would be foolish to believe that rising GDP growth will be accompanied by inflation. Indeed, inflationary pressures tend to moderate further in the first year of recovery as producers benefit from higher worker productivity. In this case, participants in the fixed-income markets fear that the Federal Reserve will no longer be accommodative and ease interest rates. Thus, healthy economic growth may simply signal the end of a friendly Fed and the end of a falling interest rate environment rather than inflationary pressures.

The equity market reaction will make more sense to the casual observer. Participants in the stock market prefer to see healthy economic growth because it spurs gains in corporate profits, whereas a weak economic environment renders poor earnings. Stock prices fall on economic (GDP) weakness and rise on economic (GDP) strength, assuming that GDP growth is not accompanied by inflationary pressures. If it is accompanied by rising prices, participants in the equity markets are as unhappy to see robust economic growth as are the fixed-income market players.

Foreign exchange market participants favor a healthy economic environment to appreciate the dollar as long as strong economic activity points to rising interest rates and increases the demand for the dollar. However, if strong economic activity signals inflationary pressures, the dollar will not appreciate. Weak economic activity leads to falling interest rates and a decline in the demand for the dollar. Thus a negative reaction in the fixed-income market is a positive reaction in the foreign exchange market.

There is an exception. If GDP increases because inventories are rising at the same time that final sales are falling, participants in the fixed-income market will view the figures as signaling weakness and interest rates will not rise. Final sales reflect aggregate demand in the economy. A decline in demand combined with rising inventories indicates that the

Watch Out For: The key elements to watch for in the GDP figures are final sales and the change in business inventories. As mentioned earlier, those will give you a clue on the next quarter's activity. In addition, keep in mind that the advance, or initial, GDP report for any quarter is based partly on forecasts of business inventories and net exports. Thus, if those two categories show unexpected activity (in either direction of weakness or strength), it is best to look at them cautiously and wait for the next revision of GDP before committing to a view. GDP revisions are common. Total growth estimates often are revised by as much as one percentage point from the advance estimate to the final estimate two months later. Sometimes the estimates made by the Bureau of Economic Analysis leave total growth virtually unchanged whereas the composition of GDP is changed. Revisions in the total growth rate are more relevant than revisions to the composition of growth unless the change comes in inventories. As mentioned previously, the inventory changes, coupled with final sales growth, give clues on future production gains or cuts. For example, the BEA initially estimated that real GDP grew at a 1.4 percent rate in the second quarter of 1992. The first revision showed no change in the growth rate (although the composition of growth was revised), and the second revision showed an insignificant change to a 1.5 percent rate of gain in the second quarter, from the first. As expected, the largest revisions came in inventories and net exports between the initial report and the first revision. Table 2.5 summarizes the advance, preliminary, and final growth rates of GDP and its components for the second quarter of 1992. Typically, the revisions between the first estimate and the final estimate tend to be larger than those shown in this table.

It is also useful to check what portion of final sales gains was due to increases in the private sector relative to the public sector. Put differently, did GDP rise because investment and consumption expenditures increased, or were the gains coming from increased spending by the government sector? Not only is government spending dependent on fiscal policy, but it could also bunch up from time to time. There is no reason to expect smooth increases or decreases in government expenditures from quarter to quarter. As a result, a first-quarter rise could easily be followed by a second-quarter drop. Federal government spending on nondefense goods can cause large shifts from quarter to quarter because of the CCC payments to farmers. As explained earlier, these payments are virtually transfer payments and are not counted as GDP growth since they are offset in inventories. They are, however, counted in final sales. As a result, final sales will surge when CCC payments to

Table 2.5 Annualized Growth Rates for 1992: Q2
(relative to Q1)

	Advance	Preliminary	Final
Real GDP	1.4	1.4	1.5
Personal Consumption Expenditures	−0.3	−0.2	−0.1
Durable goods	−2.7	−3.0	−2.1
Nondurable goods	−1.6	−1.6	−1.5
Services	1.0	1.3	1.2
Nonresidential Fixed Investment	13.5	15.3	16.1
Structures	−2.1	−4.0	−0.8
Producers' durable equipment	20.7	24.4	24.1
Residential Investment	8.7	8.9	12.6
Change in Business Inventories*	1.0	9.2	7.8
Net Exports*	−35.9	−44.7	−43.9
Exports of goods and services	−3.8	−0.9	−1.4
Imports of goods and services	6.3	15.9	14.7
Government Purchases	0.3	−0.6	−1.2
Federal	0.3	−1.7	−2.7
Nondefense	5.2	3.3	3.3
Defense	−1.6	−3.7	−5.2
State and local	0.1	0.1	−0.2
Real Final Sales	0.3	−0.4	−0.1

*Billions of 1987 dollars.

Source: U.S. GDP Summary Data, Market News Service Inc., September 24, 1992.

farmers increase, and they will rise when CCC payments decline. Between 1989 and 1992, the quarterly changes in CCC payments were fairly small by historical standards. During this period, the largest shift occurred in the first quarter of 1991 when CCC payments rose by $3 billion (in real terms). This occurred during the recession, and real final sales fell at a 4.2 percent rate during the quarter. However, excluding CCC payments, real final sales fell at a larger 4.8 percent rate. Thus, the true decline in final sales would have depicted a worse picture of the economy if it hadn't been for the rise in CCC payments during that quarter.

inventory buildup is undesired and production cuts are in order. Neither stock prices nor the foreign exchange value of the dollar will rise on such news and may post declines instead.

THE INCOME SIDE

National income is to the income side of the accounting system what gross domestic product is to the product side. While familiar to the economist, national income does not have a famous identity associated with it as does the product side. The income side of the accounts measures the income accrued to the factors of production of U.S. residents whether they are located here or abroad. This means that while the Commerce Department has shifted its focus from national product, it hasn't shifted its focus away from national income. Consequently, we are concerned with the income accruing from the use of American-owned land, labor, and capital whether it is located in the United States or abroad.

National Income

While the national income identity may not be "famous," it can be summarized as follows: national income (NI) is the sum of compensation to employees (COMP), proprietors' income (PROP), rental income (RENT), net interest income (NETINT), and corporate profits (PROF). This equation would read as follows:

$$NI = COMP + PROP + RENT + NETINT + PROF$$

It makes sense that national income should equal GDP because people have to "earn" the money to be able to spend it. Furthermore, GDP measures output and national income shows what was "spent" to produce that output. Theoretically, at least, national income equals national product. While this linkage is very clear in the introductory textbooks, it isn't totally true in the real world because many factors can't be assumed away as they are in the classroom. As a result, national income is a few steps removed from GDP. The calculation is as follows: First, add net factor income to GDP to get back to GNP; then subtract capital consumption (depreciation of durable goods and structures) to arrive at *net* national product (NNP). Next, subtract indirect business taxes, business transfer payments, and a statistical discrepancy from NNP; add subsidies less current surplus of government

Table 2.6   Components of National Income and Relative Shares

	Percentage of National Income					
	1979	1987	1988	1989	1990	1991
Compensation of Employees	73.4	73.1	73.0	73.0	73.7	74.6
Wages and salaries	61.6	61.2	61.0	60.9	61.4	61.9
Supplements to W&S	11.8	11.8	11.9	12.1	12.3	12.7
Proprietors' Income	8.9	8.4	8.1	8.2	8.2	8.1
Farm	1.2	0.8	0.8	0.9	0.9	0.8
Nonfarm	7.7	7.6	7.3	7.2	7.3	7.3
Rental Income of persons with CCAdj*	0.4	0.1	0.1	−0.3	−0.3	−0.2
Corporate Profits with IVA** & CCAdj	9.9	8.7	9.1	8.5	8.1	7.6
Profits before tax ("Book")	12.8	7.8	8.7	8.1	8.0	7.4
Profits after tax	8.5	4.4	5.3	5.2	5.0	4.9
Net Interest	7.4	9.8	9.7	10.7	10.3	9.9

* CCAdj = Capital consumption adjustments.
** IVA = Inventory valuation adjustment.
  W&S = Wages and Salaries
Source: Data are from Commerce Department publications.

enterprises to NNP, and finally arrive at national income. Table 2.6 shows relative shares of the major components of national income.

Did You Know?   "Business transfer payments" signify bad debt.

Compensation

Compensation of employees is by far the largest component of national income accounting for 75 percent. Compensation can be divided into its component parts: wages and salaries, employers' contributions for social insurance, and other labor income. "Other labor income" includes such fringe benefits as employers' contributions to pension funds.

Compensation is cyclical. When economic activity moderates and workers are either laid off or work fewer hours, wages and salaries grow at a slower pace. Because it is conventional to look at national income (and its components) in current dollars rather than real (inflation-adjusted) dollars, it is unusual to see outright declines in total compensation.

Conversely, when economic activity is expanding, compensation growth will accelerate. However, even though workers are laid off during recessions, it is common to see compensation's share of national income rise relative to the profits' share of national income because producers don't tend to lay off as many workers as the decline in production dictates. This leads to a drop in productivity per worker and a plunge in corporate profits. The reverse is true during economic upturns. Productivity per worker increases when the pickup in production is greater than the increase in employment. Profits rebound smartly. Table 2.6 shows this relationship. Compensation's share of national income was relatively stable between 1979 and 1989, but began to rise in the recession years 1990 and 1991.

Proprietors' Income

Proprietors' income accounts for about 8 percent of national income. This includes income of farmers, the self-employed, and small business owners who are sole proprietors or in partnerships. The earnings of tax-exempt cooperatives are included here as well as income-in-kind. Proprietors' income is also cyclical, rising more rapidly during economic expansions, and more slowly during recessions. Proprietors' income is more stable than corporate profits, however, over the business cycle. In addition, quarterly movements are compounded by government subsidies to farmers in the form of CCC payments. Commodity Credit Corporation payments are offset in the product side through the inventory component; the income side includes an offset in a category called "subsidies less current surplus of government enterprises." In this way, government transfer payments, which these are, don't create phantom income gains in the aggregate report.

Rental Income

Rental income is the third component of national income and hardly accounts for anything these days. The 1992 NIPA benchmarks showed that rental income was negative in every quarter beginning in 1989 through the first quarter of 1992. This category includes the income of persons from the rental of real property, except the income from property of those in the real estate business. It also includes the imputed net rental income of owner-occupants of nonfarm dwellings.

The drop in rental income might be caused by any number of factors. Plausible explanations for negative rental income include the combination of devastation in U.S. property from natural disasters (Hurricane

Hugo and the San Francisco area earthquake in 1989) along with the sharp depreciation of housing values in the late 1980s in many regions of the country. The uninsured losses of residential and business property from Hurricane Andrew in August 1992 reduced rental income of residents and businesses by a combined $23 billion at an annualized rate. As a result, rental income fell to $−13.1 billion in August, down sharply from July's level of rental income of $8.5 billion. Despite the negative impact of Hurricane Iniki in Hawaii in September 1992, rental income turned positive again in the same month.

Net Interest Income

Net interest income accounted for 11 percent of national income in 1991. Net interest income is equal to interest paid by business less interest received by business, plus interest received from foreigners less interest paid to foreigners. Interest payments on mortgage and home improvement loans are counted as interest paid by business, because homeowners are treated as a business in the national income and product accounts. This category also includes imputed interest payments as counterentries to imputed charges in the product side of the NIPA.

Net interest income is strongly affected by interest rates. It grows rapidly when interest rates are high or rising and moderates significantly when rates are declining. To a lesser degree, the strength of the economy will also impact this figure as more homes are purchased during economic booms than during recessions. The share of net interest income relative to national income dropped in 1991 and 1992 bringing its share to those levels reached in the mid-1980s.

Corporate Profits

Corporate profits are the final major component of national income. There are several measures of profits including "corporate profits with inventory valuation and capital consumption adjustment," "profits before taxes," and "profits after taxes." The profit measure can be summarized quite simply by saying it includes the income of organizations treated as corporations in the NIPA. The capital consumption adjustment deals with differences in depreciation allowances used for accounting purposes and income tax purposes. Similarly, the inventory valuation adjustment deals with the difference in measuring the cost of inventory replacement. Thus, subtracting the inventory valuation and capital consumption adjustments from the first profit measure gives the second profit measure, which is often termed "book profits." Profits that include inventory valuation and capital consumption adjustments are called "operating" or "economic" profits. They are the profits from current production.

Profits are highly sensitive to the business cycle. They grow during economic expansions and fall sharply during recessions. Profits, like the other income measures, are analyzed in nominal dollars so an inflationary environment will show an increase in measured profits. Profit gains due to price increases are not the same as those due to volume increases. The sensitivity of profits to the business cycle is evidenced in Table 2.6, which shows the 1991 share (when the United States was in recession) was down sharply from the 1979 share (when the United States was not in recession).

When converting income figures to the national concept, which incorporates the property of U.S. residents wherever they live, the corporate profits figures are related to production on which U.S. residents have a claim. Profits shown on a domestic basis would include the income earned in the United States by foreigners but would exclude the income earned by U.S. corporations operating abroad.

The description of national income was simplified in this text by mentioning only major components. There are some subcategories among major components, which are shown in Table 2.7, but these are not necessary to understand economic indicators.

You will note one major difference in this discussion of national income versus gross domestic product. The former is always analyzed in current or nominal dollars. Users of national income data do not look at

Table 2.7   National Income by Type of Income
(billions of dollars)

	1989	1990	1991	Q3:91	Q4:91	Q1:92	Q2:92
National Income	4249.4	4468.3	4544.3	4555.5	4599.0	4679.5	4716.4
Compensation of Employees	3100.2	3291.3	3390.9	3407.0	3433.7	3476.3	3506.3
Wages and salaries	2586.4	2742.9	2812.2	2824.4	2845.0	2877.6	2901.3
Government	478.5	514.8	543.5	544.3	546.4	554.6	561.4
Other	2107.9	2228.1	2268.7	2280.1	2298.6	2323.0	2339.9
Supplements to wages & salaries	513.8	548.4	578.7	582.6	588.7	598.7	605.0
Employer contributions for social insurance	261.9	277.4	290.4	292.0	293.7	299.4	301.5
Other labor income	251.9	271.0	288.3	290.6	295.0	299.3	303.5

Table 2.7   (Continued)

	1989	1990	1991	Q3:91	Q4:91	Q1:92	Q2:92
Proprietors' Income with							
IVA* and CCAdj**	347.2	366.9	368.0	367.1	377.9	393.7	398.4
Farm	40.2	41.7	35.8	29.5	37.9	40.1	38.5
Proprietors' income							
with IVA	48.3	49.5	43.4	37.1	45.4	47.5	45.8
CCAdj	−8.1	−7.8	−7.6	−7.6	−7.5	−7.4	−7.3
Nonfarm	307.0	325.2	332.2	337.6	340.0	353.6	359.9
Proprietors' income	281.1	310.0	318.7	322.4	325.6	339.1	344.8
IVA	−1.2	−0.8	−0.3	−0.5	−0.1	−0.8	−1.0
CCAdj	27.2	16.0	13.8	15.6	14.4	15.2	16.1
Rental Income of Persons							
with CCAdj	−13.5	−12.3	−10.4	−10.3	−6.6	−4.5	3.3
Rental income of persons	44.2	44.6	47.5	47.0	54.7	51.7	60.0
CCAdj	−57.7	−56.9	−57.9	−57.3	−61.3	−56.2	−56.6
Corporate Profits with							
IVA and CCAdj	362.8	361.7	346.3	341.2	347.1	384.0	388.4
Corporate profits							
with IVA	325.4	341.2	337.8	331.9	333.1	360.7	361.4
Profits before tax	342.9	355.4	334.7	336.7	332.3	366.1	376.8
Profits tax liability	141.3	136.7	124.0	127.0	125.0	136.4	144.1
Profits after tax	201.6	218.7	210.7	209.6	207.4	229.7	232.7
Dividends	134.6	149.3	146.5	145.1	143.9	143.6	146.6
Undistributed							
profits	67.1	69.4	64.2	64.5	63.4	86.2	86.1
IVA	−17.5	−14.2	3.1	−4.8	0.7	−5.4	−15.5
CCAdj	37.4	20.5	8.4	9.3	14.1	23.3	27.0
Net Interest	452.7	460.7	449.5	450.5	446.9	430.0	420.0
Addenda:							
Corporate profits							
after tax with IVA							
and CCAdj	221.5	225.1	222.3	214.2	222.2	247.6	244.3
Net cash flow with							
IVA and CCAdj	439.3	444.0	458.8	452.5	464.6	490.1	488.9
Undistributed profits							
with IVA and CCAdj	86.9	75.7	75.8	69.0	78.3	104.0	97.7
Consumption of fixed							
capital	352.4	368.3	383.0	383.5	386.3	386.1	391.2
Less: IVA	−17.5	−14.2	3.1	−4.8	0.7	−5.4	−15.5
Equals: Net cash flow	456.9	458.1	455.6	457.3	463.9	495.6	504.3

* IVA = Inventory valuation adjustment.
** CCAdj = Capital consumption adjustments.

Source: Bureau of Economic Analysis, U.S. Department of Commerce, *Survey of Current Business,* September 1992.

Watch Out For: Growth in national income closely approximates the growth in nominal or current dollar gross domestic product. If there are going to be any quirks in the data, they will appear in some of the components of national income.

Capital consumption (not a component of national income, but a factor subtracted from gross national product to get net national product) typically runs at about 11 percent of GNP: The depreciation of fixed capital in the country is relatively stable over time. However, destruction of residential and nonresidential structures from natural disasters must be reflected in the national income accounts. When Hurricane Hugo hit in the third quarter of 1989, capital consumption jumped 4.6 percent during the quarter (not at an annualized rate) relative to quarterly increases of 1.9 percent in the previous two periods. Hurricane Andrew, which devastated parts of Florida in August 1992, and Hurricane Iniki, which devastated parts of Hawaii in September 1992, caused capital consumption to jump 9.3 percent in the third quarter of 1992.

Why is this important? First, it is useful to know the extent of damage of such events to the economy and its infrastructure. But, this will also impact corporate profits for the quarter. If the capital consumption eats a larger share of the national product, less will be left over in terms of net national product and national income (from which corporate profits are derived).

Two other factors could affect corporate profits: proprietors' income and compensation. The portion of proprietors' income that gets skewed by CCC payment to farmers will either reduce or increase profits depending on the movement of CCC payments. When farm income jumps sharply during a quarter due to CCC payments from the government, profits will be down. In contrast, when farm income declines sharply during a quarter when CCC payments are reduced, profits will rise.

The same holds true for compensation: When it rises, profits fall, and vice versa. But compensation and profits are both cyclical—growth accelerates during an economic expansion and declines during a recession. More significant are the quirks here. Employers' contributions to social insurance taxes are included in total compensation. During the past decade, increases in social insurance taxes were concentrated in the first quarter of the year. Thus, whenever the employers' share of social insurance taxes are increased, profits are likely to suffer.

Finally, economists and market participants usually look at quarterly growth rates in the components of the national income accounts: GDP, personal consumption expenditures, national income; whereas they view corporate profits on a year-over-year basis because the quarterly pattern tends to be highly volatile.

the inflation-adjusted figures (although they do look at "real" disposable income). On the other hand, they typically ignore current dollar gross domestic product and always discuss real (inflation-adjusted) figures.

To be consistent, all economic data should be adjusted for inflation. Aside from using national income components as cash flow measures, there is no good reason for this discrepancy. The only reason is "convention."

Market Reaction   Participants in the financial markets typically don't react to figures for national income or its components. Equity market players are concerned with corporate profits, and stock prices are likely to rise on positive economic news. Participants in the foreign exchange and the fixed-income markets have their hands full with the GDP data and are unlikely to react to profits alone.

Key Points

- Gross domestic product—GDP—is the most comprehensive measure of goods and services produced on U.S. soil (regardless of who owns the factors of production).
- GDP is measured by spending on personal consumption expenditures, investment, net exports, and government.
- Financial market behavior to this economic indicator is often restrained since it is usually old news.
- Breaking this figure down to final sales and inventories suggests future behavior of the economy.
- National income measures the income accruing to the factors of production owned by U.S. residents living either here or abroad.
- National income is equal to compensation of employees, proprietors' income, rental income, net interest income, and corporate profits.
- Financial market participants generally ignore the income side of the accounts, although stock market investors anxiously await corporate profits data.
- Table 2.8 summarizes the NIPA series and their approximate dates of release.

Table 2.8   Indicators of the National Income and Product Accounts Provided by the Bureau of Economic Analysis

Approximate Date	Indicator	Data for
Jan 25–30	Gross domestic product	Q4(adv)
	National income	Q4(adv)
Feb 25–30	Gross domestic product	Q4(prelim)
	National income	Q4(prelim)
	Corporate profits	Q4(prelim)
Mar 25–30	Gross domestic product	Q4(final)
	National income	Q4(final)
	Corporate profits	Q4(final)
Apr 25–30	Gross domestic product	Q1(adv)
	National income	Q1(adv)
May 25–30	Gross domestic product	Q1(prelim)
	National income	Q1(prelim)
	Corporate profits	Q1(prelim)
June 25–30	Gross domestic product	Q1(final)
	National income	Q1(final)
	Corporate profits	Q1(final)
July 25–30	Gross domestic product	Q2(adv)
	National income	Q2(adv)
Aug 25–30	Gross domestic product	Q2(prelim)
	National income	Q2(prelim)
	Corporate profits	Q2(prelim)
Sep 25–30	Gross domestic product	Q2(final)
	National income	Q2(final)
	Corporate profits	Q2(final)
Oct 25–30	Gross domestic product	Q3(adv)
	National income	Q3(adv)
Nov 25–30	Gross domestic product	Q3(prelim)
	National income	Q3(prelim)
	Corporate profits	Q3(prelim)
Dec 25–30	Gross domestic product	Q3(final)
	National income	Q3(final)
	Corporate profits	Q3(final)

CHAPTER 3

The Consumer Sector

Featured Indicators	Auto Sales
	Johnson Redbook
	Retail Sales
	Chain Store Sales
	Personal Consumption Expenditures
	Personal Income
	Personal Saving Rate
	Consumer Installment Credit
	Consumer Sentiment

Consumer spending accounts for two-thirds of GDP. Consequently, it's reasonable to expect government and private agencies to publish an abundance of indicators detailing some aspects of personal consumption expenditures. The majority of the consumer sector indicators are reported monthly although a couple are available more often. The more frequently the indicator is reported, the more it is beloved by financial market participants, but the more careful they must be in interpreting it. The equity, fixed income, and foreign exchange markets are constantly moving, as traders revise their expectations of economic activity based on economists' forecasts, market rumors, or actual economic reports. As a result, the more frequent the economic data, the more readily the market can incorporate new economic information.

This chapter describes the indicators of consumer behavior most closely monitored by financial market participants, the media, and government policy-making agencies such as the Federal Reserve Board.

Some indicators get more attention than others. At times, the market or media focus of a particular series is justified; at other times it's overdone.

HIGH-FREQUENCY INDICATORS

Auto Sales

The most frequently reported indicator of consumer spending is 10-day unit auto sales. The major auto manufacturers of domestically produced cars report their sales for the first 10 days, the middle 10 days, and the last 10 days of each month. These sales figures are available on the third business day following each 10-day period: Sales for the first 10 days of any month are usually reported on the thirteenth of the month; sales for the middle 10 days, on about the twenty-third; and for the last 10 days, on the third business day of the subsequent month.

Auto manufacturers report their raw sales data for the 10-day period compared with the same period in the previous year. This means that the preceding year's sales are just as important to the calculation as the current year's sales figures. Although these figures are useful in a general sense, market participants and economists would rather know how sales are behaving compared with the most recent period. Were more cars sold in the middle 10-day period of the month than in the first 10-day period? Were car sales stronger throughout the month of May than in the month of April? The current level of sales reflect the current pace of the economy. Year-to-year changes are often irrelevant. There is another problem to consider. Auto makers report the yearly change in sales on a daily sales rate basis. That means you must know the number of selling days during the reporting period. Table 3.1 shows that there were eight selling days in the May 21–31, 1992, period versus nine selling days during the same period in 1991. So although the total number of cars sold in the 1992 period was 237,400, less than the 261,362 sold in the 1991 period, the rate still rose 2.2%. The industry standard is to calculate the percentage change in the daily rate: Auto makers sold an average of 29,675 cars per day in 1992 versus 29,040 cars per day in 1991, resulting in a year-over-year gain of 2.2%.

The raw sales figures reported by auto makers are volatile from period to period, and there is a general trend toward higher sales as the month progresses, possibly because salespeople and dealers may be given greater incentives to sell cars toward the end of the month if car

Table 3.1   Ten-Day Auto Sales, May 21–31

	1992	1991	% Change*
General Motors	107,509	109,058	10.9
Ford	56,396	56,345	12.6
Chrysler	24,289	33,206	−17.7
Honda	18,863	25,373	−16.4
Nissan	5,734	6,238	3.4
Toyota	17,140	21,156	−8.9
Mazda	2,739	5,579	−44.8
Mitsubishi	2,419	2,754	−1.2
Subaru	2,311	1,653	57.3
Total	237,400	261,362	2.2

* On a daily sales rate basis for eight selling days in the 1992 period and nine in the 1991 period.

Source: Summary of Ten-Day Auto Sales, *Market News Service, Inc.,* June 3, 1992.

sales are anemic. So if a person were to compare each 10-day period of most months, sales would increase as the month progresses with the highest sales level occurring in the final 10-day period. In May 1992, 130,700 cars were sold in the first 10 days; 196,300 cars were sold in the second 10-day period; and 237,400 cars were sold in the last 10-day period. This is a typical pattern. From these raw figures, you can't really tell if car sales were robust or lackluster.

As a result, the Bureau of Economic Analysis (BEA), a division of the U.S. Department of Commerce, releases seasonal adjustment factors for 10-day auto sales. Thus, we can divide the raw auto sales data for the 10-day period by a seasonal factor and yield a *seasonally adjusted annual rate* (SAAR). The seasonal adjustment factor blows up the current level of sales to an annual rate and takes into account normal seasonal behavior at the same time. In the last 10 days of May (1992), 237,400 domestically produced cars were sold. Dividing 237,400 cars by the BEA seasonal adjustment factor of 37.66 gives a seasonally adjusted annual rate of 6.3 million units. Applying seasonal factors to the other two periods in May yields a seasonally adjusted annual rate of 5.8 million units in the first 10 days, and a 6.7 million unit rate in the second 10 days. This makes all 10-day sales figures comparable. It now becomes evident that auto sales were rather anemic in the first 10 days in May, picked up in the middle 10 days, and fell back slightly at the end of the month. The raw sales data do not tell that same story (see box, "Seasonal Adjustment").

Seasonal Adjustment

The seasonal adjustment process can be relatively complicated because it uses complex statistical methods. Although it is not imperative to understand the actual computational methods, the theoretical concept of seasonal adjustment is relevant and crucial.

An obvious example is that retail sales spurt in November and December as consumers do their Christmas shopping; and even taking the after-Christmas discounted sales into account, retail sales plunge in January and February. A report of unadjusted data stating that retail sales rose 2 percent in December would not tell you much about consumer spending because you wouldn't know exactly how much of that rise was due to normal seasonal influences.

If you know that retail sales rise every year in December and decline every year in January, you could take sales out of December and add sales to January. The monthly fluctuations would be smoother and you would know if Christmas sales were stronger or weaker than normal.

The term *normal* is associated with a complex mathematical formula that essentially takes into account the most recent five years of data and gives appropriate weighting to various years during that five-year period. The process is an ongoing one; seasonal factors are adjusted annually to reflect new information.

It is most difficult to determine seasonal factors for frequently reported data such as weekly numbers including money supply, new claims for unemployment insurance, and 10-day auto sales.

What about structural changes in the economy? These can play havoc with seasonal adjustment factors also. For example, the baby boom generation of the postwar years led to a baby bust generation. The changing demographic structure caused blips in the employment statistics. During the 1960s and 1970s, many teenagers entered the labor force in May and June when school let out and dropped out of the labor force in August or September when school reopened. Many years of this same pattern caused seasonal adjustment factors to expect sharp labor force increases in May and June, and equally sharp decreases in August and September to reverse the process.

Baby boomers were all in the labor force by the early 1980s. At that point, the baby bust generation, a much smaller group, began entering the labor force. Thus, fewer people than "expected" would enter the labor force in May and June, and the seasonally adjusted labor force would decline during those months. A drop in the labor force often meant a corresponding drop in the unemployment rate. The reverse would happen in August and September. The seasonally adjusted labor force would rise again, and this would lead to a rise in the unemployment rate.

Cyclical variation might also affect seasonal adjustment factors. Imagine an economic downturn that begins in the second half of the year and lasts through the end of the following year. In terms of retail sales, spending tends to increase the closer it is to Christmas. Since the economy is in recession, retail sales remain suppressed in the second half of the year for two years. Because the seasonal adjustment process utilizes five years of data to calculate seasonal factors, the two years of anemic retail sales during the recession will suppress the seasonal factors for the second half of the year. Thus, in the coming years without recession, seasonal factors will be lower, thereby increasing the seasonally adjusted level of sales.

The seasonal adjustment process is not set in stone. Most seasonally adjusted data are calculated by a process called the X-11 Arima procedure. Even so, the series can be modified by seasonally adjusting totals or individual components. A good example comes from the Labor Department's seasonal adjustment of the unemployment rate. The Labor Department calculates the seasonally adjusted unemployment rate using *eight* different variations. In some months, the different variations can yield a range of estimates. For example, in September 1992, the unadjusted civilian unemployment rate stood at 7.2 percent, and the official procedure showed that the seasonally adjusted rate stood at 7.5 percent. Yet, the remaining seven variations yielded a seasonally adjusted rate ranging from 7.3 percent to 7.6 percent. These variations due to methodology differences in seasonal adjustment illustrate just how silly it is to stress small, insignificant changes in economic series.

Unseasonal behavior can cause problems with all sorts of figures. A warm January will create a housing boom, whereas a rainy July can create a housing bust.

In explaining unexpected movements in economic indicators, economists have learned to blame many statistical quirks on seasonal adjustment factors. Generally, they are justified in doing so.

Even after adjusting for seasonal variation, any number of other factors can cause 10-day auto sales to move in a sawtooth pattern from one 10-day period to the next: Instead of introducing new car models in early fall, the historical pattern, auto makers might introduce new models in the winter or spring; or auto makers could try to entice buyers with incentives on certain models to bolster sales or market share. In August and September 1985, which was the first time auto makers induced consumers to buy cars with cut-rate financing, 10-day car sales reached 12-year highs. When these financing incentives were removed in October, car sales sank to 3-year lows. By failing to take the incentives into account, a person might have concluded that a new boom period of consumer expenditures was in store and would have been unprepared for the subsequent October plunge. Awareness of such special deals aids in understanding the dips and wiggles in the auto market.

Did You Know?   Ford has 49% interest in Hertz Corp. General Motors has equity interest in Avis, Inc. and National Car Rental Systems. Chrysler Corporation owns outright Dollar Systems, Inc., Thrifty Car Rental, Snappy Car Rental, and General Car and Truck Leasing System, Inc.

Fleet sales also cause volatility in 10-day auto sales. Fleet sales are large-quantity car purchases by auto rental companies, such as Hertz and Avis, or by corporations for employees' use. Such bulk purchases could easily boost 10-day sales in any given period. In addition, auto makers often pressure the rental companies into buying their fleets when auto sales are sluggish so that they won't have to cut production. Each of the three major domestic auto companies—General Motors, Ford, and Chrysler—either own rental companies or have equity interest in one or more of them. (In November 1992, General Motors announced their plan to sell off a significant portion of their 81.5% stake in National Car Rental Systems.[1]) Typically, fleet purchases take place in the late fall and in the early spring. From 1989 through the end of 1991, fleets were purchased three times during the year, rather than the normal two. As a result, fleet dealers were forced to sell their used cars more often during the year. At the same time, these used cars were newer and higher priced than older used cars and thus competed in the marketplace with new cars spurring the used car market but hurting new car sales. In 1992, consumer demand was on the rise again, so auto manufacturers severely curtailed the incentives previously offered to fleet dealers.[2]

Only producers of domestically made cars report 10-day sales—with the exception of Chrysler, which stopped reporting 10-day figures in 1991. At the time, Chrysler claimed it would cut costs, but company executives also recognized that foreign cars were gaining a greater share of the market and that these shares were exaggerated by 10-day sales. They wanted to avoid the comparison with transplants every 10 days. (Ward's Communications, Inc., estimates 10-day sales for Chrysler to continue the publication of those sales series.) The sales figures do include foreign makers (Toyota, Honda, Nissan, Mazda, Mitsubishi, Subaru) who produce cars in the United States. Sales of foreign cars, produced abroad, are reported on a monthly basis. Total sales of all domestic and foreign makes are released on the third business day of the following month. Although monthly auto sales are not as volatile as 10-day sales, they still are hardly a stable series.

Since auto sales are actual figures reported by auto dealers, unadjusted sales figures are never revised. The seasonally adjusted data is revised marginally from year to year because the Bureau of Economic Analysis, which computes the seasonal adjustment factors for 10-day and monthly comparisons, updates the seasonal adjustment factors annually.

Market Reaction   Participants in the fixed-income or bond market—who are forever on the lookout for a bond rally that will raise bond prices and lower interest rates—prefer to see anemic auto sales that signal economic weakness. Players in the stock and foreign exchange markets would prefer to see a rise in auto sales. In the case of the stock market, strong auto sales signal a healthy economy and good earnings in auto and related industries as well as companies in general. The foreign exchange market favors strength so that rising interest rates increase the demand for the dollar. However, if the market share of foreign-produced cars increases at the expense of domestically produced cars, the demand for foreign currencies will go up and the exchange value of the dollar will decline. Strong auto sales can provoke bond market participants to push up interest rates and thereby push down bond prices.

Johnson Redbook

The Johnson Redbook series is compiled by a unit of Lynch, Jones & Ryan, a New York brokerage firm. Johnson conducts a weekly survey of 25 retailers across the country including chain stores, discounters and department stores. This weekly indicator of retail sales is reported every Tuesday afternoon and describes sales for the previous week. Johnson Redbook figures are faxed to customers, but as is the case with all economic indicators, the data are picked up by the media.

Watch Out For: Be aware of the special factors that can move around 10-day auto sales. If sales are stronger than expected even after taking special factors into account, it could indicate a pick up in consumer demand. But you should look at the trend in sales, not just a single 10-day period. Also, if you are monitoring news continuously as it is reported, beware of the first auto manufacturer to report sales. After all, auto producers are not reporting these figures at exactly the same time of day. A sharp increase or decrease in GM or Ford sales may not carry through to the other makers. Furthermore, market share of any particular auto producer can shift from one period to the next so that extrapolating sales data of only one or two makers can give a false signal. For instance, GM's market share ranged from a high of 42.8 percent in the first 10 days of August 1992, to a low of 37.2 percent in the last 10 days of the month. Ford's market share ranged from a high of 31.6 percent in the first 10 days to a low of 24.8 percent in the last 10 days of August. Chrysler's market share ranged from a high of 12.8 percent in the last 10 days of August to a low of 7.8 percent in the first 10 days of the month. Although Chrysler may have had greater incentives to sell cars in those final 10 days, it is more likely that Chrysler's market share increased because of being artificial. Since Chrysler no longer reports 10-day sales, Ward's must estimate that auto maker's 10-day sales. The sales for the last 10 days are equal to the monthly sales levels minus the estimates made by Ward's for the first two periods. Figure 3.1 shows the monthly pattern of market share of the major auto manufacturers for selected months.

Consider the 10-day sales in light of special factors that could artificially boost or suppress them and try to distinguish whether an increase or decrease is an aberration or the beginning of a new trend. For example, Ford lowered the auto loan interest rate it charged on some of its 1992 and 1993 models in September 1992, and extended its rebate program through mid-December on 1992 model year cars. The incentive program either caused an increased demand for cars in general, or it increased Ford's market share at the expense of other auto makers.

Depending on your source of information, you may not get all the details on the auto report. For example, a news wire service such as *Market News Service* or *Reuters* usually gives raw data along with seasonally adjusted figures. So does the *Wall Street Journal* on the following day. But the financial pages of your local newspaper are not always inclined to such detail. For example, the *Chicago Tribune* reports raw data with the year-to-year percentage change, but not always with the seasonally adjusted annual rate. As already shown, the raw data doesn't tell the whole story. (When car sales do plunge in any 10-day period, feel free to use this information to negotiate a better deal if you need to buy a new car.)

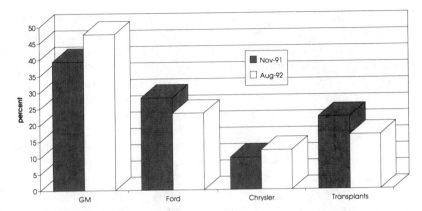

Figure 3.1 This chart reflects market shares of auto makers at two points in time. Market shares not only vary from month to month, but from one 10-day period to the next. (*Source: Market News Service, Inc.,* Ward's Communications, Inc.)

Auto sales are just one of the many sectors of the U.S. economy, and even though auto producers report 10-day sales whereas computer producers or retailers do not, auto sales are not the only major force in the economy. Indeed, market participants have recently begun to also consider truck sales, which are reported every ten days, too. It is now customary to count light motor vehicle sales (autos and light trucks) to allow for the popularity of mini-vans and jeeps. Thus, the fascination with 10-day auto sales may be somewhat overblown.

Monthly auto sales can indicate changing consumer behavior. A decline in auto sales for two or three straight months certainly suggests softness in the consumer sector possibly pointing to lower interest rates. Auto sales are also a good indicator of consumer confidence. When people are comfortable with their financial position and the economy, they are more likely to purchase a car than when they are feeling unsettled about their employment prospects.

Did You Know? Ten-day auto sales became a significant economic indicator in the 1940s when the U.S. War Control Board wanted a way to monitor the economy and the use of natural resources.

This spending survey originated in 1975 when the Commerce Department stopped releasing weekly retail sales figures. Financial market participants largely ignored it until early 1992 when the January retail sales release was found to confirm the trend discovered by the Johnson Redbook series. Actually, the Johnson Redbook series is similar to the chain store sales figures (described among monthly indicators) in that it corresponds to only 12 percent of retail sales: the general merchandise category. The Johnson Redbook series is preferred over the chain store sales data because it is seasonally adjusted both on a weekly and monthly basis, but economists are divided on its relevance. Joseph Liro of S. G. Warburg & Company feels that investors give this series too much weight because it only reflects a small portion of total retail spending, and the sample size of the survey is small.[3] Mitsubishi Bank economists concur with this view, claiming there is inherent volatility in weekly series; some chain stores are reluctant to participate in the survey; some stores don't track sales from Saturday to Saturday as Johnson collects them; and the weekly method does not correlate with the calendar system used by the Commerce Department.[4]

In contrast, Raymond Stone, a managing director of Stone & McCarthy Research Associates, likes the series because he has found a strong correlation between the government's retail sales figures and the Johnson Redbook series back to 1979.[5] Martin Mauro, a Merrill Lynch economist, also defends the Johnson Redbook data saying, "As long as you keep in mind its limitations, it can be quite helpful."[6]

Watch Out For: Weekly series tend to be more volatile than monthly or quarterly ones, even when they are seasonally adjusted. Thus, be cautious using this series. Although it is correlated with the Commerce Department's retail sales report, studies show that Johnson Redbook forecasts year-to-year changes better than month-to-month changes. Consequently, it will still be difficult to extrapolate monthly changes in the retail sales data.

Looking at the trend in the Johnson Redbook series may be a good idea but don't use it to forecast specific monthly changes in retail sales. Typically, economic series tend to move together over time, but not always by the same magnitude each month. Thus, increases reflected in the Johnson Redbook series will loosely move with chain store sales and retail sales over time.

Market Reaction Bond traders react to the Johnson Redbook data, so it is worth keeping an eye on the series. The market reaction will be similar to auto sales: If retailers post higher sales, suggesting healthy or improving economic growth, bond prices will fall and cause yields to rise; a weak report signals economic sluggishness and allows interest rates to fall. The market reaction to the Johnson Redbook series appears limited to the bond market and muted compared with more established series such as the employment situation.

MONTHLY INDICATORS

Among the indicators of consumer spending behavior, auto sales and the Johnson Redbook series are the only high-frequency indicators. The remaining indicators are reported monthly.

Retail Sales

Sales of nondurable and durable consumer goods are reported between the eleventh and fifteenth of each month for the previous month. This series is published by the Commerce Department's Bureau of the Census and is derived from a sample of establishments of all sizes and types across the country. Because the sales figures come from a sample and not all businesses report their sales in a timely fashion, they are subject to substantial revision for several months after the initial report. In addition, annual revisions also take place every spring for the previous five years to include new data for seasonal adjustment purposes. Finally, every five years, the Bureau of the Census conducts the Census of Retail Trade to further complete the details of the data such as gauging the product mix at the various types of business (e.g., department store, grocery store).

Three components make up the probability sample for retail sales estimates. Companies whose 1982 sales were greater than a certain cutoff were chosen to report their sales figures every month. These 2,000 stores account for roughly 40 percent of total retail sales. The second component of retail sales comes from about 30,000 establishments that are separated into three panels and are asked to report their sales only once every three months. This group makes up about 56 percent of total retail sales. The remaining 6 percent comes from retailers who represent areas not covered by the other two components. Participation in the retail sales survey is voluntary. In the late 1980s, the nonresponse rate was roughly 20 percent. Sampling data rather than using actual figures is the reason revisions occur so often and to such large magnitudes.

Retail sales are reported in current, or nominal, dollars; that is, they are not adjusted for inflation. Auto sales constitute the largest single component of retail sales, about 20 percent of the total. Although monthly auto sales are not as volatile as 10-day auto sales, they still jump around from month to month, and the wild fluctuations can obscure the underlying trend. The dollar value of auto sales reflects the quantity of cars sold as well as the price of the car. This changing mix of expensive versus less expensive autos gets reflected here, an important factor because price times quantity equals dollar value. Even when the quantity of car sales increases, the auto price can be low if consumers buy cheap cars rather than expensive cars. As a result, the price times quantity equals a low dollar value and holds down the growth in retail auto sales. Conversely, fewer cars may be sold, but if consumers purchase expensive cars, this puts upward pressure on the dollar value of sales. Thus, monthly changes in unit auto sales frequently don't correspond to monthly changes in the dollar value of sales, as shown in Figure 3.2.

That's why economists and financial market participants talk about *retail sales excluding autos.* By removing the volatile component of the

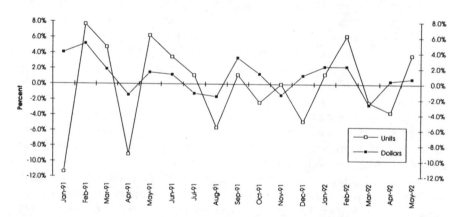

Figure 3.2 Monthly changes in auto sales are volatile and the two auto series—unit sales and retail dollar sales—are not strictly correlated each month. *(Source: Survey of Current Business.)*

series, you can assess the underlying spending behavior of consumers. The auto sales portion of retail sales also includes truck sales. Such sales were not an important consideration during the 1970s, but the introduction and popularity of minivans in the 1980s have contributed to the significance of truck sales as more than a statistical quirk. So "retail sales ex autos," really means retail sales excluding autos *and trucks,* because it refers to the category "auto dealers."

Sales are categorized by types of stores, not by types of goods. For example, sales of VCRs purchased at a department store are classified as a department store sale under the nondurable goods category even though the VCR is a durable good. The major durable goods categories for retail sales are building materials stores, furniture and appliance stores, auto dealers, and "other" durable goods. The major categories of nondurable goods include general merchandise stores (department stores fall under this category), food stores, apparel stores, eating and drinking places, gasoline service stations, drugstores, liquor stores, and mail order. The popularity of mail-order spending by consumers is evidenced by the rise in relative share attributed to the "other nondurables" category. Table 3.2 shows that spending on "other nondurables" accounted for 5 percent of total retail sales in 1988 and rose to 7.9 percent in the first part of 1992.

Because retail sales are reported in nominal or current dollars, unusual price increases or decreases can affect the monthly change in retail sales. For example, when gasoline prices are skyrocketing or plunging, total retail sales will react accordingly. However, a person looking at the real (inflation-adjusted) retail sales report might not see unusual changes from month to month. During the summer of 1990, the stage was being set for the Persian Gulf conflict, and oil prices went up. An increase in oil prices rapidly translates to an increase in gasoline pump prices. In August 1990, retail sales excluding autos rose 0.9 percent from July, apparently a healthy gain. What really happened is that sales at gasoline service stations jumped 9 percent during the month because of higher gasoline prices. Excluding gas station sales, retail sales rose a more modest 0.2 percent in August. Similarly, sharp price changes in food can cause large increases or decreases in food store sales where the real (inflation-adjusted) movement is minor. Real (inflation-adjusted) retail sales data are available with a one-month lag. However, the figures are not officially reported by any of the government statistical agencies. You have to call the Commerce Department for the figures rather than wait for them to be reported and made available in a government news release.

Table 3.2 Retail Sales

Seasonally Adjusted Millions of Dollars	% of Total 1988	Current	Jan 92	Feb 92	Mar 92	Apr 92	May 92	June 92	July 92	Aug 92
Retail Sales	100	100	157,808	159,753	157,873	158,385	159,111	158,982	160,582	159,728
Excluding auto group	77.8	79.0	124,645	125,815	124,815	125,105	125,707	125,566	126,981	126,511
Durable Goods	37.8	36.2	56,919	57,961	57,122	57,442	57,643	57,686	58,190	57,279
Building materials	5.2	5.4	8,497	8,757	8,692	8,722	8,721	8,574	8,608	8,373
Auto dealers	22.2	21.0	33,163	33,938	33,058	33,280	33,404	33,416	33,601	33,217
Furniture	5.7	4.8	7,628	7,660	7,677	7,609	7,549	7,683	7,879	7,670
Other	4.6	4.9	7,631	7,606	7,695	7,831	7,969	8,013	8,102	8,019
Nondurable Goods	62.2	63.8	100,889	101,792	100,751	100,943	101,468	101,296	102,392	102,449
General merchandise	11.4	12.1	19,328	19,731	19,030	18,947	19,053	19,025	19,602	19,649
(Dept. stores)	9.6	9.6	15,304	15,606	15,050	14,977	15,180	15,076	15,415	15,602
Food stores	20.5	20.2	32,049	31,920	31,823	32,139	31,968	32,200	32,389	32,903
Gasoline stations	6.7	6.5	10,165	10,210	10,229	10,249	10,497	10,539	10,568	10,358
Apparel	5.2	5.2	8,057	8,277	8,137	8,199	8,318	8,445	8,577	8,492
Eating and drinking	9.8	10.3	16,736	16,904	16,715	16,403	16,420	15,843	15,906	15,720
Drug stores	3.7	4.1	6,461	6,525	6,528	6,537	6,491	6,459	6,531	6,564
Other	5.0	7.9	12,117	12,350	12,269	12,439	12,594	12,734	13,006	12,810

Source: Bureau of Economic Analysis, Department of Commerce, *Survey of Current Business*, September 1992.

Market Reaction   Players in the fixed-income market favor a drop in retail sales, or at least weakness in the figures because that points to a sluggish economy. Interest rates then decline thereby boosting bond prices. If retail sales rise sharply, bond market participants will push up interest rates and push down bond prices.

Equity market professionals prefer to see retail sales increase. Strong consumer spending figures indicate a healthy economy and that bodes well for corporate profits. Stock prices, especially those related to the retail sector, are likely to rise on this. If retail sales decline, or show only a paltry gain, stock prices will fall or at best not show any upward momentum.

Foreign exchange market participants also favor a healthy spurt in retail sales because it points to a strong U.S. economy and suggests a rise in interest rates. Rising U.S. interest rates relative to the rest of the world lead to a rise in demand for the dollar. If retail sales decline, however, interest rates are likely to drop, and the softer demand will then cause the dollar to fall. Moreover, retail sales could be reflecting higher sales of imported goods, too. A greater demand for imports signals an increased demand for foreign currency at the expense of the dollar.

Watch Out For: Look at the detailed retail sales report to see if any single category was the major culprit for the rise or fall in total retail sales. Retail sales excluding autos can provide a first approximation in ignoring volatile components. A broadly based increase or decrease in retail sales is a good indication of the strength or weakness in the consumer sector. There is one caveat however. If the *broadly based increase follows a broadly based decline* from the previous month, there is probably a problem with seasonal adjustment factors. In that case, take the average of the two months to gauge consumer spending. It is always wise to examine at least a three-month trend; never take one month's report at face value. Also, retail sales tend to be revised frequently. Look at the current three- and six-month trend after all revisions have been taken into account; don't compare the most recent change in retail sales with the levels of retail sales reported two months ago.

Looking at a three- and six-month trend in retail sales is useful because even after "dumping" the auto portion of the report, you will still find some volatility in the figures. Always check gas stations, food stores, building material stores, and furniture stores for "lumpy" behavior.

Chain Store Sales

The major department stores report their sales in the first week of the month for the most recent four- or five-week period. For example, May sales would be reported in early June. Notice that sales cover the "most recent four- or five-week period," not a calendar month. The chain stores report the sales levels relative to the previous year. For a retail equity analyst making stock recommendations of specific retail stores, the annual comparison might be useful. However, if you are using the store sales to give you a more general outlook on current consumer spending behavior, the year-over-year comparison is not always helpful and can sometimes even be misleading. Also, if you are waiting for chain store sales as they are released, don't expect the data to be reported in the aggregate. Each chain store will report their company's figures during the course of the morning. You will have to calculate the aggregate level of sales yourself. Table 3.3 lists the major chain stores.

Table 3.3   Department Store Sales
(millions of dollars)

Store	Total Sales Levels		Total Yearly Change (%)	Comparable Stores Yearly Change (%)
	June 92	June 91		
Wal-Mart Stores, Inc.	4,277	3,489	23.0	8.0
Sears Merchandise	2,130	2,170	−1.7	−2.6
Kmart Corp.	2,394	2,340	2.3	0.5
J.C. Penney	1,107	987	12.2	11.2
Dayton-Hudson	1,520	1,380	9.9	2.1
May Department Stores	933	864	8.0	3.3
Woolworth Corp.	483	496	−2.5	0.6
The Limited	585	537	9.0	−4.0
The Gap	242	205	18.0	5.0
Caldor Corp.	203	173	17.1	11.6
U.S. Shoe	199	214	−6.9	−1.2
Neiman-Marcus	167	144	16.3	11.9
Edison Brothers	137	120	14.2	na
Charming Shoppes	109	92	18.0	9.0
Jamesway	87	105	0.0	0.0
Best Buy	88	87	48.0	14.0
Merry-Go-Round	71	60	19.0	1.0
Dollar General	82	66	24.6	18.5
Total	14,814	13,529	9.5	

Source: U.S. Stores Report June Sales Data, *Market News Service, Inc.,* July 9, 1992.

Because special factors can so easily affect any one month's sales, it is difficult to make sense of the yearly comparison. For example, natural disasters in major metropolitan areas might have suppressed sales in the previous year. A person who wants to compare September 1990 sales to the previous year had better be aware of the earthquake that rocked the San Francisco area in September 1989 before getting excited about a jump in sales for the (1990) month. A year-over-year comparison could show a sizable gain that does not carry through for the month-to-month comparison.

Aside from retail stock pickers, financial market participants only look at the chain store sales to preview the total retail sales report that will be released by the Commerce Department a week or two later. Department store sales are only about 10 percent of total retail sales. It seems a long shot to use chain store sales to predict retail sales. The main problem with this practice is the difficulty in translating raw store sales into seasonally adjusted department store sales that will correspond with the government report. In fact, they often don't match from month to month. However, if you are using the chain store sales simply as a guideline in a trendlike fashion, they may be useful. For example, an exceptionally strong rise in chain stores might indicate that consumers went on a general shopping spree during the month. It could point to strength in all categories of retail sales. Similarly, very anemic chain store sales could point to general consumer apathy.

Since the chain store sales are raw figures reported by the stores, the data are not revised. Furthermore, the data are not adjusted for seasonal variation so seasonal adjustment factors need not be revised either.

Did You Know?   The difference between chain stores and department stores is that chain stores are department stores having the same ownership and selling the same merchandise, such as Sears and Kmart; department stores also can be single-location stores found only in one town or city. Thus, chain stores are a subset of department stores.

Market Reaction   The reaction to chain store sales is similar to other consumer indicators: strong sales portend a healthy economy and rising interest rates, whereas sluggish sales suggest a weak economy and falling interest rates. The strength of the market reaction to chain store sales will depend on market sentiment and the availability of other economic indicators. If more reliable indicators are readily available, the market reaction to chain store sales will be muted. Chain store sales

Watch Out For: As a trader keeping a close eye on the chain store sales reports as they roll off the screen, be wary of trading the figures because they can be misleading. To make sense of the year-to-year comparison, you must know exactly what happened a year ago. Retailers often issue the annual gain over "comparable stores" if the number of stores increased or decreased since the previous year. Nevertheless, the figures remain murky. Chain store sales will be more useful when all stores are moving in tandem and by a similar magnitude.

An additional problem is that you are likely to get diverse opinions about the figures from economists and retail analysts. Retailers are always disappointed with their sales figures—if department store sales increase 5 percent on a year-over-year basis, the retailers would have preferred a 10 percent rise; if sales increased 10 percent, the retailers would have liked 15 percent. Chain store sales figures will only be useful to you if you are interested in a particular retailer and have an equity position in one or more retailers. Otherwise, the data are another minor indicator of consumer spending.

are more closely monitored by participants in the fixed-income and stock markets than by players in the foreign exchange market.

Personal Consumption Expenditures

Personal consumption expenditures are released four to five weeks after the end of each month (e.g., January data are released about the fourth week of February) by the Bureau of Economic Analysis (BEA), a division of the Commerce Department. Consumption expenditures are reported in current (nominal) and real (inflation-adjusted) dollars. They are also adjusted for seasonal variation, and the figures are annualized.

Personal consumption expenditures are derived partly from the Census Bureau's retail sales report, although a significant number of additional sources also provide input. These figures are then fed directly into GDP; that is, they are the "C" portion of the $C + I + G + X - M$ equation. Just as in the quarterly figures, personal consumption expenditures include durable goods, nondurable goods and services. Table 3.4 shows the major BEA categories. Unpublished BEA reports show more detail and can make interesting party chatter. For obvious reasons, motor vehicles, furniture, and appliances are considered to be durable goods, as are boats

Table 3.4 Personal Consumption Expenditures by Type

	% of Total		Jan 92	Feb 92	Mar 92	Apr 92	May 92	June 92	July 92	Aug 92
	1988	Current								
Billions of Current Dollars										
Personal Consumption										
Expenditures	100.0	100.0	4007.8	4030.4	4030.3	4039.9	4052.6	4078.7	4101.4	4092.0
Durables	13.3	11.7	469.1	475.5	463.5	462.6	468.6	480.2	479.7	480.3
Nondurables	32.6	31.6	1272.3	1280.6	1269.5	1274.0	1280.3	1278.6	1289.4	1291.4
Services	54.2	56.8	2266.4	2274.3	2297.3	2303.3	2303.7	2319.9	2332.3	2320.3
Billions of Constant Dollars (1987)										
Personal Consumption										
Expenditures	100.0	100.0	3291.7	3295.6	3280.4	3280.4	3284.8	3300.4	3313.5	3315.1
Durables	13.6	13.1	433.8	437.7	425.6	423.9	427.6	438.6	437.6	437.5
Nondurables	32.7	31.8	1052.7	1055.2	1040.9	1044.4	1048.8	1043.6	1051.6	1050.7
Services	53.7	55.0	1805.2	1802.7	1813.9	1812.1	1808.4	1818.2	1824.3	1826.9
Implicit Price Deflators (1987 = 100)										
Personal Consumption										
Expenditures			1.218	1.223	1.229	1.232	1.234	1.236	1.238	1.234
Durables			1.081	1.086	1.089	1.091	1.096	1.095	1.096	1.098
Nondurables			1.209	1.214	1.220	1.220	1.221	1.225	1.226	1.229
Services			1.255	1.262	1.266	1.271	1.274	1.276	1.278	1.270

Source: Bureau of Economic Analysis, Department of Commerce, *Survey of Current Business*, September 1992.

and pleasure aircraft, jewelry, watches, books, and maps. But, oddly enough, "durable" toys are also included in this category.

Did You Know?   The measurement and sampling errors from the retail sales data are transferred to the personal consumption figures. Moreover, retail sales are separated by type of store, not by type of product, increasing the likelihood of error. The Bureau of Economic Analysis must map sales by type of business to type of product using the Census of Retail Trade, which is only undertaken every five years. Federal Reserve Board economist David Wilcox explains that it is important to be cognizant of these errors in measurement and sampling when doing empirical research.[7]

Chapter 2 mentions that food, clothing and shoes, gasoline and oil, fuel oil, and coal are among the components of nondurable goods. In addition, there are tobacco products, cleaning supplies, drugs, and reassuringly, "nondurable" toys and sports supplies. This list is not exhaustive but gives a flavor of the detail.

Since services account for roughly half of consumer spending, it is not surprising that the number of minor classifications equals durables and nondurables combined. Under the major category of housing, you will find spending on hotels and college dormitories in addition to rent. The major category of household operation incorporates electricity, gas, telephone, domestic service, personal property insurance and postage among others. The transportation category includes road and bridge tolls, motor vehicle repair, car insurance, railway, bus, and airline flights. Medical care is relatively self-explanatory including services of physicians, dentists, hospitals, and nursing homes. In addition, health insurance is included in the category. Personal care services include cleaning, storage, and repair of apparel as well as barbershops, beauty parlors, and health clubs. Personal business services includes brokerage charges and investment counseling, bank service charges, expense of handling life insurance, legal services, and funeral and burial expenses. Trade union dues and employment agency fees also fall under the category of personal business services.

Economists like to see the personal consumption expenditures data because these figures are directly incorporated into GDP (although even most economists don't bother with the vast detail). Since consumer spending is two-thirds of GDP, economists have two-thirds of their forecast. Financial market participants don't care very much about this indicator because it gives little, if any, new information about the consumer. Personal consumption expenditures provide extra detail, which is not included in retail sales. However, spending on services tends to be less volatile than spending on durable or nondurable goods. You can think of services as taking care of everyday business: You take your clothes to the dry cleaners, you get a haircut periodically, you pay your annual insurance premiums, you ride the train to work each day. You are unlikely to deviate from these daily tasks and habits. As a result, spending on consumer services is more stable and consistent than spending on nondurable or durable goods: People do not purchase clothing and automobiles daily. There is, however, a more practical explanation for the monthly stability. The BEA, which compiles the data, does not have actual figures for most of these categories. Thus, the Bureau estimates them using a judgmental trend. It would be pointless to induce volatility in the service component unnecessarily.

A few components in the services category do change from month to month. Spending on electricity and spending on brokerage commissions are two such major categories. The first is related to the weather. If it is extraordinarily warm in the summer, people use their air conditioners more frequently and this increases electricity usage. If it is very cold during the winter, more natural gas is consumed for heating. Moreover, the BEA is able to collect timely data on such usage from the Edison Electric Institute and the Energy Information Administration. Brokerage commissions are dependent on the stock market. For example, unusual activity in the stock market in the form of a strong bull market or a strong bear market such as the stock market crash of 1987 can induce high volumes. Here, the Bureau of Economic Analysis gets commissions per share and volume traded from the Securities and Exchange Commission, the New York Stock Exchange, and the National Association of Securities Dealers.

The other components of consumer services spending do not really reflect actual monthly purchases but are BEA estimates on housing costs, transportation costs, medical costs, and so forth. Therefore, monthly spending gains in this category tend to be quite smooth. As a major component of total consumer expenditures (more than half), services spending makes total consumer spending gains positive from month to month on a nominal (current) dollar basis.

Market Reaction   All in all, financial market participants (either in the fixed income, equity, or foreign exchange markets) don't tend to react forcibly to monthly data on personal consumption expenditures due to its predictability.

Watch Out For: The only noteworthy aspects of this report are the following: auto sales, electricity usage, and stock volume. Auto sales, as part of durable goods, match unit sales figures, not retail sales volume. This factor causes differences between monthly retail sales and personal consumption expenditures. Thus, if you were to add the durable and nondurable goods component of personal consumption expenditures and compare it with retail sales, the monthly changes would not necessarily match. However, excluding autos from both series would make the relationship closer.

Spending on services will blip when electricity usage is unexpectedly different from its normal seasonal behavior. Stock volume will blip in bull or bear markets. These figures are known before the BEA publishes consumption expenditures and are usually taken into account by economists who forecast the data. Check for aberrations in these components when the changes in personal consumption expenditures are different from expectations.

Personal Income

The Bureau of Economic Analysis releases personal income together with personal consumption expenditures about four to five weeks after the end of the month. Personal income is seasonally adjusted, is quoted in nominal dollars, and is annualized.

Personal income comprises several components: wages and salaries (the largest component), other labor income (basically reflecting fringe benefits), proprietors' income (farm and nonfarm), rental income, dividend income, personal interest income, and transfer payments. Payments for social security insurance are subtracted from wages and salaries. Table 3.5 illustrates the relative importance of each category.

A few components in this series could cause some volatility in the data. For example, the government pays subsidies to farmers from time to time in the form of CCC (Commodity Credit Corporation) payments. These are reflected in farm income. The problem is that the subsidy payments are always annualized in the income data although they are not seasonally adjusted. A subsidy payment of $1 billion during the month balloons into $12 billion at an annual rate. Thus, it is quite common to see monthly changes of $10 billion to $20 billion in farm income. That reflects one-fourth of total farm income. Table 3.5 shows increases

Table 3.5 Personal Income

	% of Total		Jan 92	Feb 92	Mar 92	Apr 92	May 92	June 92	July 92	Aug 92
	1988	Current								
Billions of Current Dollars										
Wages and Salaries	59.9	57.8	2852.8	2884.9	2895.0	2890.6	2907.6	2905.7	2910.5	2928.5
Private	48.9	46.6	2300.0	2329.9	2339.0	2332.0	2346.3	2341.6	2345.1	2361.9
Government	11.0	11.2	552.8	555.0	556.0	558.6	561.3	564.1	565.4	566.6
Other labor income	5.7	6.0	297.8	299.2	300.7	302.1	303.6	305.0	306.4	307.9
Proprietors' income	8.0	7.9	379.5	395.5	405.9	406.7	395.3	393.3	394.8	389.6
Farm	0.8	0.7	30.5	40.7	49.0	48.1	36.1	31.4	30.7	24.2
Nonfarm	7.2	7.2	349.0	354.8	356.9	358.6	359.2	361.9	364.1	365.4
Rental income	0.1	0.0	-4.2	-6.2	-3.2	-1.2	3.3	8.0	8.5	-13.1
Dividend income	2.7	2.7	133.6	133.8	134.2	135.4	136.6	137.9	139.5	141.3
Personal interest income	14.3	13.5	693.1	684.4	676.9	676.0	675.2	674.4	670.4	666.7
Transfer payments	14.1	17.1	835.5	844.3	848.2	854.2	860.9	864.1	869.3	872.2
Less Social Security	4.8	5.0	244.9	247.3	248.2	249.8	249.8	249.9	250.4	251.8
Personal income	100.0	100.0	4943.2	4988.6	5009.5	5015.5	5032.7	5038.5	5049.0	5041.3
Less taxes	12.9	12.4	621.8	627.9	609.0	614.7	617.6	619.0	623.8	630.3
Disposable Income	87.1	87.6	4321.4	4360.7	4400.5	4400.8	4415.1	4419.5	4425.2	4411.0
Less personal outlays	83.2	83.3	4131.4	4153.8	4153.8	4162.7	4174.9	4200.9	4223.1	4213.6
PCE	80.9	80.8	4007.8	4030.3	4030.3	4039.9	4052.6	4078.7	4101.4	4092.0
Interest paid by consumers	2.3	2.2	113.4	113.3	113.3	112.4	111.9	111.8	111.4	111.3
Personal transfers to foreigners	0.1	0.2	10.2	10.2	10.2	10.4	10.4	10.4	10.3	10.3
Personal saving	3.8	4.3	190.0	206.9	246.7	238.1	240.2	218.6	202.1	197.4
Saving rate			4.4%	4.7%	5.6%	5.4%	5.4%	4.9%	4.6%	4.5%

Source: Bureau of Economic Analysis, Department of Commerce, *Survey of Current Business*, September 1992.

of nearly $10 billion per month in February and March of 1992. Decreases in May and June of the same year reverse the gain. To avoid this volatility, economists favor looking at personal income exclusive of the farm sector.

Transfer payments and government wages and salaries are two other categories that can cause occasional blips in personal income. Transfer payments include Social Security payments to retirees. Every year in January, Social Security recipients receive a cost-of-living adjustment. Government employees also receive a cost-of-living adjustment in January, and this will add to total wages and salaries.

Historically, rental income has been a relatively stable component of personal income from month to month, unless some region of the country suffers a major natural disaster. In 1989, rental income plunged with destruction caused by hurricanes and earthquakes. The impact of Hurricane Andrew (August 1992) on rental income was huge, causing rental income to plunge from $8.5 billion in July to $−13 billion in August. Rental income turned positive again in September but was held down by roughly $5 billion dollars due to damages caused by Hurricane Iniki in Hawaii.

Although personal income gives market participants an idea how much money consumers have to spend on necessities and luxuries, *disposable personal income* is a better indicator. Subtracting personal income taxes shows the difference between disposable income and personal income.

Personal income is a coincident indicator of the economy because growth accelerates with expansions and decelerates with business cycle downturns. Personal income is reported in nominal (current) dollars, but disposable income is usually monitored in real (inflation-adjusted) dollars. It is also a coincident indicator of the economy. Real disposable income typically rises with expansions and declines with contractions. When real disposable income *declines* during a recession, it makes sense that *consumer spending* should also decline during the period.

Market Reaction   Financial market participants are likely to respond mildly to personal income data. Increases in personal income generally point to increases in consumer spending and gains in economic activity overall. That bodes poorly for the fixed-income market because bond traders fear that economic expansions are inflationary. Consequently, bonds are likely to fall in price and rise in yield. Decelerating or falling personal income growth portends weakness in consumer spending and is favorable news to bond traders because it suggests recession and a deceleration of inflationary pressures or potential Fed easing. This would cause bond prices to rise and yields to decline.

Stock market participants view personal income as well as personal consumption expenditure growth favorably. Strong consumer spending points to healthy corporate profits. Thus, stock prices are likely to rise when personal income growth increases and fall when personal income growth declines.

The foreign exchange professional will take the same perspective as the equity trader. Rising personal income growth bodes well for the economy pointing to higher interest rates and therefore an increase in the demand for dollars. This will raise the exchange value of the dollar. Sluggish gains in personal income or outright declines (which are unusual) clearly portend economic weakness. Consequently, interest rates would fall and lead to a drop in the demand for the dollar (pushing down its value in the foreign exchange market).

Watch Out For: Special factors which can skew growth in personal income come mainly from two government-related sources. Every January, government workers and Social Security recipients receive cost-of-living adjustments. Economists and financial market participants have learned to anticipate these annual adjustments.

Farm income can spurt or plunge in any given month depending on the amount of subsidy payments made by the Commodity Credit Corporation (see box on the CCC in Chapter 2 for more detail). Commerce Department economists know in advance when subsidy payments are allocated and will tell you if you call them. Thus, business economists who regularly forecast economic indicators have a sense about movements in farm income. But surprises can still occur. Always look at farm income as a main source of volatility in total personal income.

As mentioned earlier, natural disasters can skew rental income. Look to this component as a source of volatility as well, in periods of hurricanes and earthquakes.

Finally, when workers of major corporations or industries receive unexpected bonuses, it will boost income in the wages and salaries component. For example, the Clinton Administration's plan to increase taxes on high income individuals caused many corporations to pay out annual bonuses in December 1992 rather than January or February 1993. This caused income to spurt in December, but grow more slowly again early in the year.

Personal Saving Rate

Economists also search for clues of shifts in spending behavior by the personal saving rate, a by-product of the income and consumption data that is released at the same time. Although this rate is an important indicator of the consumer sector, it isn't very reliable on a monthly basis. Personal savings are calculated as a residual; that is, savings are simply the difference between disposable income and personal outlays. (Personal outlays are personal consumption expenditures, interest paid by consumers to business, and transfer payments to foreigners.) Conceptually, it makes sense that whatever isn't spent is saved. However, the use of credit causes the reported saving rate to be understated. For example, automobile purchases are generally financed. However, the Bureau of Economic Analysis enters the full purchase price of the car plus the interest payments amortized over the life of the loan as spending on consumer durables in a specific month. Thus, when auto sales surged in August 1987, the saving rate fell to 3.2 percent from 6.4 percent in January of the same year. In March 1989, auto sales plunged; at the same time wages and salaries were boosted by bonus payments to auto workers. This brought the saving rate to 5.5 percent, its highest level in two years (when it had also been boosted by special factors).

In the same vein, unusual income or tax payments can cause aberrant behavior in the saving rate. In January, when Social Security recipients receive increases in their monthly payments, the saving rate will be higher for a few months until that extra income is absorbed into the spending stream. Conversely, tax payments could lead to reverse behavior. In April 1987, tax payments surged, and the saving rate fell to 1.1 percent for the month.

Market Reaction   Financial market participants don't generally react to the saving rate. Even after accounting for its monthly volatility from its residual status, people can be unsure how to deal with increases or decreases in the saving rate. For example, the saving rate falls when consumers are feeling confident about the economy and are spending fast and furiously. The saving rate will rise when consumers lose confidence in the economy and stop spending. However, it has been argued for quite some time that Americans don't save enough. A rising saving rate can also be associated with increasing investment alternatives. If consumers are saving more and spending less, more money becomes available for lending at lower interest rates, which is favorable for capital investment purposes.

Watch Out For: When the saving rate falls sharply, look for unusual gains in durable goods spending, or a spurt in tax payments. Several factors can cause the saving rate to rise sharply: a decline in durable goods spending, a cost-of-living adjustment in government wages and salaries, a cost-of-living adjustment in Social Security payments, and a jump in tax payments. Since the saving rate is a residual, never take one month's level at face value.

Consumer Installment Credit

The net change in consumer installment credit is reported by the Federal Reserve Board between five and six weeks after the end of the month. This series is based on data from monthly surveys from several sources: monthly surveys of commercial banks, monthly surveys of consumer finance companies, monthly surveys of savings and loan associations (from the Federal Home Loan Bank Board), monthly surveys of credit unions, and monthly surveys of retail sales (from the Bureau of the Census). The joke among traders is that economists frequently must forecast the release date of this indicator as well as its direction. The Fed sets a tentative release date for consumer credit but often revises it at the last minute. The figures are reported in current dollars and on a seasonally adjusted basis. (Unadjusted data are also readily available.) Although from one month to the next, consumer installment credit is revised only marginally, the series undergoes annual benchmark and seasonal adjustment revisions.

Changes in credit outstanding are available by major credit type (auto, revolving, and other), or by major credit holder (commercial banks, finance companies, credit unions, savings institutions, retailers, gasoline companies, pools of securitized assets). Table 3.6 shows the relative importance of each category. Until 1992, mobile home credit was available as a separate category. With the release of the April 1992 figures, the Federal Reserve Board rolled the mobile home credit into the "other" category.

To some extent, the change in consumer installment credit could reflect consumer spending, consumer confidence, and consumer debt burdens, but how does a person distinguish among these factors? Not easily. In the early 1980s, the Fed reported the extension of new credit,

Table 3.6 Consumer Installment Credit
(millions of dollars)

	% of Total		Jan 92	Feb 92	Mar 92	Apr 92	May 92	June 92	July 92
	1989	Current							
Total	100.0	100.0	728,618	728,395	727,404	723,822	722,928	722,650	721,528
Major Credit Type (seasonally adjusted)									
Auto	40.7	35.9	263,134	261,659	262,125	260,376	259,834	257,240	257,761
Revolving	27.8	33.9	244,288	245,974	245,259	245,905	246,220	247,372	247,229
Other	31.5	30.2	221,196	220,762	220,020	217,541	216,874	218,038	216,538
Major Credit Holder (not seasonally adjusted)									
Commercial banks	47.0	45.3	335,320	330,464	327,697	326,205	324,791	324,171	323,790
Finance companies	19.1	16.3	119,206	120,280	118,353	118,364	116,138	116,690	116,968
Credit unions	12.8	12.7	91,894	91,469	91,164	91,339	91,605	92,237	92,054
Savings institutions	7.9	5.1	39,448	38,479	37,142	36,499	36,224	35,618	35,084
Retailers	6.1	5.4	41,567	40,015	39,454	39,553	37,824	37,438	37,219
Gasoline companies	0.5	0.6	4,377	4,151	3,988	4,094	4,193	4,360	4,506
Pools of securitized assets	6.7	14.5	101,482	101,024	103,293	102,622	107,645	109,064	108,655

Source: Federal Reserve Bulletin, November 1992, Board of Governors of the Federal Reserve System, Washington, DC.

and the liquidation of old credit to reflect a net change in total consumer installment credit. In that case, an increase in extensions would surely indicate increases in consumer spending and probably a degree of consumer confidence. Individuals would extend their credit obligations only if they anticipated being able to repay their debts. A slowdown or decline in liquidations (repayments) would suggest that consumer incomes were being stretched to their limit and a drop in spending might soon follow. Unfortunately, the Federal Reserve Board was unable to continue to publish this detail and has reported only the net change in consumer installment credit for several years. That leaves market participants with the problem of having to *assume* that changes in credit are due to more credit usage (and greater spending) or a drop in repayments. (As the saying goes, economists are quite adept at making assumptions.)

For the most part, when consumer credit increases, it suggests gains in consumer spending and a sense of optimism about the economy. This will happen during economic expansions. When consumer credit decreases, it suggests decreased consumer spending, possibly coupled with a sense of pessimism about future economic activity. This often happens during recessions. Without the breakdown on extensions and liquidations of credit, it is necessary to look at the consumer installment credit data in conjunction with other economic indicators for better analysis. For example, increases in consumer credit coupled with increases in auto sales and retail sales clearly point to consumer optimism and healthy economic activity. Conversely, if retail sales and auto sales decline, but consumer credit increases, consumers may not be repaying their debt as rapidly. It could signal lackluster economic activity along with some cautious consumer behavior. Finally, declines in consumer credit coupled with increases in retail sales or auto sales, suggest that consumers are repaying their loans more rapidly than they are undertaking new loans. This could also indicate squeamishness about the economy.

Another measure that can be helpful in interpreting changes in credit outstanding is the ratio of consumer installment credit to disposable income, more commonly known as the debt-to-income ratio. (The terms *consumer credit* and *consumer debt* are used interchangeably.) The debt-to-income ratio will rise during an expansion as consumers feel comfortable about their future financial obligations and increase their spending on credit. The debt-to-income ratio will stabilize or decline during recessions as consumer spending, especially on durable goods, falls sharply. However, as a Federal Reserve study points out, changes in the debt-to-income ratio do not have a simple relation to changes in the circumstances of individual households. Using the 1983 and 1986 Surveys of Consumer Finances, Federal Reserve analysts found that many households faced changing debt burdens over time: Those families with heavy debt burdens in 1983 had lightened their burdens by 1986, whereas those families with light debt burdens in 1983 had heavier burdens in 1986.[8] As shown in Figure 3.3, the debt-to-income ratio was on a rising trend throughout this period, not reflecting this behavior at all.

Consumer installment credit has shown an increasing trend over time. Studies by the Federal Reserve Board revealed this pattern is mainly due to the increased usage of installment credit for convenience. Often, consumers pay their balance in full each month. Demographics is another factor that likely has increased the use of consumer credit. The life-cycle theory of consumer spending states that consumers spend more in the early years of their life and less in the later years. At the same time, the slower income growth in the earlier years means that current income flows do not meet consumption demands. As a result, consumers finance the gap by borrowing. During the 1970s and 1980s, baby boomers came on the market to spend

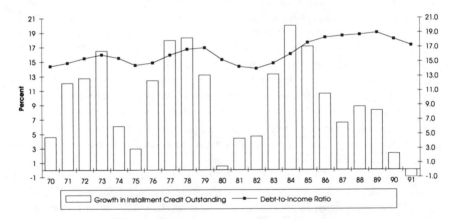

Figure 3.3 Consumer installment credit declined in 1991 for the first time in more than 30 years (although only 20 years are depicted on this chart.) Note the cyclical behavior of consumer installment credit growth—with significant moderation in years of recession. Despite the downward trend in the debt-to-income ratio, it remains high by historical standards. (*Source:* Data are from Commerce Department and Federal Reserve publications.)

and borrow. The use of consumer installment credit skyrocketed during those two decades. The 1986 Survey of Consumer Finances confirmed this view. Families whose heads were aged 25 to 55, had the highest usage of consumer credit along with the highest payment levels. In addition, the theory states that earnings peak in the middle years of an individual's lifetime, which allows savings for retirement and repayment of debt. Nonetheless, consumer spending growth continues its upward path during this period. Consequently, many households who are using consumer installment credit may very well have the financial assets to more than cover their debt burdens. Looking at the debt-to-income ratio alone obscures this fact.

Despite the rising secular trend, consumer installment credit is sensitive to the business cycle. Barring any special factors, such as the 1980 credit controls instituted by the Fed, credit outstanding will increase when the economy is expanding and will decrease (or increase at a slower rate) when the economy is in recession. This behavior is more easily explained by looking at the major types of installment credit: auto, revolving, and other (which includes mobile homes). If consumers are purchasing fewer durable goods, such as cars, during a recession, then consumer installment credit will also decline. As Table 3.6 shows, auto credit makes up 36 percent of consumer credit outstanding. A decline in retail sales, which includes furniture and other household appliances, would point to a drop in revolving credit, too. However, revolving credit may not decline since consumers might repay less of their monthly debt even if they are making fewer purchases during a recession. It is unclear how the catchall "other" category should behave because it includes loans for mobile homes, education, boats, vacations, recreational vehicles, motorcycles, tax payments, and home improvements along with loans that are not collateralized at all. On the surface, at least part of the "other" category representing discretionary items—mobile homes, boats, vacations, recreational vehicles, and motorcycles—seems to indicate a decline in credit during a recession.

Market Reaction   Financial market participants don't usually react to this economic indicator. It is old news by the time it is reported, having followed all the other consumer indicators. Other economic indicators would have already revealed whether the economy was in an expansionary or contractionary phase during the month. Also, the indicator is usually reported late in the afternoon and generally goes unnoticed by market participants, who are getting ready to go home.

Did You Know?   Financial market participants may ignore this figure, but many economists don't. *New York Times* reporter Robert Hershey surveyed several economists and asked them which "offbeat" indicators they monitored.[9] Three of the nine economists cited some form of consumer credit as an indicator to watch. No other indicator was mentioned more than once.

First Chicago's Chief Economist, James Annable claimed that increases in the bank's credit card operations (revolving credit) in the months following the stock market crash of 1987 reassured him that the crash would not lead to a recession.

Using a variation of this indicator, Sears economist Carolyn Scott monitors the ratio of net credit change to disposable personal income. According to Ms. Scott, this gauge tends to show smaller movements when approaching economic peaks and troughs. She said that it flashed caution signals in 1989.

Another variation is used by James F. Smith, a University of North Carolina professor. He monitors the change in nonauto credit as an indicator of discretionary purchases.

Consumer Sentiment

Two private institutions undertake monthly surveys of consumer confidence: (1) the Conference Board and (2) the University of Michigan Survey Research Center. The Conference Board releases its information on the last Tuesday of the month, whereas the Survey Research Center reports on the first day of the month. There is one caveat. The University of Michigan Survey Research Center reports preliminary interim results to its clients on a confidential basis at mid-month. Usually, the results are leaked to the press and become common knowledge among financial market participants.

You might think that consumer sentiment is consumer sentiment and the two measures of consumer confidence should be identical. Actually, the two surveys are somewhat different in their approaches as well as in their technical calculation. In general, consumers are asked about their current attitudes toward the economy as well as their opinions about the outlook for the economy 6 or 12 months hence. In addition, they are asked if they intend to invest in housing or to purchase such major items as cars and household appliances. The Conference Board's Consumer Confidence Index and the Index of Consumer

Sentiment produced by the Survey Research Center at the University of Michigan tend to move together over the business cycle. The series will diverge at economic peaks, however, with the Conference Board series posting greater confidence. Conference Board economist, Fabian Linden attributes the high level of consumer confidence in the 1987 to mid-1990 period to low unemployment rates. When the economy fell into recession in 1990, the Consumer Confidence Index fell more sharply than the University of Michigan's Index of Consumer Sentiment because of its question on employment in the current period as well as employment prospects in the future period.

University of Michigan Survey The Survey Research Center at the University of Michigan has conducted the Surveys of Consumers since 1946. Initially, the Surveys were annual events, soon became quarterly, and since 1978 have been conducted monthly. Each month, the survey contains 25 core questions that cover three broad areas of consumer sentiment: (1) personal finances, (2) business conditions, and (3) buying conditions. The population samples are designed to be representative of all U.S. households except Alaska and Hawaii. Every month, the Survey Research Center interviews 500 consumers by telephone. The scores of questions are summarized so as to develop three indexes: the Index of Consumer Sentiment, the Index of Consumer Expectations, and the Index of Current Economic Conditions.

The Index of Consumer Sentiment is derived from the following five questions:[10]

1. We are interested in how people are getting along financially these days. Would you say that you (and your family living there) are *better off* or *worse off* financially than you were *a year ago?*

2. Now looking ahead—do you think that *a year from now* you (and your family living there) will be *better off* financially, or *worse off*, or just about the same as now?

3. Now turning to business conditions in the country as a whole—do you think that during the *next twelve months* we'll have *good* times financially, or *bad* times, or what?

4. Looking ahead, which would you say is more likely—that in the country as a whole we'll have continuous good times during the *next five years* or so, or that we will have periods of widespread *un*employment or depression, or what?

5. About the big things people buy for their homes—such as furniture, a refrigerator, stove, television, and things like that. Generally speaking, do you think now is a *good* or *bad* time for people to buy major household items?

The Index of Current Economic Conditions uses Questions 1 and 5; the Index of Consumer Expectations uses Questions 2, 3, and 4. The Survey's three main indexes are based to the year 1966 = 100. The Index of Consumer Expectations is one of the 11 series in the Commerce Department's Index of Leading Indicators.

Some of the questions asked by the Survey Research Center concern consumer expectations of interest rates, unemployment, consumer price inflation, assessments of changes in the national economy, buying conditions for homes, and buying attitudes for motor vehicles (cars and light trucks). According to their own research, correlations between the consumer expectations and the actual figures are at least 0.75, and sometimes higher. This means that the survey series and the actual data move together 75 percent of the time. Typically, consumer expectations lead the actual data by roughly two quarters. With respect to the national economy, there was no lead time.[11]

Conference Board Surveys   The Conference Board surveys, *Consumer Attitudes* and *Buying Plans*, were first produced in 1967, on a bimonthly basis; in 1977 they switched to a monthly basis. The Conference Board survey is 10 times larger than the University of Michigan's Survey covering a representative sample of 5,000 households. The survey is conducted by NFO Research, Inc., of Connecticut, which mails a questionnaire to an entirely different sample of individuals each month, representing all geographic regions, age groups, and income levels. The survey consists of two segments. One segment reflects consumers' appraisal of current conditions and their expectations of the future. Three series come from these questions: the Consumer Confidence Index, the Present Situation Index, and the Expectations Index. Another section deals with plans to buy homes, autos, and major household appliances yielding the Buying Plans Index as well as the percentage of households intending to make such purchases the next six months. The Conference Board also releases separately consumer confidence information for nine major geographic regions. The Conference Board uses a base year of 1985 = 100. In contrast to the Michigan Survey, the Conference Board seasonally adjusts all the statistical series included in its survey.

The Consumer Confidence Index combines an appraisal of the present situation along with an appraisal of conditions six months in the future. For the Present Situations Index, consumers are asked questions regarding business conditions and employment: Are jobs plentiful; are jobs not plentiful; are jobs hard to get? The Expectations Index asks the same questions about business conditions and employment and adds a question about income: Will business conditions be the same, better or worse in six months? Will there be more jobs, fewer jobs, or the same number of jobs six months in the future? Do you expect your income to increase, decrease, or remain the same in six months?

The Buying Plans Index includes plans to buy automobiles, homes, or appliances. Consumers are also asked whether they intend to take a vacation within the next six months. It makes sense to ask consumers about their plans to buy durable goods because these are relatively infrequent purchases. Similarly, vacations are generally high-expense items that require some planning (even though the expenditure would probably be classified under the services portion of consumption expenditures). Vacation plans are not incorporated in the Buying Plans Index. The home purchase component is weighted half as much as the intentions to buy cars or home appliances because of its greater volatility.

Consumer confidence is a coincident indicator of the economy. Typically, consumers feel confident about the economy during an expansion and pessimistic about the economy during a recession. According to Fabian Linden of the Conference Board, the Confidence Index "only suggests the general direction and approximate degree of likely changes, but not the precise magnitude. . . . it also fails to indicate with any precision the time frame of changes."[12] Thus, the claim by some economists that consumer confidence can predict consumer spending on a month-to-month basis is not supported by the expert opinion of the architect of these series. Fabian Linden of the Conference Board states that the Buying Plans Index "has failed to demonstrate a convincing capacity to forecast consumer demand for specific products included with a consistency sufficiently reliable to allow for marketing decision-making."[13] Furthermore, he claims "the aggregate buying intentions index should be considered only as a broad gauge of general shifts in the consumers' disposition to spend."[14]

When consumer spending and consumer confidence are plotted on the same chart, they are likely to show similar dips and wiggles as a trend. A more detailed monthly chart will show that they do not move in tandem or by the same magnitude every month (see Figure 3.4).

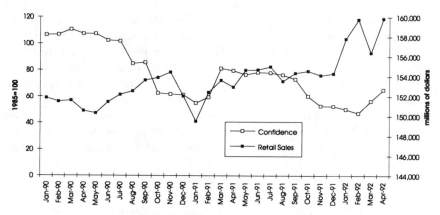

Figure 3.4   Although there are some similar behavioral trends between confidence and spending, the Conference Board Confidence Index cannot predict month-to-month changes in retail sales. *(Source: Market News Service, Inc., Survey of Current Business.)*

The consumer confidence series were quite fashionable in the financial markets in 1990 and 1991. Most likely, this was because Fed Chairman Greenspan cited them once or twice as indicators that he monitors. When a Federal Reserve chairman talks, market participants listen.

Watch Out For: Every monthly change in the consumer confidence numbers will not be mirrored in the actual spending figures such as retail sales, personal consumption expenditures, or housing starts. Thus, look at the trend in the direction of the consumer confidence series rather than at just a one-month change. Moreover, both the Index of Consumer Sentiment (Michigan Survey) as well as the Consumer Confidence Index (Conference Board) tend to move in similar directions over time but may diverge in any one month. The Conference Board series tends to increase more rapidly at business cycle peaks when employment prospects improve. Also, the Conference Board surveys an entirely different group of individuals each month. The consistency wouldn't be the same as in the Michigan Survey, which talks to the same group each month.

Wait for actual spending data to cement your views on the economy. True confidence shows up at the cash register, either at a department store or at the auto dealer.

Market Reaction In the past few years, the markets have reacted strongly to consumer confidence surveys. This reaction is similar to that of actual consumer spending. Bond traders favor a drop in consumer confidence because it signals a weaker economy and points to lower bond yields (but higher bond prices). Conversely, the bond prices will drop (and yields will rise) if consumer confidence increases.

Participants in the stock market don't favor a drop in consumer confidence because that means lower corporate profits. Lower corporate earnings should lead to a dip in the stock market.

A pessimistic consumer won't make a foreign exchange market participant happy either. Pessimism signals a weak economy and low interest rates, leading to a drop in the value of the dollar. An optimistic consumer is favorable in that interest rates will rise and the demand for dollars will rise, pushing up the foreign exchange value of the dollar.

Key Points

- Some consumer indicators are more volatile than others. It is always preferable to analyze the trend in the series rather than a one-month change.
- A strong consumer sector signals a healthy economy, which can lead to inflation and higher interest rates.
- Consumer indicators that point to robust spending are bearish for the fixed-income market; bullish for the stock market; and favor a strong exchange value of the dollar.
- Consumer indicators that point to sluggish spending are bullish for the fixed-income market; bearish for the stock market; and unfavorable for the foreign exchange value of the dollar.
- Personal consumption expenditures are the most comprehensive and appropriate indicator of consumer spending when you are monitoring just one indicator.
- Personal income is the indicator most likely to reflect consistent consumer behavior over time.
- Personal consumption expenditures and personal income are *not* the indicators of choice for financial market participants who tend to favor high-frequency indicators.
- Table 3.7 summarizes the consumer indicators, their approximate dates of release, and source agencies.

Table 3.7 Indicators of Consumer Spending

| | Approximate | | | |
Month	Day	Indicator	Data for	Source Agency
Jan	1 to 3	Middle 10-day auto sales	Dec 11–20	Ward's Communications, Inc.
	3 to 9	Chain store sales	Dec	Various stores
	3 to 6	Late 10-day and monthly auto sales	Dec	Ward's Automotive
	Every Thurs	Johnson Redbook Index	Wk end previous Sat	Lynch, Jones & Ryan
	6 to 9	Consumer installment credit	Nov	Federal Reserve Board
	11 to 15	Retail sales	Dec	Bureau of the Census
	13 to 15	Early 10-day auto sales	Jan 1–10	Ward's Communications, Inc.
	23 to 26	Middle 10-day auto sales	Jan 11–20	Ward's Communications, Inc.
	Last Tues	Consumer confidence	Jan	Conference Board
	23 to 1	Personal income	Dec	Bureau of Economic Analysis
	23 to 1	Personal consumption expenditures	Dec	Bureau of Economic Analysis
	23 to 1	Personal saving rate	Dec	Bureau of Economic Analysis
	Last day	Consumer sentiment	Jan	Univ. of Michigan Survey Center
Feb	3 to 9	Chain store sales	Jan	Various stores
	3 to 6	Late 10-day and monthly auto sales	Jan	Ward's Communications, Inc.
	Every Thurs	Johnson Redbook Index	Wk end previous Sat	Lynch, Jones & Ryan
	6 to 9	Consumer installment credit	Dec	Federal Reserve Board
	11 to 15	Retail sales	Jan	Bureau of the Census
	13 to 15	Early 10-day auto sales	Feb 1–10	Ward's Communications, Inc.
	23 to 26	Middle 10-day auto sales	Feb 11–20	Ward's Communications, Inc.
	Last Tues	Consumer confidence	Feb	Conference Board
	23 to 1	Personal income	Jan	Bureau of Economic Analysis
	23 to 1	Personal consumption expenditures	Jan	Bureau of Economic Analysis

Table 3.7 *(Continued)*

Month	Approximate Day	Indicator	Data for	Source Agency
Feb	23 to 1	Personal saving rate	Jan	Bureau of Economic Analysis
	Last day	Consumer sentiment	Jan	Univ. of Michigan Survey Center
Mar	3 to 9	Chain store sales	Feb	Various stores
	3 to 6	Late 10-day and monthly auto sales	Feb	Ward's Communications, Inc.
	Every Thurs	Johnson Redbook Index	Wk end previous Sat	Lynch, Jones & Ryan
	6 to 9	Consumer installment credit	Jan	Federal Reserve Board
	11 to 15	Retail sales	Feb	Bureau of the Census
	13 to 15	Early 10-day auto sales	Mar 1–10	Ward's Communications, Inc.
	23 to 26	Middle 10-day auto sales	Mar 11–20	Ward's Communications, Inc.
	Last Tues	Consumer confidence	Mar	Conference Board
	23 to 1	Personal income	Feb	Bureau of Economic Analysis
	23 to 1	Personal consumption expenditures	Feb	Bureau of Economic Analysis
	23 to 1	Personal saving rate	Feb	Bureau of Economic Analysis
	Last day	Consumer sentiment	Mar	Univ. of Michigan Survey Center
Apr	3 to 9	Chain store sales	Mar	Various stores
	3 to 6	Late 10-day and monthly auto sales	Mar	Ward's Communications, Inc.
	Every Thurs	Johnson Redbook Index	Wk end previous Sat	Lynch, Jones & Ryan
	6 to 9	Consumer installment credit	Feb	Federal Reserve Board
	11 to 15	Retail sales	Mar	Bureau of the Census
	13 to 15	Early 10-day auto sales	Apr 1–10	Ward's Communications, Inc.
	23 to 26	Middle 10-day auto sales	Apr 11–20	Ward's Communications, Inc.
	Last Tues	Consumer confidence	Apr	Conference Board
	23 to 1	Personal income	Mar	Bureau of Economic Analysis

Table 3.7 *(Continued)*

Month	Approximate Day	Indicator	Data for	Source Agency
Apr	23 to 1	Personal consumption expenditures	Mar	Bureau of Economic Analysis
	23 to 1	Personal saving rate	Mar	Bureau of Economic Analysis
	Last day	Consumer sentiment	Apr	Univ. of Michigan Survey Center
May	3 to 9	Chain store sales	Apr	Various stores
	3 to 6	Late 10-day and monthly auto sales	Apr	Ward's Communications, Inc.
	Every Thurs	Johnson Redbook Index	Wk end previous Sat	Lynch, Jones & Ryan
	6 to 9	Consumer installment credit	Mar	Federal Reserve Board
	11 to 15	Retail sales	Apr	Bureau of the Census
	13 to 15	Early 10-day auto sales	May 1–10	Ward's Communications, Inc.
	23 to 26	Middle 10-day auto sales	May 11–20	Ward's Communications, Inc.
	Last Tues	Consumer confidence	May	Conference Board
	23 to 1	Personal income	Apr	Bureau of Economic Analysis
	23 to 1	Personal consumption expenditures	Apr	Bureau of Economic Analysis
	23 to 1	Personal saving rate	Apr	Bureau of Economic Analysis
	Last day	Consumer sentiment	May	Univ. of Michigan Survey Center
June	3 to 9	Chain store sales	May	Various stores
	3 to 6	Late 10-day and monthly auto sales	May	Ward's Communications, Inc.
	Every Thurs	Johnson Redbook Index	Wk end previous Sat	Lynch, Jones & Ryan
	6 to 9	Consumer installment credit	Apr	Federal Reserve Board
	11 to 15	Retail sales	May	Bureau of the Census
	13 to 15	Early 10-day auto sales	June 1–10	Ward's Communications, Inc.
	23 to 26	Middle 10-day auto sales	June 11–20	Ward's Communications, Inc.
	Last Tues	Consumer confidence	June	Conference Board

Table 3.7 *(Continued)*

Month	Approximate Day	Indicator	Data for	Source Agency
June	23 to 1	Personal income	May	Bureau of Economic Analysis
	23 to 1	Personal consumption expenditures	May	Bureau of Economic Analysis
	23 to 1	Personal saving rate	May	Bureau of Economic Analysis
	Last day	Consumer sentiment	June	Univ. of Michigan Survey Center
July	3 to 9	Chain store sales	June	Various stores
	3 to 6	Late 10-day and monthly auto sales	June	Ward's Communications, Inc.
	Every Thurs	Johnson Redbook Index	Wk end previous Sat	Lynch, Jones & Ryan
	6 to 9	Consumer installment credit	May	Federal Reserve Board
	11 to 15	Retail sales	June	Bureau of the Census
	13 to 15	Early 10-day auto sales	July 1–10	Ward's Communications, Inc.
	23 to 26	Middle 10-day auto sales	July 11–20	Ward's Communications, Inc.
	Last Tues	Consumer confidence	July	Conference Board
	23 to 1	Personal income	June	Bureau of Economic Analysis
	23 to 1	Personal consumption expenditures	June	Bureau of Economic Analysis
	23 to 1	Personal saving rate	June	Bureau of Economic Analysis
	Last day	Consumer sentiment	July	Univ. of Michigan Survey Center
Aug	3 to 9	Chain store sales	July	Various stores
	3 to 6	Late 10-day and monthly auto sales	July	Ward's Communications, Inc.
	Every Thurs	Johnson Redbook Index	Wk end previous Sat	Lynch, Jones & Ryan
	6 to 9	Consumer installment credit	June	Federal Reserve Board
	11 to 15	Retail sales	July	Bureau of the Census
	13 to 15	Early 10-day auto sales	Aug 1–10	Ward's Communications, Inc.

Table 3.7 *(Continued)*

Approximate				
Month	Day	Indicator	Data for	Source Agency
Aug	23 to 26	Middle 10-day auto sales	Aug 11–20	Ward's Communications, Inc.
	Last Tues	Consumer confidence	Aug	Conference Board
	23 to 1	Personal income	July	Bureau of Economic Analysis
	23 to 1	Personal consumption expenditures	July	Bureau of Economic Analysis
	23 to 1	Personal saving rate	July	Bureau of Economic Analysis
	Last day	Consumer sentiment	Aug	Univ. of Michigan Survey Center
Sep	3 to 9	Chain store sales	Aug	Various stores
	3 to 6	Late 10-day and monthly auto sales	Aug	Ward's Communications, Inc.
	Every Thurs	Johnson Redbook Index	Wk end previous Sat	Lynch, Jones & Ryan
	6 to 9	Consumer installment credit	July	Federal Reserve Board
	11 to 15	Retail sales	Aug	Bureau of the Census
	13 to 15	Early 10-day auto sales	Sep 1–10	Ward's Communications, Inc.
	23 to 26	Middle 10-day auto sales	Sep 11–20	Ward's Communications, Inc.
	Last Tues	Consumer confidence	Sep	Conference Board
	23 to 1	Personal income	Aug	Bureau of the Census
	23 to 1	Personal consumption expenditures	Aug	Bureau of the Census
	23 to 1	Personal saving rate	Aug	Bureau of the Census
	Last day	Consumer sentiment	Sep	Univ. of Michigan Survey Center
Oct	3 to 9	Chain store sales	Sep	Various stores
	3 to 6	Late 10-day and monthly auto sales	Sep	Ward's Communications, Inc.
	Every Thurs	Johnson Redbook Index	Wk end previous Sat	Lynch, Jones & Ryan
	6 to 9	Consumer installment credit	Aug	Federal Reserve Board
	11 to 15	Retail sales	Sep	Bureau of the Census
	13 to 15	Early 10-day auto sales	Oct 1–10	Ward's Communications, Inc.

Table 3.7 *(Continued)*

Month	Approximate Day	Indicator	Data for	Source Agency
Oct	23 to 26	Middle 10-day auto sales	Oct 11–20	Ward's Communications, Inc.
	Last Tues	Consumer confidence	Oct	Conference Board
	23 to 1	Personal income	Sep	Bureau of Economic Analysis
	23 to 1	Personal consumption expenditures	Sep	Bureau of Economic Analysis
	23 to 1	Personal saving rate	Sep	Bureau of Economic Analysis
	Last day	Consumer sentiment	Oct	Univ. of Michigan Survey Center
Nov	3 to 9	Chain store sales	Oct	Various stores
	3 to 6	Late 10-day and monthly auto sales	Oct	Ward's Communications, Inc.
	Every Thurs	Johnson Redbook Index	Wk end previous Sat	Lynch, Jones & Ryan
	6 to 9	Consumer installment credit	Sep	Federal Reserve Board
	11 to 15	Retail sales	Oct	Bureau of the Census
	13 to 15	Early 10-day auto sales	Nov 1–10	Ward's Communications, Inc.
	23 to 26	Middle 10-day auto sales	Nov 11–20	Ward's Communications, Inc.
	Last Tues	Consumer confidence	Nov	Conference Board
	23 to 1	Personal income	Oct	Bureau of the Census
	23 to 1	Personal consumption expenditures	Oct	Bureau of the Census
	23 to 1	Personal saving rate	Oct	Bureau of the Census
	Last day	Consumer sentiment	Nov	Univ. of Michigan Survey Center
Dec	3 to 9	Chain store sales	Nov	Various stores
	3 to 6	Late 10-day and monthly auto sales	Nov	Ward's Communications, Inc.
	Every Thurs	Johnson Redbook Index	Wk end previous Sat	Lynch, Jones & Ryan
	6 to 9	Consumer installment credit	Oct	Federal Reserve Board
	11 to 15	Retail sales	Nov	Bureau of the Census

Table 3.7 *(Continued)*

Month	Approximate Day	Indicator	Data for	Source Agency
Dec	13 to 15	Early 10-day auto sales	Dec 1–10	Ward's Communications, Inc.
	Last Tues	Consumer confidence	Dec	Conference Board
	23 to 1	Personal income	Nov	Bureau of Economic Analysis
	23 to 1	Personal consumption expenditures	Nov	Bureau of Economic Analysis
	23 to 1	Personal saving rate	Nov	Bureau of Economic Analysis
	Last day	Consumer sentiment	Dec	Univ. of Michigan Survey Center

CHAPTER 4

Investment Spending

Featured Indicators   **Advance Durable Goods**
Manufacturers' Shipments,
    Inventories, and Orders
Business Sales and Inventories
Construction Expenditures
Housing Starts and Permits
Sales of New and Existing
    Single-Family Homes
Plant and Equipment Expenditure
    Survey

There are fewer indicators of investment spending than there are of consumer spending because investment spending accounts for only about one-fifth of gross domestic product. Despite its smaller contribution to GDP, investment spending is significant because the volatility inherent in investment spending exacerbates the business cycle. Growth in investment expenditures outpaces GDP growth during a cyclical upswing but also declines more sharply during recessions.

This chapter describes major economic indicators monitored by financial market participants, the media, and policy-making agents in the federal government. Not all indicators get the same amount of attention from the various groups. In general, most of these indicators are not followed as intimately as the consumer indicators.

MONTHLY INDICATORS

There are roughly five (sets of) monthly indicators for investment spending. On the whole, they tend to be less stable than consumer indicators, especially on a monthly basis. It's useful to remember that these are large-ticket items (airplanes, houses, factory plants) that must be financed, not goods that can be paid in cash.

Advance Durable Goods

The Bureau of Census, within the Department of Commerce, produces an advance report of manufacturers' shipments, new orders, and unfilled orders of durable goods about three to four weeks after the end of the month. Shipments, new orders, and unfilled orders are seasonally adjusted and denominated in current dollars. (That is, they are not adjusted for inflation.) Unlike many other economic indicators, the figures are not annualized either: Reported orders and shipments are the monthly levels. For instance, to get an annualized rate, the monthly level would be multiplied by twelve.

These data include (new and unfilled) orders and shipments for such categories as fabricated metals, primary metals, electrical and nonelectrical machinery, and transportation. This report is called "advance" because it is an early release of the manufacturers' shipments, inventories, and orders release including information on nondurable goods as well as durable goods. The revisions of this "advance" report can be significant and might alter the initial economic scenario depicted by the figures. A preliminary estimate might show lackluster performance in the manufacturing sector, whereas the revised data might show a more robust economy. For example, on July 24, 1992, new orders for manufacturers' (advance) durable goods were initially reported to have risen 2.3 percent in June. One week later, the more complete manufacturers' report showed a 2.7 percent gain. On September 2, 1992, figures were released for July, but June data were revised once again to reflect a 2.8 percent rise. The levels of new orders for May had also been revised up, so that June levels were higher by an additional 0.1 percentage point. Thus, between the end of July and the beginning of September, the level of new orders for June was 0.6 percentage points higher than initially reported. This specific example does not show a particularly large revision. Nonetheless, the June rise in durable goods orders was following a decline in May of 2.2 percent. The initial estimate thus showed that the May drop was simply offset by the June rise. However, the subsequent revisions, however, showed that the rise in orders in June more than offset the decline, possibly pointing to an upward trend in the series.

The durable goods report is divided into broad categories such as defense and nondefense goods; capital goods and noncapital goods; nondefense capital goods and defense capital goods. Nondefense capital goods, including such diverse items as blast furnaces and computers, are an indicator of capital spending. Noncapital goods are generally of the household variety: automobiles, refrigerators, and other appliances. As mentioned in Chapter 2, however, automobiles are classified in all sectors of GDP including capital spending. Portions of new and unfilled orders for durable goods are included in the Commerce Department's Index of Leading Indicators.

New orders for durable goods orders jump around from month to month, as shown in Figure 4.1. Economists often joke that it's easy to forecast durable goods orders: See what happened last month and reverse the sign. During economic expansions, the declines are smaller than the increases, and during recessions, the declines are larger than the gains. The main reason for this erratic pattern of behavior is that durable goods orders include many sectors, such as transportation equipment, in which the order of even one piece of equipment is so large that an absence or

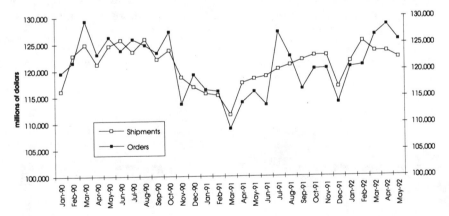

Figure 4.1 This chart depicts monthly levels of orders and shipments of manufacturers' durable goods. Note how the trend in shipments tends to be somewhat more stable than the trend in orders. (*Source:* Data are from Department of Commerce publications.)

noncontinuation of that order is noticeable. The transportation category, for example, includes military and civilian aircraft which are high-dollar items. Moreover, when placing such orders, companies generally purchase more than one plane at a time. If 20 planes are ordered in February, for example, and no airplanes are ordered in March, February orders will surge, but March orders will plummet.

Economists prefer to exclude volatile components from series and analyze the series excluding that component. Over the course of several years, economists have persuaded financial market participants and the financial press to look at durable goods orders excluding transportation; durable goods orders excluding defense; nondefense capital goods orders; and nondefense capital goods orders excluding aircraft. All these categories exclude the most unstable components to clarify the underlying trend of investment demand (see Figure 4.2).

Shipments of durable goods can be divided into the same categories as orders. Whereas the orders are leading indicators of production three to six months hence, the shipments are indicators of current production and sales of manufactured goods. Shipments tend to be more stable than orders. Companies can order multiple products, but producers make them one at a time. Thus, an order for 20 airplanes gets spread over many months in terms of production so that shipments may reflect the delivery of one airplane at a time.

Unfilled orders don't always attract attention, even among economists. When unfilled orders are rising, it suggests that manufacturers

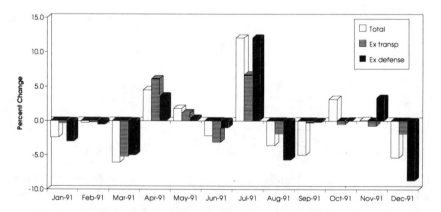

Figure 4.2 The three series of orders give very different pictures of manufacturing activity. (*Source:* Data are from Commerce Department publications.)

are busy and aren't producing fast enough to keep pace with incoming orders. On the other hand, a falling level of unfilled orders suggests that manufacturers are producing more quickly than new orders are coming in. Unfilled orders tend to rise when the economy is expanding and to decline when the economy is contracting. The level of unfilled orders never goes down to zero; a backlog exists even during a recession. Luckily, production doesn't have to come to a complete halt during a recession even though the pace of production can fall dramatically, because manufacturers work down their unfilled orders.

It is ironic that the series for new orders of durable goods is the one that gets the most attention (relative to shipments and unfilled orders), because it is calculated as a residual. New orders are computed from figures on unfilled orders (which are net of cancellations) and shipments. Technically, the Census Bureau begins with the level of unfilled orders at the end of the current month; it adds shipments for the month; it subtracts unfilled orders for the previous month. The remainder is equal to new orders for the month.

Market Reaction Strictly speaking, fixed-income market participants will consider a rise in orders and shipments indicative of economic strength; a decline in durable orders and shipments signals weakness. As a result, strong orders and shipments lead to rising interest rates, whereas weak orders and shipments portend lower rates. Shipments are much less relevant to the markets than orders, however, because shipments represent present conditions and orders represent future conditions. Financial market professionals are future oriented.

Equity market players, along with foreign exchange market professionals, prefer economic strength over weakness and would favor strong durable orders over declines in the series. Those in the stock market are looking for growth in corporate profits, whereas those in the foreign exchange market are looking to push up the foreign exchange value of the dollar on rising interest rates. A decline in orders could lower the value of the dollar if interest rates fall. Economic growth is unfavorable to fixed-income market professionals because it either signals inflationary pressures (during economic expansions) or the end of Federal Reserve easing (during recoveries). Neither foreign exchange or equity market professionals want to see economic growth accompanied by inflation. But, foreign exchange professionals tend to prefer high interest rates, so they would be relieved to see the end of a period of Federal Reserve easing.

Financial market participants certainly know that durable goods orders move in a sawtooth pattern. Since economists have bombarded them with various exclusions to keep in mind, market participants also realize that they could look at subcomponents of the report. As a result, the market reaction to durable goods orders is often inconsistent. That is, sometimes the markets will trade on these figures and sometimes they won't. It depends on their *mood.* If the market psychology is negative (bond prices are falling, bond yields are rising), fixed-income market professionals may view a rise in durable goods orders negatively using the rise in orders to confirm their views of a strong economy. If market psychology is positive (bond prices are rising, bond yields are falling), they will ignore a gain in durable goods orders and cite their inherent volatility. Whenever possible, they will point to the portion of the report confirming their view: total orders excluding transportation; total orders excluding defense; orders of nondefense capital goods.

Watch Out For: Analyze the advance report for special factors. Defense orders are typically erratic even if they are generally following a downward trend or an upward trend. Check these first. You really want to see how the private economy is growing. Defense spending depends on fiscal policy. You can get a better feel of fiscal policy by looking at the federal budget balance. If the unusual spurt or plunge in durable orders is not due to defense, check the transportation sector for aircraft orders. Market participants remove these, not because they are meaningless, but because they tend to be uneven. It's unusual to see aircraft orders rise continuously month after month: It's just not a sustainable pattern. Even though aircraft orders were generally strong between 1985 through 1990, with the greatest level of orders in 1989, increases did not occur in each and every month during that five-year trend.

For the most part, durable goods orders are a good indicator of future production and shipments—with one exception. New orders, shipments, and production of automobiles occur simultaneously in the same month. Because data on the production of autos are available before the advance durable goods release, there is less interest in orders and shipments of cars than of items in other categories. Since autos are in the transportation category, this is another good reason to exclude transportation from the total.

At a secondary level of importance, determine whether the increase in total orders was concentrated in consumer durable goods or capital equipment. Both sectors help the manufacturing sector when they are in an increasing mode and hurt the manufacturing sector when they are in a declining mode. However, investment type goods can expand the production capacity of the United States, essentially increasing the nation's economic pie. Put differently, increases in investment can raise our standard of living in the long run. In that case, you would prefer to see increases in nondefense capital goods over increases in noncapital goods because the noncapital goods are consumer goods for current consumption. Also, be sure you compare shipments and unfilled orders in addition to the new orders category.

Ignore durable goods orders on a one-month basis. Rather than analyze the figure monthly, it is more prudent to analyze the figures over a three-month period. If you do look at the long-term trend of orders and shipments, then do *not* exclude the volatile categories such as aircraft, because they also add to domestic production and economic growth. Put the durable goods report in a broader perspective by comparing these figures with other economic indicators, such as industrial production or the purchasing managers' index. In a April 17, 1988 *New York Times* article featuring indicators that economists love to hate, economist Lacy Hunt, described the report as "doubtable goods."

Manufacturers' Shipments, Inventories, and Orders

About one week after the advance (and partial) report on durable goods, the Census Bureau releases the entire report on manufacturers' goods. The monthly survey of manufacturers has a response rate of roughly 55 percent. This complete report includes figures on nondurable goods as well as durable goods. Nondurable goods, which make up roughly half the total, don't tend to be as unstable as durable goods. No single category in the nondurable goods component could cause a monthly spike such as that caused by aircraft orders. Petroleum, however, is a nondurable goods category that could cause monthly fluctuations, in nominal terms, because of price changes. As shown in Table 4.1, new orders and unfilled orders of detailed nondurable goods categories are not officially published. Table 4.1 shows volatile shipments for tobacco products and petroleum and coal products over this three-month time period. This volatility in tobacco products is not meaningful due to the small weight attributed to the category.

In the past, the component "nondefense capital goods" was the closest category aligned with the producers' durable equipment portion of GDP. Consequently, economists put it on the "watch list." Approximately in 1991, the Census Bureau began publishing a series of orders

Table 4.1 Manufacturers' Orders, Shipments, and Inventories

	Relative Importance 1991*	New Orders (% change)			Shipments (% change)			Inventories (% change)			Unfilled Orders (% change)		
		Dec 91	Nov 91	Oct 91	Dec 91	Nov 91	Oct 91	Dec 91	Nov 91	Oct 91	Dec 91	Nov 91	Oct 91
All Manufacturing Industries	100.0	-3.7	0.1	2.1	-3.4	0.0	0.9	-0.6	-0.1	-0.3	-0.6	-0.5	-0.5
Durable goods	50.4	-5.3	0.1	3.2	-4.8	0.0	0.7	-0.9	-0.2	-0.6	-0.6	-0.5	-0.5
Stone, clay, and glass	2.0	3.1	-8.2	-0.7	-1.8	-0.6	-1.8	0.1	1.2	-0.6	0.0	-3.4	2.4
Primary metals	4.6	-5.3	0.1	-2.3	-2.1	-0.9	-0.7	-1.2	-0.9	-0.7	-2.1	-0.6	-1.1
Fabricated metals	5.6	-3.1	0.4	2.0	-4.0	0.4	2.5	-1.3	0.3	-0.1	-0.3	-0.8	-0.8
Machinery and equipment	8.6	-2.9	0.6	-4.8	-3.6	0.7	1.0	-1.7	-0.9	-0.3	-1.0	-1.3	-1.2
Electronic machinery	7.1	2.9	1.5	1.9	-0.1	1.9	-0.2	-0.7	-0.3	-0.6	0.9	-0.3	-0.2
Transportation	12.9	-14.8	2.4	15.1	-11.4	-2.2	1.5	-1.2	0.3	-1.1	-0.4	0.0	-0.6
Instruments and products	4.4	-6.0	-10.8	4.7	-3.0	1.1	1.0	0.3	-1.0	-0.4	-2.5	-2.1	0.1
Nondurable Goods	49.6	-2.0	0.0	1.0	-2.0	0.0	1.1	0.0	0.2	0.4	0.6	0.7	0.8
Food and kindred products	13.7	not available			-1.2	0.7	0.6	0.0	0.1	1.0	not available		
Tobacco products	1.1	not available			-21.5	17.2	-3.0	2.8	-3.1	0.1	not available		
Textile mill products	2.4	not available			-1.5	-1.4	1.2	0.4	-1.4	0.2	not available		
Paper and allied products	4.4	not available			0.5	-1.2	-0.4	0.2	0.6	1.3	not available		
Chemicals and allied products	10.2	not available			-0.5	-2.2	0.9	0.1	0.9	0.3	not available		
Petroleum and coal products	5.7	not available			-6.0	1.0	2.9	-3.7	0.5	-3.1	not available		
Rubber and plastic products	3.7	not available			-1.7	-2.1	0.6	-0.6	0.2	0.1	not available		
Special Categories													
Nondefense capital goods	13.0	-18.4	12.3	2.4	-7.0	0.4	1.9	-0.6	-0.1	-0.7	-1.0	0.6	-0.9
Nondefense cap goods excluding aircraft	10.6	-2.1	-0.4	-3.3	-3.7	0.1	1.0	-0.7	-1.2	-1.0	-0.8	-0.3	-0.6
Producers durable equipment	31.3	-10.8	2.1	1.5	-6.5	-0.1	1.9	-0.6	0.1	-0.4	-1.1	0.3	-0.4

*Based on shipments.

Source: Bureau of the Census, Department of Commerce. *Manufacturers' Shipments, Inventories, and Orders: 1982–1991* (Current Industrial Reports) June 1992.

and shipments called "producers' durable equipment," which align closely with the quarterly GDP component also called "producers' durable equipment." This series is a better indicator of the GDP component than the nondefense capital goods series that was formerly used. Although it still doesn't have the following attracted by the nondefense capital goods classification, it is a better indicator of capital spending in terms of its relationship to GDP. Thus, monthly shipments of producers' durable equipment closely approximate the category of the same name reported in current quarter GDP and provide a good clue on the amount of capital spending for equipment that actually shows up in GDP. Moreover, the orders version also does a good job of predicting future gains in producers' durable equipment in the next quarter or two. Because gross domestic product is measured in real (inflation-adjusted) terms, it is necessary to adjust the monthly shipments and orders data for price fluctuations as well.

In addition to a more complete and detailed report of shipments, new orders, and unfilled orders, the manufacturers release also includes data on inventories. Inventories tend to grow with the economy, accelerating with healthy sales growth and moderating with slower sales demands. The key factor in inventory investment is to distinguish between intended and unintended inventory buildup. One way to monitor inventories is to look at the relationship between inventories and sales. Otherwise, there is no way of knowing whether the current inventory buildup is sufficient for the current pace of sales. The inventory-to-sales ratio is a common indicator of inventory management that provides this perspective. A rising inventory-to-sales ratio in an expanding economy can be viewed favorably; whereas a rising ratio during a recession signals production cutbacks.

Market participants can monitor inventories by stage of fabrication: materials and supplies, work-in-process, and finished goods. They each account for roughly one-third of total inventories. A sharp and sustained rise in inventories of finished goods can signal unintended inventory accumulation coming from a decline in consumer demand.

Market Reaction Typically, financial market participants will keep their eyes on the durable goods orders data reported in the previous week. It is not unusual to see revisions to the figures even after only one week. As shown in an earlier example, durable goods orders were initially reported to rise 2.3 percent in June but were revised one week later to show a 2.7 percent gain.

Once again, shipments will get less attention. Market participants will watch unfilled orders, but only to justify their positions. Economists tend to be more vigilant of the unfilled orders series. New orders are a residual based on actual unfilled orders data, so it would make sense to pay greater attention to unfilled orders.

Financial market participants tend to look at the inventory data at turning points in the economy. If the economy is expanding and demand is rising, then increases in inventories point to continued growth and signal a desired buildup. If the economy is contracting and demand is falling, then increases in inventories point to an undesired buildup. Traders in the fixed-income market will rally the bond market whenever they see signs of economic contraction (bond prices will rise, yields will fall) because it could signal the beginning of some Federal Reserve easing moves. In contrast, they don't like signs of healthy economic growth (bond prices will fall, yields will rise) because the Fed will stop easing when the economy shows clear signs of upward momentum. Also, inflationary pressures could potentially arise.

Players in the equity market much prefer economic growth because it spurs corporate earnings. As a result, stock prices will increase when

---

Watch Out For: Check for revisions to durable goods orders and shipments. If either is rising or falling by 5 or 10 percent, a revision of 1 percent will not be meaningful, so don't worry about it. However, if orders or shipments only moved 1 percent in either direction, a revision to that extent is certainly significant. In addition, look at the pattern or trend of growth in orders. It is interesting how convention determines the mode of analyzing figures. Headlines reported on the news wire services will release the percent change in orders, shipments, and inventories. With inventories and unfilled orders, that's fine because the series tend toward some stability from month to month. With respect to the trend growth rate in new orders, it would be more beneficial to see a three-month moving average of the level. Monthly growth rates are too volatile to be meaningful.

Look at the inventory-to-sales ratio to see if there are signs of unintended stockpiling. The inventory-to-sales ratio will rise as shipments moderate. One-month changes are not significant, but look for developing trends.

orders, shipments, and inventories are rising. Foreign exchange market professionals also like to see healthy economic growth because interest rates will rise and the foreign exchange value of the dollar will tend to increase. Thus, the value of the dollar will rise with increases in shipments, inventories, and orders. If increased growth in the manufacturing sector is accompanied by inflation, neither stock prices nor the foreign exchange value of the dollar are likely to rise.

Business Sales and Inventories

The Bureau of the Census reports business sales and inventories about six weeks after the end of the month. Business sales are the sum of manufacturing, retail trade, and wholesale trade figures that have already been reported earlier in that month. Consequently, the sales portion of this release is old news. Parts of the business inventories figures are new, however. Manufacturing inventories are reported as discussed earlier. Wholesale trade inventories are reported about five weeks after the end of the month. Financial market participants ignore these figures and generally economists ignore them as well. Retail trade inventories are reported for the first time with this release. They correspond to the retail sales data discussed in Chapter 3.

Market Reaction   The market reaction to this report is mild, although at business cycle turning points, the markets will react to business inventories. Inventory accumulation during a sluggish economic period suggests producers will have to unload unwanted inventories and production will suffer. Declines in production are favorable news for the bond market participant because they indicate possible recession and lower interest rates. Production declines are not favorable news to stock market participants nor to foreign exchange players looking for a strong dollar. A weak economy means lackluster earnings. Low interest rates indicate capital flows to the United States will be reduced and a drop in demand for the dollar will ensue.

Inventory liquidation portends future rebuilding of inventories and increases in production. Bond market participants will not be happy as interest rates climb while bond prices sag. In contrast, stock market players will view the potential rise in production favorably as corporate earnings move upward. Similarly, foreign exchange players favor the potential for upward momentum in the economy and in the dollar.

Watch Out For: At this point, most data in this report have been analyzed and taken apart several times. It's hard to find new quirks. The only portion of the release that is new relates to retail trade inventories, so look at the breakdown between total retail inventories and retail inventories excluding autos. A large auto buildup could portend a drop in auto production or possible rebates in the offing.

The only other time this report is interesting is after the Bureau of Economic Analysis has reported a preliminary estimate of GDP. The initial estimate includes an estimate for inventories. Once you know the BEA assumptions for inventory change and the actual monthly inventory change, you can estimate the potential revision to the GDP estimate that will be forthcoming in the next scheduled release.

Construction Expenditures

The Bureau of the Census reports construction expenditures about five weeks after the end of the month. These data are revised dramatically in subsequent months (significantly more than durable goods orders) and move easily from the positive to the negative and back again to the positive camp with each monthly revision. Just like durable goods orders, construction expenditures are more descriptive when they are broken down into smaller categories: private residential construction, private nonresidential construction, and public construction, such as highways and streets, and military facilities. (The public sector will be discussed in Chapter 6.) As shown in Table 4.2, this information is reported in current dollars (not adjusted for inflation) as well as in real (inflation-adjusted) dollars. Like most economic indicators, the figures are seasonally adjusted and annualized.

The conventional practice is to report the nominal growth rates first. The real (inflation-adjusted) growth rates are reported almost as an afterthought. So many of the monthly economic indicators are only available in nominal terms that financial market participants have become accustomed to them. Yet, when they discuss U.S. economic growth, the inflation-adjusted numbers are what they are after. In any case, whether looking at real or nominal data, participants still examine the three major parts: private residential, private nonresidential, and public construction.

Table 4.2 Construction Expenditures

	Current Dollars			Real (1987) Dollars		
	Dec 91	Nov 91	Oct 91	Dec 91	Nov 91	Oct 91
Total	407.4	408.4	410.3	365.6	365.7	366.6
Private Construction	295.0	295.7	297.5	264.5	264.6	265.6
Residential Buildings	167.3	168.2	168.3	150.5	151.0	150.6
New housing	119.2	118.9	118.3	107.3	106.7	105.9
Single unit	106.2	104.9	104.1	95.6	94.2	93.2
Multi units	13.0	14.0	14.2	11.7	12.5	12.7
Nonresidential						
Buildings	89.2	89.0	91.1	80.4	80.0	81.7
Industrial	22.4	21.6	21.5	20.2	19.5	19.3
Office	18.7	19.5	21.2	16.8	17.5	19.0
Hotels/Motels	4.4	4.6	4.5	4.0	4.1	4.0
Other commercial	22.6	22.8	23.5	20.3	20.5	20.9
Religious	3.6	3.6	3.4	3.2	3.3	3.1
Educational	3.9	3.7	4.0	3.5	3.3	3.6
Hospital/institutional	9.8	9.0	9.0	8.8	8.1	8.1
Miscellaneous	3.9	4.1	4.3	3.5	3.7	3.8
Public Construction	112.4	112.7	112.8	101.0	101.1	101.0

Source: Construction Reports, Bureau of the Census, Department of Commerce, February 1992.

In the past, nonresidential construction expenditures were somewhat procyclical but lagged other sectors of the economy; that is, spending on nonresidential structures would begin to recover after the overall economy recovered. In the expansion following the 1981–1982 recession, nonresidential construction grew rapidly early in the recovery, partly because of tax laws implemented in 1981. The potential impact of tax law changes on investment in nonresidential structures could be just as large as the impact coming from interest rate changes. A rapid and early recovery of nonresidential structures won't be repeated after the 1990–1991 recession. Overbuilding from the late 1980s could potentially hold down the growth in nonresidential structures through the first half of the 1990s, or even longer.

Historically, residential construction was countercyclical; that is, spending on residential structures would increase when interest rates were relatively low near the trough of a business downturn. Since 1980, residential construction has become more closely aligned with the

Table 4.3 Monthly Percentage Changes in Construction Expenditures

Date Reported	Aug 92	July 92	June 92	May 92	Apr 92	Mar 92	Feb 92	Jan 92
10/1/92	−0.8	0.2	−0.3	0.1				
9/1/92		−0.6	−0.4	0.7	0.4			
8/3/92			−1.5	0.1	0.4	2.4		
7/1/92				0.2	0.2	2.4	1.2	
6/1/92					−0.3	1.8	0.7	2.2

Source: Data are from Commerce Department publications.

business cycle, although it does begin to recover somewhat sooner than the overall economy because interest rates are lower when demand for capital equipment is still low or declining. The sensitivity of construction expenditures to interest rates has been mitigated somewhat in the 1980s and early 1990s because of the popularity of adjustable rate mortgage loans that were not previously available.

Market Reaction On the whole, financial market participants ignore construction expenditure data, which have a reputation for instability and frequent revision. Table 4.3 shows revisions in 1992. Unlike durable good orders, which market players watch to some extent, construction expenditures are old news. They don't have any element as a leading indicator of future economic activity. Although residential structures tend to pick up before the rest of the economy during a recession, and moderate before the rest of the economy during an expansion, other indicators report the same information in a more timely fashion. Housing starts, for instance, come out roughly three weeks earlier.

Housing Starts and Permits

Housing starts are a good monthly indicator of housing activity. The Bureau of the Census reports housing starts and permits about two to three weeks after the end of the month. Permits are considered to be a leading indicator of starts and the economy in general, and are included in the Index of Leading Indicators published by the Commerce Department. Housing starts and permits tend to move in tandem from month to month, and only rarely do permits lead starts by any significant amount. Since 1984, the figures on housing starts and permits

Watch Out For: Keep an eye on the pattern of growth in real private nonresidential structures. These figures are directly incorporated into GDP by the Bureau of Economic Analysis even though they undergo frequent revisions. If you follow this pattern, you won't be surprised by changes in this component of gross domestic product. In addition, these figures will help you decipher the direction of GDP revisions. The Bureau of Economic Analysis doesn't have a complete set of actual data when putting together the preliminary estimate of GDP. As a result, analysts must make some assumptions for the last month of each quarter, and these assumptions are available to the public (for a nominal fee). This way you will be able to incorporate the revisions as actual data are released. Finally, these are the only statistics available for nonresidential structures on a monthly basis. (It's this news or no news.)

For the same reason that you monitor real nonresidential construction spending, you should watch real residential construction. The pattern of growth in residential construction is also fed directly into gross domestic product. Keeping track of the monthly pattern will help you to gauge residential investment spending when the quarterly numbers are reported. However, other housing statistics (described in the following section) used for estimating the strength of the housing sector are somewhat more timely and usually show smaller revisions.

have come from a universe of 17,000 places in the United States that require construction permits.

Housing starts and permits include single- and multifamily units. Single-family housing starts are the lion's share of the total, as shown in Figure 4.3. In the past, single-family housing starts were more sensitive than multifamily housing starts to changes in interest rates. Multifamily housing units, which include townhouses, condominiums, and apartment buildings, are also affected by subsidized housing, changes in tax laws, and speculative investment building. If housing permits are at all a leading indicator of starts, it would be for the multifamily sector. Technically, a start is defined as "an excavation beginning for the footing or foundation of a residential building." In plain English, a housing start is nothing more than the first shovel of dirt to break ground. A brick doesn't have to be laid.

The Bureau of the Census expanded this definition with the release of the September 1992 figures reported in October of that year. According to Erica Annarella, a survey statistician with the Bureau of the

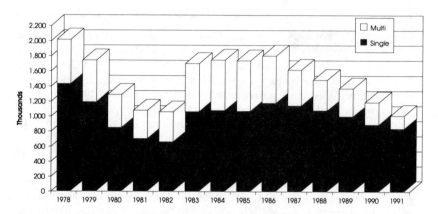

Figure 4.3 Single-family housing starts hold a greater share of total housing activity. (*Source: Housing Market Statistics,* National Association of Home-builders, December 1992.)

Census, the new definition also includes a dwelling that is being totally rebuilt on an existing foundation.[1] A house that has lost part of its superstructure, such as a roof, would not be counted as a new start.

The multifamily sector is divided into two groups: houses of two to four units, and buildings with five or more units. The latter sector is larger. In addition, housing starts and permits are available on a regional basis.

Did You Know? According to Erica Annarella of the Commerce Department's Bureau of the Census, Hurricane Andrew (which devastated parts of Florida in August 1992) prompted the change in definition. However, a similar issue was raised earlier in the year when a fire destroyed a large number of homes in Oakland, California. Commerce Department officials don't believe this new definition will have a large effect on the series except in cases of natural disasters. Ms. Annarella said that the Commerce Department does not have its own estimate for the rebuilding that will occur in Florida because of Hurricane Andrew. However, she cited an American Red Cross estimate of 75,000 badly damaged or destroyed houses, and the Building Association of South Florida estimate of 100,000 heavily damaged or destroyed homes.[2]

Market Reaction Participants in the fixed-income market view a rise in housing starts unfavorably because it signifies economic growth.

They will push down bond prices, causing yields to rise. When housing starts decline, bond and money market traders will view this favorably, pushing up prices, and causing bond yields to fall.

In contrast, an increase in housing starts will cheer equity market professionals. A healthy economy provides potentially robust corporate earnings. Similarly, foreign exchange market professionals will favor the rise in housing starts that brings about the bond market reaction of higher interest rates. Although rising interest rates are unfavorable for bond market professionals, they are a positive factor for the foreign exchange markets because they push up the foreign exchange value of the dollar. A drop in housing starts bodes poorly for stock prices and for the dollar because it signals weak domestic growth.

Financial market reaction to housing starts data is not as strong as the reaction to some other figures, but it can move the markets when the changes are significant and compatible with market psychology. Housing starts typically lead the economy out of recession, so they are closely monitored at turning points of the business cycle: at the early stages of recovery, when market participants assess the magnitude of strength of the recovery; and at expansion peaks, when market participants anticipate declines in housing activity. In the middle of an expansion or a recession, housing starts are virtually ignored. Economists generally don't view this indicator as a good overall measure of economic activity.

Sales of New and Existing Single-Family Homes

Sales of new and existing single-family homes are another indicator of housing demand. These are reported about four to five weeks after the end of the month, although new and existing home sales are not reported on the same day. New single-family home sales are published by the Bureau of the Census; existing single-family home sales are compiled by the National Association of Realtors. Both new and existing home sales are reported on a seasonally adjusted basis at an annualized rate.

The reports issue figures on the number of homes sold, homes for sale, and the month's supply of unsold homes. An inventory of unsold new homes is reasonable to count. In terms of existing home sales, however, the supply is almost infinite. Technically, anyone can decide to sell his or her house if offered the right price even if the home isn't officially on the market at the time.

Watch Out For: Look at the gains in the single-family market separately from the increases in the multifamily market. The single-family sector reflects consumer demand, whereas building in the multifamily sector may be more speculative. Also, the single-family sector will show more stable trends from month to month. Historically, the multifamily sector has been more likely to show the effects of "special factors." In the 1970s and early 1980s, subsidized housing boosted the total, but the level of such housing fell sharply later in the 1980s. The effects of tax law changes mainly affected buyers of apartment buildings for speculative or investment purposes rather than resident homeowners. Tax law changes in the mid-1980s made speculative housing investment less profitable pushing down further the level of multifamily units.

Demographic factors such as age and marital/family status of the population play a major role, with long-term impacts on total housing construction. Consequently, these will not change from month to month, but over a period of years. The housing boom of the late 1970s could never be repeated in the early to mid-1990s because of the altered structure of the population.

Once you have looked at the breakdown by type of structure, you'll also want to check the regional distribution if starts jump unexpectedly or plunge sharply. Housing starts have a strong seasonal component, and during the winter months, construction comes to a standstill in many parts of the country. Thus, a large increase during one of the winter months should be viewed skeptically, especially if it occurs in the Midwest or Northeast. Similarly, a rainy July could curtail starts in the summer. For instance, housing starts jumped sharply from December 1991 through March 1992 coinciding exactly with the Federal Reserve's cut in the discount rate, bringing it to its lowest level in 30 years. Consequently, mortgage rates also fell during that period. The winter months of January, February, and March also happened to be unusually warm for the season. Housing starts plunged again in April, however, and remained virtually unchanged through the spring and summer months. Although uncertainty about the economy no doubt contributed to the sluggish behavior of housing starts, so did the irregular seasonal adjustment factors. The anemic spring and summer compensated for the exceptionally strong winter.

Economist Frederick Sturm explained the quirk in the June 12, 1992, issue of *Perspectives,* a weekly Fuji Securities, Inc., newsletter, "Since most of the first quarter's astonishing growth was fair-weather fluff, attributable to an unseasonably warm and mild winter, April's purge was little more than a healthy corrective."

Vagaries in the weather can cause the growth in housing permits to exceed starts. If bad weather prevents housing construction, but not paperwork, an increase in permits portends a rise in starts in the subsequent month. Multifamily construction adds a domino effect: A contractor gets a permit for a 50-unit apartment complex in July, but heavy rains prevent excavation from starting until August; a 50-unit building counts as 50 starts.

Economists at the Census Bureau are well aware that weather patterns can distort economic activity but don't have any methods for analyzing the actual impact. In an April 17, 1988 *New York Times* article, an unidentified official was quoted as saying, "But every so often, we contact the Weather Service to see if anything out of the ordinary has happened in a particular area."

Also look at the detail in the housing statistics and distinguish between long-term trends and one-time aberrations. With unexpected increases or decreases, see whether the movements are broadly based among the regions as well as by type (single-, versus multifamily units). Starts that increase in only one region of the country might indicate a strong regional economy while suggesting weakness in the rest of the country. The regional variation in economic activity is easily visible by the activity in the housing sector. During the 1980s, the level of new housing starts peaked as follows: 1983 in the South, 1986 in the Northeast and the West, and 1987 in the Midwest. In the current cycle, new housing starts plunged 61.4 percent from peak to trough in the Northeast, 55.7 percent in the South, 47.4 percent in the West, and "only" 21.8 percent in the Midwest. This takes into account the annual level of housing starts with the annual trough in 1991.

Whether you are interested in aggregate housing activity or regional breakdowns, look at more than one month's housing figures: These can be volatile from month to month for the reasons discussed earlier.

There aren't too many breakdowns for analysis of single-family homes, but looking at the level of sales on a regional basis will show some regional disparity. The sales of new and existing homes peaked in 1986 in the Northeast and the Midwest, and in 1988 in the South and West; but sales of new homes did not move in tandem in all regions of the country. In the Midwest, sales of new homes peaked in 1989, two years after the peak in housing starts, and three years after the peak in sales of existing homes. In the South, sales of new homes peaked in 1985, two years after the peak in housing starts and three years before the peak in existing home sales. In the West, sales of new and existing homes peaked in 1988, two years after the peak in housing starts. Finally, sales of new and existing homes in the Northeast peaked in 1986, the same year as starts.

The other information in this report is the median and average sales price of new and existing homes. These prices are used in the calculation of affordability measures along with income and interest rates. Typically, prices will move in the opposite direction of sales, which seems to make sense in terms of the economic theory that there is an inverse relationship between the price and quantity demanded for any good. Actually, the average and median prices of new and existing homes tend to rise as sales fall because higher income families are more likely to be able to afford to buy a home during economic downturns (see Table 4.4). The rise in the price reflects the shift to more expensive homes. Between 1981 and 1991, the median price of new homes rose 74.2 percent, whereas the median price of existing homes rose 51.1 percent. The greater affordability of existing homes could explain why new homes accounted for 13.6 percent of total home sales in 1991, down from 15.3 percent of total sales in 1981.

Table 4.4   Single-Family Homes: New and Existing

	Sales (thousands of units)		Prices (average) (thousands of dollars)	
	New	Existing	New	Existing
Jan 91	406	2,900	148.6	123.1
Feb 91	490	3,090	147.8	121.1
Mar 91	497	3,180	156.4	125.1
Apr 91	505	3,270	150.8	129.0
May 91	511	3,480	145.4	130.8
June 91	513	3,480	145.9	130.6
July 91	505	3,260	148.2	132.2
Aug 91	522	3,190	141.8	130.9
Sep 91	499	3,120	147.3	127.8
Oct 91	526	3,150	147.4	126.4
Nov 91	578	3,230	141.7	124.9
Dec 91	578	3,310	143.0	127.3
Jan 92	667	3,220	144.2	130.5
Feb 92	627	3,490	144.8	128.8
Mar 92	555	3,510	144.8	130.2
Apr 92	546	3,490	145.0	130.6
May 92	554	3,460	146.0	130.6
June 92	583	3,350	146.6	133.7
July 92	613	3,450	138.1	132.2
Aug 92	623	3,310	143.7	132.2

Source: Housing Market Statistics. National Association of Home Builders, December, 1992, Washington, DC.

Market Reaction   Home sales are old news to the market by the time they are reported. Home sales often move in the same direction as housing starts, so if the latter have already shown market participants that the demand for housing has increased or decreased during any given month, home sales are almost irrelevant.

Watch Out For: The combination of home sales with the stock of unsold homes can indicate future housing construction. When home sales are rising strongly and the stock of unsold new homes is falling, it signals a need to replenish the supply of new homes, and starts could pick up in ensuing months. Conversely, if new home sales are declining, while the stock of unsold new homes is increasing, it portends a drop in hew housing construction in coming months.

For the most part, sales of new and existing homes move in tandem. If sales of existing homes are rising more rapidly than sales of new homes, existing homes are probably less expensive. If sales of new homes are rising more rapidly than sales of existing homes, the relative price differential between new and used homes may have shrunk.

Home sales, like housing starts, tend to be more meaningful during turning points of the economy. For example, home sales will recover before other economic sectors when interest rates are low near the trough of the business cycle.

Watch for unexpectedly large changes. Home sales tend to follow the same seasonal pattern as housing starts. As a result, unusually warm weather during winter months can cause a temporary spurt in home sales, especially in the Midwest or Northeast. Similarly, unusually rainy seasons in the spring or summer months can hold down home sales temporarily. In addition, it can be useful to put the home sales data in perspective with the housing starts figures as well as the current level of mortgage rates.

Despite the rule of thumb that new and existing home sales move in tandem, along with housing starts, it is not a hard and fast rule. For instance, housing starts rose from January through March 1992 with the biggest one-month spurt in March. In contrast, sales of new homes peaked in January 1992 and then declined steadily in June. Sales of existing homes fell in January 1992, rose in February, and peaked in March before decreasing steadily through the first half of the year. Thus, in this particular instance, the movement in housing starts, new home sales, and existing home sales did not match up at all from one month to the next.

QUARTERLY INDICATORS

Plant and Equipment Expenditure Survey

The Bureau of the Census conducts surveys five times a year to estimate actual capital spending as well as planned expenditures for the
upcoming year. The October–November survey of each year gives the
first glimpse of the year to come. Figures are seasonally adjusted and
available in nominal dollars. Since 1990, total industry figures have also
been reported in constant (1987) dollars.

Actual and planned figures are quarterly and annual. The annual
data are calculated as an average of the four quarters, and benchmark
revisions are incorporated every five years. The most recent benchmark
revision was completed in 1990 revising estimates for capital expenditures back to 1978. (Economic history is often rewritten as new information becomes available.)

The Capital Spending Survey, as it is also known, is conducted by mail
for manufacturing and nonmanufacturing industries. The nonmanufacturing industries include mining, transportation, public utilities, and
commercial and other. Capital expenditures include new plants, machinery, and equipment that are depreciated. Capital expenditures in
farming, real estate, the professions, and nonprofit institutions are not
included here. (That's too bad because I spent a fortune on computer and
office equipment when I started my business!)

The October–November survey, which provides the first glimpse of
the upcoming year, is reported in late December. These plans are then
revised in subsequent surveys. For example, businesses were first
asked to estimate 1992 expenditures in October–November 1991. These
figures were reported on December 18, 1991. At the same time, the
Census Bureau also reported actual figures for the third quarter of
1991. Fourth quarter (1991) actuals were reported April 9, 1992, along
with a revised estimate of 1992 expenditures. On June 4, 1992, first
quarter (1992) actuals were reported along with another revision for
1992 planned expenditures.

Table 4.5 shows the actual annual expenditures for 1990 and 1991
and the planned expenditures for 1992. Notice the revisions in planned
expenditures. The table shows "all industries" in nominal and real dollars. The Bureau of the Census uses the quarterly implicit price deflator
for nonresidential fixed investment (from the national income and
product accounts) and extrapolates (forecasts) a price deflator for

Table 4.5 New Plant and Equipment Expenditures by
Business in Current Dollars
(% change from preceding year)

| | Actual | | Planned for Each Year as Reported in the Periods Shown | | |
| | | | 1992 | | |
	1990	1991	Oct-Nov 91 Survey	Jan-Mar 92 Survey	Apr-May 92 Survey
All Industries	5.0	−0.6	5.4	4.6	4.7
1987 dollars	3.3	−1.0	5.7	5.9	6.0
Manufacturing	4.8	−4.7	−0.1	−0.4	−2.4
Durable Goods	0.0	−5.6	3.0	0.3	−3.6
Primary metals	1.2	−10.8	−9.1	−5.1	−14.5
Fabricated metals	5.3	−8.1	0.5	3.5	−12.7
Electrical machinery	7.7	−4.6	7.0	4.3	−2.6
Nonelectrical machinery	−6.3	−6.8	1.7	−10.0	−8.3
Transportation equipment	−4.4	−3.5	6.7	−1.3	0.6
Stone, clay, and glass	−17.9	−12.1	1.8	6.8	15.9
Other durables	6.2	0.1	4.9	11.3	3.7
Nondurable Goods	8.7	−4.0	−2.4	−1.0	−1.5
Food including beverage	3.0	6.5	5.9	7.4	6.3
Textiles	−3.2	−9.9	2.5	8.9	0.4
Paper	6.1	−29.6	−11.2	−7.5	−2.9
Chemicals	11.7	4.0	5.8	8.6	6.9
Petroleum	15.6	3.4	−14.4	−11.8	−10.3
Rubber	−8.2	−1.2	4.3	6.2	12.3
Other nondurables	6.0	−14.4	11.7	4.2	−4.3
Nonmanufacturing	5.1	1.6	8.4	7.3	8.4
Mining	7.3	1.4	−5.5	−8.9	−10.4
Transportation	14.0	5.7	18.3	7.7	8.2
Public utilities	1.4	−1.0	8.3	7.2	9.5
Commercial and other	5.3	2.0	8.0	8.0	8.9

Source: "Plant and Equipment Expenditures and Plans." Bureau of the Census, Department of Commerce, June 1992.

planned expenditures. Table 4.6 shows the quarterly detail of actual and planned expenditures for the various industries in nominal dollars only. All figures are seasonally adjusted.

How well does the Plant and Equipment Survey forecast? First of all, that depends on what you want to forecast: actual plant and equipment

Table 4.6   New Plant and Equipment Expenditures by
Business in Current Dollars*
(billions of dollars, quarters seasonally adjusted at annual rates)

	1990	1991	1992	Q1:92	Q2:92	Q3:92	Q4:92
All Industries	532.6	529.2	553.9	536.5	558.5	557.6	562.9
1987 dollars	498.1	493.0	522.6	503.7	526.1	527.0	533.7
Manufacturing	192.6	183.6	179.2	174.2	185.2	179.6	177.8
Durable Goods	82.6	78.0	75.2	74.5	76.6	74.4	75.2
Primary metals	12.2	10.9	9.3	9.8	10.0	8.9	8.4
Fabricated metals	4.4	4.0	3.5	3.6	3.7	3.5	3.3
Electrical machinery	22.0	21.0	20.5	20.8	21.1	20.3	19.7
Nonelectrical machinery	13.7	12.7	11.7	10.4	12.5	12.5	11.3
Transportation equipment	17.9	17.3	17.4	17.4	16.6	16.4	18.9
Stone, clay, and glass	3.3	2.9	3.4	3.1	3.2	3.2	3.9
Other durables	9.2	9.2	9.5	9.4	9.5	9.4	9.7
Nondurable Goods	110.0	105.7	104.0	99.7	108.6	103.2	102.6
Food including beverage	16.4	17.4	18.5	19.2	19.1	17.7	18.1
Textiles	2.2	2.0	2.0	1.9	2.0	2.0	1.9
Paper	16.5	11.6	11.3	11.4	10.8	11.2	11.8
Chemicals	20.6	21.5	22.9	21.5	23.7	23.3	23.2
Petroleum	34.8	36.0	32.3	29.4	34.8	34.1	30.7
Rubber	3.5	3.4	3.9	4.0	3.8	3.9	3.8
Other nondurables	16.1	13.8	13.2	12.3	14.4	13.0	13.0
Nonmanufacturing	340.0	345.6	374.7	362.3	373.3	377.9	385.1
Mining	9.9	10.0	9.0	8.8	9.5	9.1	8.5
Transportation	21.5	22.7	24.6	21.6	25.4	25.7	25.5
Public utilities	67.2	66.5	72.8	68.8	73.0	74.0	75.5
Commercial and other	241.4	246.4	368.3	263.0	265.3	269.2	275.7

* Data for 1990, 1991, and Q1:1992 are actual; others are planned expenditures.

Source: "Plant and Equipment Expenditures and Plans," Bureau of the Census, Department of Commerce, June 1992.

expenditures or business fixed investment as estimated in the national income and product accounts. According to a study by two economists at the Federal Reserve Bank of Cleveland, the success rate is mediocre in both cases. The Plant and Equipment Survey does a better job forecasting its own future—actual plant and equipment expenditures— than predicting changes in business fixed investment. Gerald Anderson and John Erceg of the Cleveland Fed also found that the annual plans are much better predictors than the plans for quarterly expenditures.[3] Furthermore, and this should be no surprise, the survey improves when comparing plans from the first survey taken in the previous year with the last survey taken at the end of the current year.

Planned expenditures can be different from actual expenditures for many reasons including management's reaction to current economic conditions or inability to get financing for projects. Thus, the last survey can still yield an estimate that is off the mark.

Timing and definitional differences cause the gap between changes in plant and equipment expenditures and business fixed investment even on an annual basis. Nonetheless, the two series track well over time. The absolute error, however, averaged 4.3 percent over the past 20 years, so use these figures with a grain of salt. Also, keep in mind that the Plant and Equipment Survey tends to overstate capital expenditures during recessions and to understate the strength in capital spending during expansions.

Market Reaction   Financial market participants don't tend to react very strongly to this report. This may have to do with timing. The most important release in terms of new information occurs in late December when planned expenditures are available for the first time reflecting the coming year. Markets are generally thin around holiday periods. In subsequent quarters, revisions are less important unless they differ significantly from the first report.

Watch Out For: Look at the magnitude of change in this series, which could be confirming evidence for the monthly reports on new orders that come either from the Census Bureau or from the National Association of Purchasing Managers.

Key Points	■ Volatility is the main characteristic shared by the indicators of investment.
	■ Revisions occur with great frequency in these investment series. Make sure to look at the trend in the data rather than at a one-month change.
	■ Financial market reaction to indicators of investment is somewhat more restrained than reaction to other economic indicators such as those describing the consumer sector or inflation.
	■ Investors who must limit the indicators they monitor will find it best to keep track of housing starts and total manufacturers' shipments, inventories, and orders.
	■ Table 4.7 summarizes the investment indicators, their approximate dates of release, and source agencies.

Table 4.7   Indicators of Investment Spending

Approximate				
Month	Day	Indicator	Data for	Source Agency
Jan	1 to 5	Construction spending	Nov	Bureau of the Census
	1 to 6	Mfg. shipments, inventories, and orders	Nov	Bureau of the Census
	12 to 16	Manufacturing and trade sales, inventories	Nov	Bureau of the Census
	16 to 22	Housing starts and permits	Dec	Bureau of the Census
	25 to 28	Existing home sales	Dec	National Association of Realtors
	23 to 30	Durable goods shipments and orders	Dec	Bureau of the Census
	28 to 3	New home sales	Dec	Bureau of the Census
Feb	1 to 5	Construction spending	Dec	Bureau of the Census
	1 to 6	Mfg. shipments, inventories, and orders	Dec	Bureau of the Census

Table 4.7 *(Continued)*

Approximate		Indicator	Data for	Source Agency
Month	Day			
Feb	12 to 16	Manufacturing and trade sales, inventories	Dec	Bureau of the Census
	16 to 22	Housing starts and permits	Jan	Bureau of the Census
	23 to 30	Existing home sales	Jan	National Association of Realtors
	25 to 28	Durable goods shipments and orders	Jan	Bureau of the Census
	28 to 3	New home sales	Jan	Bureau of the Census
Mar	1 to 5	Construction spending	Jan	Bureau of the Census
	1 to 6	Mfg. shipments, inventories, and orders	Jan	Bureau of the Census
	12 to 16	Manufacturing and trade sales, inventories	Jan	Bureau of the Census
	16 to 22	Housing starts and permits	Feb	Bureau of the Census
	23 to 30	Durable goods shipments and orders	Feb	Bureau of the Census
	25 to 28	Existing home sales	Feb	National Association of Realtors
	28 to 3	New home sales	Feb	Bureau of the Census
Apr	1 to 5	Construction spending	Feb	Bureau of the Census
	1 to 6	Mfg. shipments, inventories, and orders	Feb	Bureau of the Census
	12 to 16	Manufacturing and trade sales, inventories	Feb	Bureau of the Census
	16 to 22	Housing starts and permits	Mar	Bureau of the Census
	23 to 30	Durable goods shipments and orders	Mar	Bureau of the Census

Table 4.7 *(Continued)*

Approximate				
Month	Day	Indicator	Data for	Source Agency
Apr	25 to 28	Existing home sales	Mar	National Association of Realtors
	28 to 3	New home sales	Mar	Bureau of the Census
May	1 to 5	Construction spending	Mar	Bureau of the Census
	1 to 6	Mfg. shipments, inventories, and orders	Mar	Bureau of the Census
	12 to 16	Manufacturing and trade sales, inventories	Mar	Bureau of the Census
	16 to 22	Housing starts and permits	Apr	Bureau of the Census
	25 to 28	Existing home sales	Apr	National Association of Realtors
	23 to 30	Durable goods shipments and orders	Apr	Bureau of the Census
	28 to 3	New home sales	Apr	Bureau of the Census
June	1 to 5	Construction spending	Apr	Bureau of the Census
	1 to 6	Mfg. shipments, inventories, and orders	Apr	Bureau of the Census
	12 to 16	Manufacturing and trade sales, inventories	Apr	Bureau of the Census
	16 to 22	Housing starts and permits	May	Bureau of the Census
	23 to 30	Durable goods shipments and orders	May	Bureau of the Census
	25 to 28	Existing home sales	May	National Association of Realtors
	28 to 3	New home sales	May	Bureau of the Census
July	1 to 5	Construction spending	May	Bureau of the Census

Table 4.7 *(Continued)*

Approximate				
Month	Day	Indicator	Data for	Source Agency
July	1 to 6	Mfg. shipments, inventories, and orders	May	Bureau of the Census
	12 to 16	Manufacturing and trade sales, inventories	May	Bureau of the Census
	16 to 22	Housing starts and permits	Jun	Bureau of the Census
	23 to 30	Durable goods shipments and orders	Jun	Bureau of the Census
	25 to 28	Existing home sales	Jun	National Association of Realtors
	28 to 3	New home sales	Jun	Bureau of the Census
Aug	1 to 5	Construction spending	Jun	Bureau of the Census
	1 to 6	Mfg. shipments, inventories, and orders	Jun	Bureau of the Census
	12 to 16	Manufacturing and trade sales, inventories	Jun	Bureau of the Census
	16 to 22	Housing starts and permits	Jul	Bureau of the Census
	23 to 30	Durable goods shipments and orders	Jul	Bureau of the Census
	25 to 28	Existing home sales	Jul	National Association of Realtors
	28 to 3	New home sales	Jul	Bureau of the Census
Sep	1 to 5	Construction spending	Jul	Bureau of the Census
	1 to 6	Mfg. shipments, inventories, and orders	Jul	Bureau of the Census
	12 to 16	Manufacturing and trade sales, inventories	Jul	Bureau of the Census
	16 to 22	Housing starts and permits	Aug	Bureau of the Census

Table 4.7   *(Continued)*

Approximate		Indicator	Data for	Source Agency
Month	Day			
Sep	23 to 30	Durable goods shipments and orders	Aug	Bureau of the Census
	25 to 28	Existing home sales	Aug	National Association of Realtors
ø	28 to 3	New home sales	Aug	Bureau of the Census
Oct	1 to 5	Construction spending	Aug	Bureau of the Census
	1 to 6	Mfg. shipments, inventories, and orders	Aug	Bureau of the Census
	12 to 16	Manufacturing and trade sales, inventories	Aug	Bureau of the Census
	16 to 22	Housing starts and permits	Sep	Bureau of the Census
	23 to 30	Durable goods shipments and orders	Sep	Bureau of the Census
	25 to 28	Existing home sales	Sep	National Association of Realtors
	28 to 3	New home sales	Sep	Bureau of the Census
Nov	1 to 5	Construction spending	Sep	Bureau of the Census
	1 to 6	Mfg. shipments, inventories, and orders	Sep	Bureau of the Census
	12 to 16	Manufacturing and trade sales, inventories	Sep	Bureau of the Census
	16 to 22	Housing starts and permits	Oct	Bureau of the Census
	23 to 30	Durable goods shipments and orders	Oct	Bureau of the Census
	25 to 28	Existing home sales	Oct	National Association of Realtors
	28 to 3	New home sales	Oct	Bureau of the Census

Table 4.7 *(Continued)*

Approximate				
Month	Day	Indicator	Data for	Source Agency
Dec	1 to 5	Construction spending	Oct	Bureau of the Census
	1 to 6	Mfg. shipments, inventories, and orders	Oct	Bureau of the Census
	12 to 16	Manufacturing and trade sales, inventories	Oct	Bureau of the Census
	16 to 22	Housing starts and permits	Nov	Bureau of the Census
	23 to 30	Durable goods shipments and orders	Nov	Bureau of the Census
	25 to 28	Existing home sales	Nov	National Association of Realtors
	28 to 3	New home sales	Nov	Bureau of the Census

CHAPTER 5

The Foreign Sector

Featured Indicators   Merchandise Trade Balance
                            Current Account
                            Capital Account

In 1980, real merchandise exports accounted for 6.6 percent of real gross domestic product, whereas real merchandise imports accounted for 6.2 percent. The U.S. trade balance was in surplus, and the foreign sector was not considered to be a consequential sector of the economy: Total trade in goods between the United States and foreigners contributed 12.8 percent of GDP.

In 1991, real merchandise exports accounted for 8.2 percent of gross domestic product and real merchandise imports had reached 9.5 percent. The increase of both imports and exports as a share of gross domestic product signifies that the foreign sector is now more significant than it was 10 or 15 years ago: Its contribution has increased roughly five percentage points to 17.7 percent, almost the size of U.S. government spending. The growth in trade continues to be strong and shows how the United States has developed into a more open and global economy during the past several years. U.S. consumers and businesses now purchase one-tenth of their goods from foreigners. As a consequence, the trade balance for 1991 was in deficit, as it had been throughout the prior decade. Although the foreign sector has become more relevant to U.S. markets, the list of indicators that highlight the international statistics is very short. Focusing on those indicators that financial market participants and the media monitor closely makes the list shorter still.

This chapter describes the international statistics available for scrutiny by financial market players, the media, and makers of fiscal and monetary policy.

MONTHLY INDICATOR

Merchandise Trade Balance

The Bureau of the Census releases the merchandise trade balance six weeks after the end of the month. It is reported on a seasonally adjusted basis, and the figures are available in both current dollars and constant (inflation-adjusted) dollars. The figures are not annualized but can be converted by multiplying each monthly amount by twelve. Exports are calculated on a "free alongside ship" (FAS) basis. This means that transportation costs to the port of export are included, but other transportation costs and loading fees are not. Imports are reported based on the customs value. Costs for insurance and freight (CIF), essentially, shipping costs, are not reflected. The customs value represents the price actually paid, or payable, for merchandise at the foreign port of exportation. Excluding the costs of insurance and freight from the import figures lowers the value of imports and thereby lowers the trade deficit. However, the main rationale for measuring the trade balance in such a way is that transportation costs are considered a service and not a good.

The merchandise trade balance report is rich with information. To start, it shows the pattern of growth for both exports and imports in nominal, or current, dollars, as well as in real, or constant (1987) dollars. Given a choice, economists always prefer to discuss inflation-adjusted figures rather than current dollar data because they give a better picture of the state of affairs. In the same way, the constant dollar trade balance says more about changes in the volume of exports and imports than the nominal dollar data. However, the constant dollar trade balance has only been available on a monthly basis since 1991, and some economists and financial market participants are still more comfortable thinking in terms of the nominal data. Table 5.1 shows the nominal and constant dollar figures.

Monitoring the inflation-adjusted data is more useful because monthly fluctuations in the foreign exchange value of the dollar, or in the prices of various goods, can obscure an underlying trend. For

Table 5.1   Merchandise Trade Summary
(billions of dollars, seasonally adjusted)

		Current Dollars	%	Constant (1987) Dollars	%
Exports	Jan 92	35.4671	−1.6	33.3522	−1.3
	Feb 92	37.6544	6.2	35.3034	5.9
	Mar 92	37.0847	−1.5	34.7365	−1.6
	Apr 92	36.4058	−1.8	34.3098	−1.2
	May 92	35.7179	−1.9	33.7173	−1.7
	June 92	38.1646	6.9	35.9929	6.7
	July 92	37.8055	0.9	35.7523	−0.7
	Aug 92	35.7993	−5.3	33.9078	−5.2
	Sep 92	37.8823	5.8	35.9237	5.9
	Oct 92	39.0721	3.1	37.0956	3.3
	Nov 92	38.1872	−2.3	36.3884	−1.9
	Dec 92	39.7284	4.0	37.9242	4.2
Imports	Jan 92	41.4129	−0.6	39.2477	0.0
	Feb 92	41.0773	−0.8	38.9191	−0.8
	Mar 92	42.8091	4.2	40.7637	4.7
	Apr 92	43.4940	1.6	41.4406	1.7
	May 92	42.9027	−1.4	40.8232	−1.5
	June 92	44.9569	4.8	42.3438	3.7
	July 92	45.1697	0.5	42.5342	0.4
	Aug 92	44.9735	−0.4	42.3647	−0.4
	Sep 92	46.5512	3.5	43.7187	3.2
	Oct 92	46.3239	−0.5	43.4007	−0.7
	Nov 92	45.5350	−1.7	43.0519	−0.8
	Dec 92	46.6811	2.5	44.7503	3.9
Balance	Jan 92	−5.9458		−5.8955	
	Feb 92	−3.4229		−3.6157	
	Mar 92	−5.7244		−6.0272	
	Apr 92	−7.0882		−7.1308	
	May 92	−7.1848		−7.1059	
	June 92	−6.7923		−6.3509	
	July 92	−7.3642		−6.7819	
	Aug 92	−9.1742		−8.4569	
	Sep 92	−8.6689		−7.7950	
	Oct 92	−7.2518		−6.3051	
	Nov 92	−7.3478		−6.6635	
	Dec 92	−6.9527		−6.8261	

Source: Bureau of the Census; Department of Commerce, "U.S. Merchandise Trade: December 1992," February 18, 1993.

instance, large variations often come from changes in oil prices. Given its large relative share among total merchandise imports, a sharp rise or fall in oil prices can easily swing the monthly trade balance by half a billion dollars or so, a hefty movement on a monthly trade deficit of $5 billion.

Because the merchandise trade balance is the last report the Bureau of the Census releases each month; it is not known for its timeliness. For most reports, the government generally releases statistics that describe the previous month's transactions. However, it describes transactions for two months back for the merchandise trade balance report. To make up for its lack of timeliness, the published report is extremely detailed, unlike many releases with only general summary statistics. It breaks down the merchandise trade balance of the United States by commodity group, by end-use commodities, and by trade shares with other countries. Although the summary statistics are seasonally adjusted and in constant dollars, all the detail figures are not. The trade balance by country and by commodity group is only available on an unadjusted basis. However, the end-use commodities are available on a seasonally adjusted basis in current and constant dollars.

Furthermore, the country detail separates Western Europe by "European Community," "European Free Trade Association," and "other Eastern Europe." Japan, Australia, New Zealand, and South Africa are each listed separately, and aren't included in a larger category. Among developing countries, you will find Mexico, Brazil, Egypt, and "Newly Industrialized Countries." Other developing countries include Eastern Europe, OPEC, and China. Figure 5.1 shows trade shares with major countries.

The commodity detail divides total exports and imports by agricultural commodities, manufactured goods, mineral fuels, and all others. And the end-use commodities are sorted by: foods, feeds, and beverages; industrial supplies and materials; capital goods excluding autos; autos and parts; consumer goods excluding autos; and "other." Each group is sorted by both imports and exports.

Such detail allows users to scrutinize monthly changes in the trade balance by component. Did the trade deficit worsen because exports fell, or imports rose? Are consumers buying more foreign goods or are manufacturers purchasing more capital goods from overseas? Although an increase in imports always worsens the trade balance, a rise in imports of capital goods is viewed more favorably than a gain in consumer goods because the former can increase the productive capacity of the country, but the latter are only for current consumption.

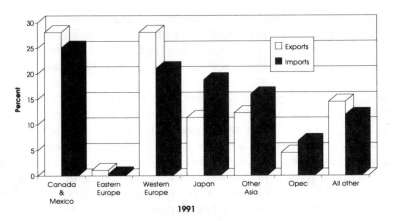

Figure 5.1 Canada and Mexico are the largest trading partners of the United States. (*Source:* Data are from Commerce Department publications.)

It is well recognized that the merchandise trade deficit is due largely to oil imports, which accounts for a major portion of our import bill. If we were to exclude oil imports from the total, the merchandise trade deficit would be cut in half. Many analysts look at the trade balance excluding oil, and other categories could be excluded as well. For example, the trade balance would show a surplus if we excluded automobiles and parts. Why don't we then? The fact of the matter is that economists can get a bit carried away in excluding components from variables. If one of the policy goals of the United States is a balanced merchandise trade account, and we know that oil is always going to be a large share of our import bill, we will just have to decrease the level of imports in other categories, such as capital equipment and automobiles.

The nature of foreign trade makes this indicator rather volatile from month to month. For example, the United States exports aircraft. A purchase of this size can skew the figures in any one month (as shown with durable goods orders and shipments.) And even oil purchases, a nondurable good, tend to be uneven because producers need to replenish reserves from time to time. Thus, it is important to look at the trade balance on a moving average basis.

Import growth is procyclical; that is, as the domestic economy expands and consumers have more income, they are more likely to spend some of the extra money on foreign goods. Holding all other factors constant, the trade balance tends to deteriorate during economic expansions. When foreign countries are experiencing rapid economic growth, their imports, (our exports) should increase at a faster pace. An increase in the growth of our exports will cause the trade deficit to narrow, or our surplus to widen. Economies across the globe sometimes experience economic expansions simultaneously. In that case, whose exports and imports will grow most rapidly? That depends on several factors based on the sensitivity of import demand to income. Historically, the sensitivity of import demand of U.S. residents has been stronger than the sensitivity of foreigners' import demand to income. As a result, we can predict that U.S. imports will probably grow faster than exports, and our trade balance will worsen.

Just like the demand for any product or service, the consumer and business demand for imports depends on more than just income and the business cycle. The prices of imported goods or services will also affect the demand for them. The price of imports can change in one of two ways: (1) The actual price of the good or service can rise or fall; or (2) the exchange value of the dollar can rise or fall, and effectively change the price of the imported good.

The exchange value of the dollar relative to other currencies is an important factor in trade flow. As the value of the dollar increases, imports become less expensive and therefore more desirable. At the same time, our exports become more expensive to foreigners and their demand tends to decline.

The picture can be muddied further. The marketing strategy of foreign corporations, may involve holding prices firm when the value of the dollar has declined, effectively making their products more expensive. Conversely, they can follow that same strategy when the value of the dollar is increasing. In this case, the price of the import may not necessarily rise as it would if it were simply responding to the foreign exchange value of the dollar. During the mid-1980s, the value of the dollar rose, so foreigners took advantage of their competitive edge and established their products in the United States. The merchandise trade deficit reached its peak in about 1987. Earlier, when the value of the dollar started to decline in the middle of 1985, economists expected that imports would drop sharply (with a time lag of 12 to 18 months) in response to higher import prices. But importers didn't rush out to raise their prices, preferring to hold on to their market share in the United States. As a result, imports didn't decline with the drop in the value of the dollar, although the rate of growth slowed significantly. The lower value of the dollar did make American products more competitive overseas, and export growth started to climb in 1987.

There are rough rules of thumb for various changes in the economic environment. First, the demand for imports moves in tandem with the business cycle, meaning that imports will grow during expansions and decline during recessions. At the same time, exports move in tandem with the business cycles of foreign economies, so the demand for our exports will grow when our major trading partners are expanding but will contract (or grow more slowly) when foreign economies are in recession.

The second rule of thumb is that trade flows are sensitive to the exchange rate. Whenever the value of the dollar increases in the foreign exchange market, consumers and businesses demand more imports because they have become relatively cheaper. The flip side of the coin says that foreigners will demand fewer U.S. exports because our goods and services have now become more expensive. A *decrease* in the value of the dollar will soften our demand for imports because they are more expensive. American exporters benefit from a decline in the value of the dollar because their products become more competitive overseas.

Did You Know?   Competition and a weak economy may prevent price pass-throughs when currencies rise relative to the dollar. "It's called margin squeeze," says Mike Hennessy of Gourmet Specialities, Hayward, California. In one case, the *Wall Street Journal* reported that another California company, Italfoods, Inc., of South San Francisco only raised their Italian cheese prices 9 percent when their costs rose 15 percent.[1]

The third rule of thumb also has to do with prices. When prices of American goods rise more rapidly than prices of foreign goods, the demand for domestically produced goods declines both in the United States and abroad. Thus, U.S. inflation bodes poorly for exports. On the flip side, inflationary pressures in foreign economies that lead to increases in the prices of imported goods will cause a drop in demand for imports.

Market Reaction   During much of the 1980s, financial market participants eyed the net merchandise trade balance (always a deficit during the period) and reacted to changes in the balance. In the past few years, markets have begun to look at the figures more closely. That is, they now look at the separate monthly changes in exports and imports.

Participants in the fixed-income market favor a deteriorating balance coming from weak exports because that points to a sluggish economy. However, they don't necessarily favor an increase in imports because that weakens the foreign exchange value of the dollar. A deteriorating dollar can lead to inflationary pressures as well as a rise in the demand for exports down the road.

Watch Out For: Market expectations surrounding the figures should give you an idea whether higher exports will be good or bad for the markets. Depending on other economic indicators, the interpretation may change. In any case, there are a few special factors that you should watch for in the merchandise trade deficit. First, as mentioned previously, you should always determine whether the change in the trade balance comes from exports or imports. Second, look at the pattern of growth in each series. A one-month blip in imports or exports is not necessarily a problem, nor the beginning of a new trend. Therefore look at a three-month moving average of each series (imports and exports.) Oil imports and agricultural exports occasionally cause monthly blips. Auto shipments from overseas can also cause occasional distortions. These have become smaller, however, since many producers of foreign cars now produce in the United States. Aircraft shipments can spur exports from time to time.

When the exchange value of the dollar is in a declining mode, the nominal trade balance will get worse before it gets better. This phenomenon is called the "*J*-curve effect." When the exchange value of the dollar declines, economic theory suggests that we should sell more exports and buy fewer imports. But, since the import figures are denominated in dollars, we need more dollars to pay for the current level of imports. Let's say that the value of the dollar depreciated by 10 percent in March. It will take several months for consumers and producers to change their demand based on the weaker dollar. At the same time, all the goods that were brought in March now cost 10 percent more, so the initial impact of a drop in the value of the dollar is to worsen the U.S. trade deficit. Conversely, when the foreign exchange value of the dollar has appreciated, economic theory suggests that we should purchase more imports. But consumers and producers will take a few more months to respond to a rise in the value of the dollar. Thus, a 10 percent appreciation in the dollar in March will lead to a drop in the trade bill. In this case, the initial impact of a dollar rise is to improve the deficit.

This is one of the reasons that constant dollar data will not lead you astray when determining underlying trends in the data. In adjusting the merchandise trade balance for inflation, the *J*-curve will not be evidenced.

Participants in the equity markets favor an improving trade balance with a robust demand for exports coupled with a lackluster demand for imports. That points to strong gains in domestic production and also bodes well for domestic sales and corporate earnings. The only stipulation is that export growth should not be strong enough to incite inflationary pressures in the domestic economy. No one likes inflation.

Foreign exchange market professionals also favor an improving trade balance caused by healthy export growth. A demand for exports points to a demand for dollars that is independent of the demand for dollars from higher interest rates. If exports grow too rapidly, fixed-income market players may worry about credit demands in an expanding economy that could cause interest rates to rise.

QUARTERLY INDICATORS

The Bureau of Economic Analysis publishes the balance of payments of the United States quarterly. The balance of payments is a summary measure of economic transactions of U.S. residents with the rest of the world. In the balance of payments measures (although not the national income and product accounts), U.S. residents include all 50 states and the District of Columbia along with U.S. territories and Puerto Rico (of course, military personnel on bases outside the United States are also U.S. residents). In general, the international accounts comprise transactions on current account and on capital account. These form the basis for the quarterly estimates of exports and imports that are part of gross domestic product.

Current Account

The current account—a comprehensive measure of a country's trade balance in goods, services, and unilateral transfers—is widely used in international comparisons of countries' relative strengths and weaknesses in international transactions. The current account is reported nearly three months after the end of the quarter. The data are released at a quarterly level (not annualized), but they are seasonally adjusted. The account is denominated in current dollars, that is, it isn't adjusted for inflation. Moreover, it is never discussed in real terms (unlike the merchandise trade balance, which is analyzed in current and constant dollars).

More specifically, the current account transactions include exports and imports of merchandise, investment receipts and payments, net military, transportation, travel, and other services. Unilateral transfers are imputed transactions. The balance of payments uses double entry bookkeeping. Consequently, an export of a good or service that is not paid for in a good, service, or income becomes a transfer. Examples of unilateral transfers are U.S. government grants and remittances, and pensions. For

Table 5.2   U.S. Current Account Summary Data
(billions of dollars, seasonally adjusted)

	Q1:91	Q2:91	Q3:91	Q4:91	Q1:92	Q2:92
Balance on merchandise trade	−18.326	−16.397	−20.174	−18.539	−17.222	−24.418
Balance on services	9.355	10.782	12.023	13.136	13.844	12.972
Balance on investment income	6.965	3.931	3.076	2.458	4.474	1.377
Unilateral transfers	14.199	4.115	−6.012	−4.273	−6.999	−7.719
Balance on current account	12.193	2.431	−11.087	−7.218	−5.903	−17.788

Source: Bureau of Economic Analysis, U.S. Department of Commerce; *Summary of U.S. International Transactions* Sept. 15, 1992.

instance, if a company pays a pension to a former U.S. resident who now lives in a foreign country permanently, it is a transfer from the U.S. accounts to that foreign country. In the same way, a person who previously lived and worked in a foreign country, but now permanently resides in the United States, may receive a pension from the foreign country that will also be a transfer payment. These are all added together to arrive at a net balance for unilateral transfers. Table 5.2 lists the major categories of the current account.

Capital Account

The balance on capital account is divided into broad categories of U.S. assets abroad and foreign assets in the United States. U.S. assets are divided into U.S. official reserves and other government assets, and private assets. This category includes direct investment in a foreign country. Direct foreign investment in the United States might include the Japanese or British purchase of U.S. land and buildings, whereas direct investment by an American corporation might be the purchase of an office building in Singapore. Foreign assets are divided into foreign official assets and other foreign assets. The account is balanced by a statistical discrepancy.

Market Reaction   Not all financial market participants will react to these international transactions statistics. In fact, players in the stock and fixed-income markets are likely to ignore them altogether. The news is old—at least three months old—and not very worthwhile in terms of predicting near-term future events.

Professionals in the foreign exchange market would find the data somewhat interesting because of the implications for the dollar. If the U.S. current account balance is deteriorating (or going into greater deficit), it means that businesses and consumers are purchasing more goods and services overseas than foreigners are purchasing American goods and services. This suggests a greater demand for currencies of foreign countries, rather than a demand for the U.S. dollar, causing the value of the dollar to decline. When the current account balance is improving (or going into greater surplus), it means that foreigners are demanding more American goods and services than we are demanding foreign products. This demand suggests that the value of the dollar will increase.

The transactions measured in the current account occurred months ago, and most likely, the greater or smaller demand for the U.S. dollar also took place during that time period. Because the current account balance is simply an information mechanism or a confirmation of what has already happened, the reaction in the foreign exchange market is likely to be subdued.

Watch Out For: Always search for special factors that could skew the underlying trends in the data. In 1991, several foreign countries reimbursed the United States for its military hardware during the Persian Gulf war. The billions of dollars of payments resulted in a U.S. current account deficit of a mere $3.5 billion dollars in 1991, compared with a deficit of $90 billion dollars in 1990. These payments obscured the underlying trends in the current account. It is true that the current account was improving as the gap narrowed on the balance of trade (for goods). However, the United States still had quite a bit of red ink.

Look at long-term trends in the current account to assess the relative competitiveness of the United States versus foreign countries. Also, these trends indicate where our standard of living is headed. During the 1980s, the trade deficit and the federal budget deficit were termed the "twin deficits." Spending by consumers, businesses, and government led to large borrowing needs and little savings. As a result, the U.S. federal budget deficit had to be financed by foreigners. How does that hurt the United States? It means that interest payments are made to foreigners, not American residents; therefore, funds leave our economy and become income abroad. Eventually, the income loss through high deficit repayments leads to a lower standard of living.

- The U.S. economy has steadily increased its reliance on trade with foreign countries during the 1980s and 1990s.
- Indicators describing foreign trade in goods, services, and capital expenditures are sparse relative to economic indicators describing other sectors of the economy.
- Indicators of foreign trade are the least timely of all economic series.
- A positive or improving trade balance is bullish for the foreign exchange market—it means a strong value of the dollar.
- A positive or improving trade balance is also bullish for the stock market because it portends strong domestic corporate profits.
- A positive or improving trade balance is bearish for the fixed-income market because it suggests healthy domestic production and portends inflationary pressures.
- Table 5.3 summarizes the foreign sector indicators, their approximate dates of release, and source agencies.

Table 5.3   Indicators of the Foreign Sector

Approximate		Indicator	Data for	Source Agency
Month	Day			
Jan	15 to 20	Merchandise trade balance	Nov	Bureau of the Census
Feb	15 to 20	Merchandise trade balance	Dec	Bureau of the Census
Mar	1 to 5	Balance of payments	Q4	Bureau of Economic Analysis
Mar	15 to 20	Current account	Q4	Bureau of Economic Analysis
Mar	15 to 20	Merchandise trade balance	Jan	Bureau of the Census
Apr	15 to 20	Merchandise trade balance	Feb	Bureau of the Census

Table 5.3   *(Continued)*

| Approximate | | | | |
Month	Day	Indicator	Data for	Source Agency
May	15 to 20	Merchandise trade balance	Mar	Bureau of the Census
June	1 to 5	Balance of payments	Q1	Bureau of Economic Analysis
June	15 to 20	Current account	Q1	Bureau of Economic Analysis
June	15 to 20	Merchandise trade balance	Apr	Bureau of the Census
July	15 to 20	Merchandise trade balance	May	Bureau of the Census
Aug	15 to 20	Merchandise trade balance	June	Bureau of the Census
Aug	25 to 30	Balance of payments	Q2	Bureau of Economic Analysis
Sep	15 to 20	Current account	Q2	Bureau of Economic Analysis
Sep	15 to 20	Merchandise trade balance	July	Bureau of the Census
Oct	15 to 20	Merchandise trade balance	Aug	Bureau of the Census
Nov	15 to 20	Merchandise trade balance	Sep	Bureau of the Census
Nov	25 to 30	Balance of payments	Q3	Bureau of Economic Analysis
Dec	15 to 20	Current account	Q3	Bureau of Economic Analysis
Dec	15 to 20	Merchandise trade balance	Oct	Bureau of the Census

CHAPTER 6

The Government Sector

Featured Indicators	Federal Budget
	Government Employment
	Public Construction
	Defense Orders, Shipments, and
	Inventories

Government expenditures on goods and services account for nearly 20 percent of gross domestic product. This category of GDP does not incorporate transfer payments and funds going to entitlement programs such as Social Security payments, unemployment insurance compensation, or food stamps and housing subsidies. As mentioned in Chapter 2, the government spending category can include such items as office equipment, military hardware, or the salaries of civilian and military workers, which are payment for services rendered. However, transfer payments can't be counted in GDP because they don't represent the production of a good or service.

Government spending is different from other sectors of the economy. Consumer spending and investment expenditures depend on such economic factors as income and interest rates. The foreign sector depends on these also, as well as on the foreign exchange value of the dollar. Government spending on goods and services are not directly related to the economy in the same manner. Federal defense purchases, for example, do not depend on U.S. economic growth in the same way that personal consumption expenditures depend on disposable income.

Therefore, you can't apply the same rules of thumb to increases or decreases in government expenditures as to declines or gains in other economic indicators. For instance, consumers spend about 95 cents of each additional dollar they earn, so if disposable income increases by 1 percent, we can surmise that consumer spending will increase by practically the same amount.

Government expenditures are based instead on fiscal policy, which is measured by the federal government's decision to purchase goods and services, pay out transfers in income or in-kind, and determine tax policy. The government may decide to spend more during recessions to spur economic activity; the government may decide to spend less during expansions to prevent inflationary pressures. But these decisions must be determined: No automatic mechanism increases government expenditures on goods and services as the economy falls into recession, nor does a mechanism curtail government expenditures on goods and services when the economy is expanding at a good clip. Fiscal policy does impact economic growth. Through the multiplier effect, increases in government spending will eventually lead to increases in consumer income and spending. It's just that the relationship is more indirect.

Although there is a lack of automatic expenditures on goods and services that are counted as government spending in GDP, the government has some automatic mechanisms in place that move counter to the business cycle. These automatic stabilizers work on the income side as well as the expenditure side of the federal government budget. The expenditures are not those counted in GDP because they are transfer payments. When the economy slides into a downturn, the government will pay more unemployment compensation or will give more subsidies such as food stamps to those in need. At the same time, federal government coffers will also suffer a decline in revenues because of lower income and corporate taxes. The U.S. tax system is such that those individuals in lower income brackets pay less taxes. When workers earn less money by working fewer hours during a week, or fewer weeks in a year, they will also have a smaller tax bill.

State and local governments also experience this decline in tax revenues during downturns and subsequent increases in tax revenues when the economy recovers. Whereas the federal government has not worked consistently toward a balanced budget, state and local governments have tended to operate in that direction. In the aggregate, state and local government revenues have exceeded outlays for the past 30 years with only minor exceptions (1959, 1961, and 1967). As a result, state and local government spending is closely tied to the business cycle—sales and income tax revenues drop during recessions and rise with expansions.

Through reduced tax revenues and increased transfer payments, the government sector of the economy will be affected by the business cycle. It is up to the decision makers whether to offset declines in the private sector by beefing up the public sector, and this decision-making process is beset by many lags so that a spending boost may not always be in place when it is needed most. Many may remember President Ford's tax rebate in the first half of 1975. As it turned out, the economy was already coming out of recession by the time that the Administration and Congress had approved a tax rebate to stimulate consumer spending and the economy. Many economists believe that a poorly timed fiscal stimulus can instigate or exacerbate inflationary pressures.

In looking at government spending as a GDP entity, we have few indicators that show the direction of this spending on a monthly basis. No single indicator is relevant in the same way that retail sales are related to personal consumption expenditures or the merchandise trade balance is related to the foreign sector. However, few indicators that are subcategories of series for other sectors of the economy suggest the level of government spending for the current period.

In contrast to most economic statistics, most of the following factors don't have a media following, nor are they closely monitored by financial market participants. If federal policymakers such as the Federal Reserve want to monitor developments in both the private sector and the public sector, they scrutinize figures known as "hidden indicators."

The only release describing government spending used by players in the financial markets is the monthly estimate of the federal budget. Oddly enough, the media often give it little attention relative to less important indicators. It is no wonder then, that a September 1992 Gallop poll found only 19 percent of those surveyed knew the expected size of the 1992 budget deficit.

MONTHLY INDICATOR

Federal Budget

The Department of the Treasury releases a monthly budget report, showing the receipts and outlays incurred by the federal government agencies. These figures are reported about three weeks after the end of each month. Neither expenditures nor receipts are adjusted for

Table 6.1 U.S. Budget Receipts by Source, Outlays by Function (billions of dollars)

	Sep	FY 1992	FY 1991
Receipts:			
Individual income taxes	55,496	476,465	467,827
Corporation income taxes	19,896	100,270	98,086
Social insurance taxes and contributions			
Employment taxes and contributions	32,597	385,491	370,526
Unemployment insurance	315	23,410	20,922
Other retirement contributions	409	4,788	4,568
Excise taxes	4,093	45,570	42,402
Estate and gift taxes	1,004	11,143	11,138
Customs	1,552	17,359	15,949
Miscellaneous	2,980	27,195	22,846
Total Receipts	118,344	1,091,692	1,054,265
Outlays:			
National defense	25,842	298,188	273,292
International affairs	1,727	16,100	15,851
General science, space, and technology	1,159	16,234	16,111
Energy	665	4,519	2,408
Natural Resources and environment	1,742	19,870	18,552
Agriculture	195	14,968	15,183
Commerce and housing credit	585	9,752	75,639
Transportation	3,618	33,747	31,099
Community and regional development	764	7,924	6,811
Education, training, employment and social services	2,233	43,586	42,809
Health	8,834	89,586	71,183
Medicare	10,309	119,024	104,489
Income security	15,175	199,395	170,846
Social Security	24,151	287,545	269,015
Veterans benefits and services	3,213	33,973	31,349
Administration of justice	1,277	14,481	12,276
General government	1,869	12,874	11,661
Interest	15,435	199,422	194,541
Undistributed offsetting receipts	−5,847	−39,280	−39,356
Total Outlays	112,943	1,381,895	1,323,757
Memorandum (outlays)			
Defense cooperation account	0,000	−4,910	−43,154
FDIC outlays			
Bank insurance fund	−1,806	3,666	7,363
Savings association insurance fund	−80	−292	−36
FSLIC resolution fund	3,253	8,469	8,556
Credit union share insurance fund	2	−233	−261
Resolution Trust Corporation outlays	−4,193	−8,934	50,758

Source: Department of the Treasury; U.S. Budget Receipts by Source, Outlays by Function Data, *Market News Service, Inc.,* New York, October 28, 1992.

seasonal variation. Furthermore, the data are not annualized like most economic statistics.

Budget receipts are some form of taxes, individual income taxes being the largest source of revenue; the second largest source is social insurance taxes and contributions. Table 6.1 shows all the other classifications of taxes and duties released regularly.

Outlays include total government expenditures: those that can be counted as GDP expenditures, and those that can't (by virtue of being a transfer payment of some sort). In fiscal year 1991, outlays for national defense were the largest government expenditure, closely followed by outlays on Social Security. Interest on the national debt and income security was the third largest expenditure despite a drop in interest rates between 1991 and 1992. However, it was closely rivaled by outlays on income security partially because the recession and lackluster recovery during this period resulted in higher transfer payments. Table 6.1 shows expenditures for all categories.

Although the budget receipts and outlays are not seasonally adjusted, they tend to follow a seasonal pattern, the magnitude of which varies from year to year. Receipts tend to rise in January, April, June, September, and December, months that correspond to quarterly tax payment dates. Outlays don't follow any discernible pattern over the year. The only exception is that agencies may spend more in August and September, the end of the fiscal year, if they still have unspent appropriated funds because they fear the funds will be taken away in the subsequent fiscal year.

Since the budget is not seasonally adjusted, always look at the current budget deficit (surplus) relative to the previous year. For instance, if the budget is in surplus every April, check to see if this year's surplus is larger than last year's. In April 1992, the budget surplus was $14.6 billion. Following a deficit of $50.7 billion in March, it would appear that the United States was on the right track. However, judging by the previous April's budget surplus of $30 billion, the 1992 surplus was less then spectacular. Figure 6.1 depicts monthly budget figures for three fiscal years.

Market Reaction Financial market professionals aren't always interested in the specifics of what was spent and what was collected. They are more interested in the total monthly budget balance, more commonly referred to as the budget deficit, since we haven't seen a surplus in any fiscal year since 1969. Even then, a surplus was an unusual occurrence. A large budget deficit is bearish for the fixed-income market.

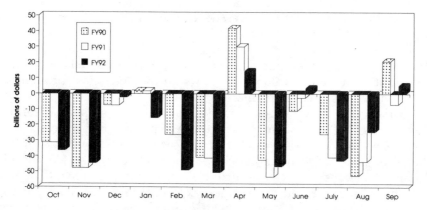

Figure 6.1 Although the federal budget is not seasonally adjusted, some patterns persist from month to month. (*Source: Market News Service, Inc.,* U.S. Treasury.)

It means more government borrowing. To finance the deficit, the United States Treasury will sell bonds (securities with maturities of more than 10 years), notes (securities with maturities of 2 to 10 years), and bills (securities that mature in 3 or 6 months or 52 weeks), through the Federal Reserve System. Treasury securities have to be bought by someone. The greater the supply of Treasury securities (which support the budget deficit) the lower the price of these securities. Low bond prices mean high yields. Thus, a large supply of Treasury securities that need to be financed suggests higher interest rates are in line to entice buyers. If there is a large supply of Treasury securities in the marketplace, corporate bonds must compete with them. A high rate of interest for Treasury securities, considered a risk-free security, means a higher rate of interest on corporate bonds, which are associated with greater risk (due to default possibilities.) This is indeed bad news for the markets.

Players in the stock market are not favorably disposed to a high budget deficit either. Since the stock market represents the equity of corporations, these companies will have to borrow funds at a higher interest rate to expand their businesses, or even to meet short-term cash management needs. Moreover, higher interest rates are associated with a lower present value for the returns of the company (see box, "Net Present Value," in Chapter 1).

Foreign exchange market professionals might be more favorably disposed toward a large budget deficit supported by an ample supply of

Treasury securities. It means higher interest rates in the United States, which in turn bring in capital from abroad. As foreigners try to buy our supply of Treasury securities, they will bid up the demand for dollars. The exchange value of the dollar will increase. However, foreigners will not be exactly happy to finance our budget deficit forever. Japanese investors were major buyers of U.S. Treasury securities during much of the 1980s, but their interest waned as our deficit continued to skyrocket.

Watch Out For: Check the various categories of receipts and outlays to see if anything in particular could have caused the current month's budget surplus to be smaller or larger than expected. For example, a particularly good report (high surplus) might reflect the postponement of payments by government agencies. A rather poor report (large deficit) might be the result of a business cycle in which the government is paying out more in transfer payments, and receiving fewer tax receipts. The July 1992 outlays on Social Security payments were higher than normal because August 1 fell on a Saturday and Social Security recipients must receive their checks by the third of every month. As a result, the August outlays for Social Security were lower than normal, allowing the July budget deficit to be overstated and the August deficit to be understated.

As the federal budget deficit increases, the U.S. Treasury has to finance it with more and more Treasury bonds. The only way to entice consumers and foreigners to buy bills, notes, and bonds is to raise the interest rate on these securities. There is another aspect to consider. Many financial market participants fear that a surge in the federal budget deficit will accelerate inflationary pressures. Many feel that larger budget deficits will induce the Federal Reserve to print money and inflate the economy to reduce the burden of the debt on the government and transfer it to taxpayers. During the 1980s the Federal Reserve Board went to great efforts to reduce inflationary pressures, and the rhetoric of the Federal Reserve continues to be one of fighting inflation. They have repeatedly stated that they don't intend to inflate the economy to reduce the deficit. It remains to be seen whether the Fed will be able to convince financial market participants, who, at least during the 1980s and early 1990s, were not fully persuaded. As a result, an inflation premium was built in the long (30-year) bond, as can be seen in Figure 6.2. The yield on 30-year Treasury bonds won't decline until financial market participants are convinced inflation has been wiped out, and/or the supply of 30-year bonds declines.

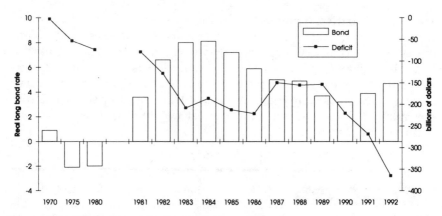

Figure 6.2 While the real interest rate was low or negative in the 1970s, bondholders made up for it in the 1980s with extraordinarily high real interest rates. Despite some improvement in the federal budget deficit in the late 1980s, the United States got deeper into red ink in the 1990s with the onset of recession and the savings and loan bailout. (*Source:* Data are from Commerce Department and Federal Reserve publications.)

HIDDEN INDICATORS

There are three hidden indicators: (1) the employment report, (2) construction expenditures, and (3) durable goods orders and shipments.

Government Employment

The first indicator reported during the month is the employment situation. The Bureau of Labor Statistics, a division of the Labor Department releases the employment situation for the previous month only one week after the end of the month. The establishment survey that measures nonfarm payroll employment includes payroll changes in federal as well as state and local government. Data are seasonally adjusted monthly levels.

The federal government portion includes only civilian federal employees in the establishment survey. In terms of the federal government, compensation is a small portion of total purchases. With respect to the state and local government figures, however, compensation is a large portion of state and local government purchases, so changes in employment could have a significant impact on total spending. After adjusting for wages, I found that employment levels at the state and local level have corresponded closely with quarterly changes in state and local government spending as measured in gross domestic product. (See Table 6.2.)

The household survey that measures total employment (and is the source of the nation's unemployment rate) also provides information on military employment, but these figures are no longer reported in the monthly news release with other household data. The figures are available in the monthly publication of the Bureau of Labor Statistics, *Employment and Earnings*. (Also, economists at the Bureau of Labor Statistics are quite accommodating in releasing data, so you can always call the agency for the figures.)

Until the early 1980s, when the United States was beset by recession and high employment rates, the Bureau of Labor Statistics regularly reported only the civilian unemployment rate. About the same time, many economists were conducting studies that suggested it would be proper to include the military in the monthly labor force statistics. The Commission for Employment and Unemployment Statistics had recommended this policy in 1979. By definition, all military personnel would be counted as employed and in the labor force. Adding these figures to the civilian labor force would put downward pressure on the total unemployment rate, because these would be workers with total job security. Thus, the total unemployment rate including military personnel was always 0.1 or 0.2 percentage points less than the civilian jobless rate. The rationale behind the inclusion of military personnel is that working in this sector is a viable choice as long as there is no draft. Despite the government's attempt to highlight the total unemployment rate rather than the civilian unemployment rate, it just didn't work. Financial market participants and the media continued to pay attention to the civilian jobless rate. Finally, the Bureau of Labor Statistics stopped releasing the total unemployment rate monthly.

All in all, the employment figures are a good indicator of monthly spending in state and local government. Although the data are virtually ignored by the markets, economists use them to forecast the government spending portion of gross domestic product.

Table 6.2 Employees on Nonfarm Payrolls by Industry
(thousands, seasonally adjusted)

	Jan 92	Feb 92	Mar 92	Apr 92	May 92	June 92	July 92	Aug 92	Sep 92	Oct 92	Nov 92	Dec 92
Government	18,457	18,461	18,507	18,542	18,546	18,538	18,606	18,682	18,650	18,623	18,685	18,700
Federal	2,981	2,981	2,989	2,986	2,984	2,972	2,927	2,959	2,967	2,942	2,940	2,973
State	4,347	4,346	4,345	4,360	4,367	4,357	4,388	4,383	4,401	4,390	4,384	4,395
Local	11,129	11,134	11,173	11,196	11,195	11,209	11,261	11,340	11,282	11,291	11,361	11,332

Source: *Monthly Labor Review*, U.S. Department of Labor, Bureau of Labor Statistics, March 1993.

Watch Out For: Keep an eye on government employment growth to discern whether the total rise in nonfarm payrolls was due to the private or public sector. Gains in government employment are not necessarily smooth from month to month, despite the ever-present seasonal adjustment mechanism. For example, during election years, local governments may hire extra workers for polling and the like, which will show up as a temporary blip. If teachers go on strike at the start of the school year, it can affect local government employment, especially since teachers tend to return to school in large numbers in August and September and the seasonal adjustment factors expect them.

The major blip in government sector employment occurs during census years. The last census was undertaken in 1990, so this particular aberration won't happen again until the year 2000. In 1990, census workers were hired during the first half of the year, raising monthly estimates of nonfarm payrolls. These same workers were fired in the second half of the year, lowering estimates of nonfarm payrolls by a similar magnitude.

Remember to check the trend in employment in addition to the monthly figures. Just as with all other economic data, the level or rate of growth can be erratic from one month to the next.

Public Construction

Construction expenditures are also reported monthly. As mentioned in Chapter 4, the Bureau of the Census reports construction expenditures about five weeks after the end of the month. The series encompasses private residential spending, private nonresidential spending, and public expenditures.

Public expenditures include spending on education buildings, highways, streets, and sewer systems, among others. Table 6.3 shows the complete report. The largest component is highways and streets. State and local governments finance most highway and street construction (even when it is subsidized by federal government funds). This component gives a good idea as to the spending on structures by state and local governments on a monthly basis. These figures are also ignored by the financial markets but are useful to economists in assessing spending on structures by state and local government, as measured by GDP.

Table 6.3   Construction Expenditures
(billions of dollars, seasonally adjusted)

	Current Dollars			Real (1987) Dollars		
	Mar 92	Apr 92	May 92	Mar 92	Apr 92	May 92
Public Expenditures	120.4	118.3	121.6	110.2	107.9	110.8
Housing/redevelopment	3.6	3.5	3.6	3.2	3.1	3.3
Industrial	1.9	1.7	1.7	1.7	1.6	1.5
Educational	25.7	23.5	24.4	23.0	21.0	21.7
Hospital	3.0	2.8	2.8	2.7	2.5	2.5
Other public buildings	21.3	21.9	23.3	19.1	19.5	20.7
Highways and streets	30.9	31.7	33.3	29.9	30.5	32.0
Military facilities	2.5	2.3	2.7	2.4	2.2	2.5
Conservation/development	6.2	5.8	5.2	5.4	5.0	4.5
Sewer systems	9.3	9.7	8.8	8.1	8.4	7.6
Water systems	5.1	4.8	4.8	4.7	4.5	4.4
Miscellaneous public	10.9	10.5	11.0	10.0	9.6	10.0

Source: Bureau of the Census, Department of Commerce, *Construction Reports.*

Watch Out For: The detail on public construction expenditures are not necessarily useful on a piecemeal basis. Nonetheless, you should always check spending on highways and streets. If is by far the largest category and is subject to more volatility from weather and seasonal adjustment problems. It corresponds to the spending on structures by state and local governments in GDP data.

Defense Orders, Shipments, and Inventories

The advance durable goods report, along with the more complete manufacturers' shipments, inventories, and orders report, also includes figures for defense. Defense orders and shipments that illustrate spending on ships, tanks, and aircraft are highly volatile from month to month. These figures don't correlate well with government spending figures as measured by gross domestic product. (I spent several years tracking the data just in case.) These figures are also ignored by the financial markets, and rightly so. Although we could look at the level of orders, shipments, inventories, and unfilled orders of defense goods, this indicator is probably the least useful (see Table 6.4).

Table 6.4   Defense Capital Goods
(millions of dollars)

	Orders	Shipments	Unfilled Orders	Inventories
Jan 91	7,685	8,171	150,544	39,213
Feb 91	8,240	8,405	150,379	39,459
Mar 91	6,274	8,388	148,265	39,013
Apr 91	7,627	8,821	147,071	39,075
May 91	9,448	8,271	148,248	38,570
June 91	7,926	8,406	147,768	38,521
July 91	8,825	8,182	148,411	38,099
Aug 91	10,960	8,965	150,407	37,340
Sep 91	5,059	8,901	146,565	38,102
Oct 91	8,462	8,661	146,365	37,512
Nov 91	4,946	8,573	142,738	37,071
Dec 91	8,425	8,270	142,893	36,230

Source: Bureau of the Census, Department of Commerce, *Current Industrial Reports,* June 1992.

Key Points

- Increases in government spending are unfavorable to the fixed-income market because increased borrowing needs will cause interest rates to rise. Higher U.S. interest rates are favorable for the value of the dollar, but not for stock prices.
- The Treasury's monthly budget tells the market about the government's spending and borrowing needs.
- Hidden indicators, reflecting government spending, don't affect the financial markets because participants don't see what is happening.
- Table 6.5 summarizes the government sector indicators, their approximate release dates, and source agencies.

Table 6.5　Indicators of Government Spending

Month	Day	Indicator	Data for	Source Agency
Approximate				
Jan	1 to 5	Public sector construction spending	Nov	Bureau of the Census
	1 to 6	Defense shipments, inventories, and orders	Nov	Bureau of the Census
	1 to 10	Government employment	Dec	Bureau of Labor Statistics
	20 to 26	Treasury budget	Dec	U.S. Department of Treasury
	23 to 30	Defense goods shipments and orders	Dec	Bureau of the Census
Feb	1 to 5	Public sector construction spending	Dec	Bureau of the Census
	1 to 6	Defense shipments, inventories, and orders	Dec	Bureau of the Census
	1 to 10	Government employment	Jan	Bureau of Labor Statistics
	20 to 26	Treasury budget	Jan	U.S. Department of Treasury
	23 to 30	Defense goods shipments and orders	Jan	Bureau of the Census
Mar	1 to 5	Public sector construction spending	Jan	Bureau of the Census
	1 to 6	Defense shipments, inventories, and orders	Jan	Bureau of the Census
	1 to 10	Government employment	Feb	Bureau of Labor Statistics
	20 to 26	Treasury budget	Feb	U.S. Department of Treasury
	23 to 30	Defense goods shipments and orders	Feb	Bureau of the Census
Apr	1 to 5	Public sector construction spending	Feb	Bureau of the Census
	1 to 6	Defense shipments, inventories, and orders	Feb	Bureau of the Census
	1 to 10	Government employment	Mar	Bureau of Labor Statistics

Table 6.5 *(Continued)*

Approximate		Indicator	Data for	Source Agency
Month	Day			
Apr	20 to 26	Treasury budget	Mar	U.S. Department of Treasury
	23 to 30	Defense goods shipments and orders	Mar	Bureau of the Census
May	1 to 5	Public sector construction spending	Mar	Bureau of the Census
	1 to 6	Defense shipments, inventories, and orders	Mar	Bureau of the Census
	1 to 10	Government employment	Apr	Bureau of Labor Statistics
	20 to 26	Treasury budget	Apr	U.S. Department of Treasury
	23 to 30	Defense goods shipments and orders	Apr	Bureau of the Census
June	1 to 5	Public sector construction spending	Apr	Bureau of the Census
	1 to 6	Defense shipments, inventories, and orders	Apr	Bureau of the Census
	1 to 10	Government employment	May	Bureau of Labor Statistics
	20 to 26	Treasury budget	May	U.S. Department of Treasury
	23 to 30	Defense goods shipments and orders	May	Bureau of the Census
July	1 to 5	Public sector construction spending	May	Bureau of the Census
	1 to 6	Defense shipments, inventories, and orders	May	Bureau of the Census
	1 to 10	Government employment	June	Bureau of Labor Statistics
	20 to 26	Treasury budget	June	U.S. Department of Treasury
	23 to 30	Defense goods shipments and orders	June	Bureau of the Census

Table 6.5   *(Continued)*

Approximate		Indicator	Data for	Source Agency
Month	Day			
Aug	1 to 5	Public sector construction spending	June	Bureau of the Census
	1 to 6	Defense shipments, inventories, and orders	June	Bureau of the Census
	1 to 10	Government employment	July	Bureau of Labor Statistics
	20 to 26	Treasury budget	July	U.S. Department of Treasury
	23 to 30	Defense goods shipments and orders	July	Bureau of the Census
Sep	1 to 5	Public sector construction spending	July	Bureau of the Census
	1 to 6	Defense shipments, inventories, and orders	July	Bureau of the Census
	1 to 10	Government employment	Aug	Bureau of Labor Statistics
	20 to 26	Treasury budget	Aug	U.S. Department of Treasury
	23 to 30	Defense goods shipments and orders	Aug	Bureau of the Census
Oct	1 to 5	Public sector construction spending	Aug	Bureau of the Census
	1 to 6	Defense shipments, inventories, and orders	Aug	Bureau of the Census
	1 to 10	Government employment	Sep	Bureau of Labor Statistics
	20 to 26	Treasury budget	Sep	U.S. Department of Treasury
	23 to 30	Defense goods shipments and orders	Sep	Bureau of the Census
Nov	1 to 5	Public sector construction spending	Sep	Bureau of the Census
	1 to 6	Defense shipments, inventories, and orders	Sep	Bureau of the Census
	1 to 10	Government employment	Oct	Bureau of Labor Statistics

Table 6.5 *(Continued)*

Approximate		Indicator	Data for	Source Agency
Month	Day			
Nov	20 to 26	Treasury budget	Oct	U.S. Department of Treasury
	23 to 30	Defense goods shipments and orders	Oct	Bureau of the Census
Dec	1 to 5	Public sector construction spending	Oct	Bureau of the Census
	1 to 6	Defense shipments, inventories, and orders	Oct	Bureau of the Census
	1 to 10	Government employment	Nov	Bureau of Labor Statistics
	20 to 26	Treasury budget	Nov	U.S. Department of Treasury
	23 to 30	Defense goods shipments and orders	Nov	Bureau of the Census

CHAPTER 7

Inflation

Featured Indicators	Crude Oil Prices
	Food Prices
	CRB Futures Price Index
	Index of Prices Received by Farmers
	Producer Price Indexes
	Consumer Price Index
	GDP Deflators
	Average Hourly Earnings
	Employment Cost Index
	Productivity and Costs

WHAT IS INFLATION?

Seldom can you put several people in a room who will be on the same side of an issue; but you could sequester a bond trader, a stock trader, a foreign exchange trader, and even several economists, and all would agree that inflation is bad. Government administration officials, Governors of the Federal Reserve Board, and Congress will also concur that inflation is bad. Even a broader constituency of consumers—lawyers, doctors, teachers, retailers, and homemakers—will be of one mind that inflation needs to be wiped out.

Although people read about inflation in the popular press, bandy the term about, and seem to be well versed on the topic, they are often not speaking about the same thing. So what is inflation anyway? A well-coined phrase describes it as "too much money chasing too few goods." The economic definition is not quite so succinct but states that inflation is an increase in the general level of prices. When I was a bank economist, a customer of the bank called to inquire about inflation. She obviously didn't know what it meant, and when I explained that inflation was caused by rising prices, she berated me for getting off the subject and huffily asked what prices had to do with inflation anyway.

When we talk about economic growth, we can point to gross domestic product as a comprehensive measure of economic activity in a country and can easily describe GDP by the sum of its components. Unfortunately, even though we can define inflation as an increase in the level of prices, there aren't any easy equations to memorize, nor is there a single measure of inflation that everyone will agree is a comprehensive and acceptable industry standard. Depending on the index, or the goods or services being measured, different rates of inflation abound. Inflation can be measured with a fixed weight or variable weight basket. Analyzing commodity prices, wages, or prices of services will yield not only different inflation rates, but also varying degrees of response to the environment.

Some commodity prices are so sensitive to the economic environment that a recession or weak growth can actually cause them to decline. Inflation then becomes *deflation*. The CRB Futures Price Index, which is a commodity index, declined about 6.0 percent between July 1990 and March 1991—during the recession. This index continued to decline during the mild recovery. It fell an additional 8% between March 1991 and February 1993 when the economy was clearly growing, albeit modestly. In contrast, a recession might affect wages and prices of services by *slowing down their rate of increase.* For instance, workers might receive annual wage increases of 3 percent a year rather than 6 percent. Compensation for professional services of lawyers or doctors may only increase 5 percent instead of 10 percent a year. The Employment Cost Index, a measure of wage inflation, was increasing at a 4.5 percent rate in the second quarter of 1990 (before the economy fell into recession), and was increasing at a 3.5 percent rate two years later, after the recession. As long as prices continue to rise, inflation has not gone away. This process of smaller price gains is *a moderation in the rate of inflation.* When prices were slowing in the mid-1980s, the term *disinflation* became popular. That term, however, implies a lack of inflation when prices are simply rising more slowly. Annual increases in the Consumer Price Index averaged 6.6 percent in the first half of the 1980s whereas they averaged 3.7 percent in the second half of the 1980s, but that does not mean inflation was wiped out, only that inflationary pressures moderated. True deflation occurs when prices actually have fallen. The last time the United States experienced extended price deflation was during the Great Depression in the 1930s. (In the postwar period, the consumer price index declined marginally on an annual basis only twice: in 1949 and 1954.)

In the labor market, a slower rate of inflation occurs, rather than outright declines in wages, because wage increases are contractual and often institutionalized. Moreover, wage contracts are long term, based on past inflation rates. It is uncommon to see someone's nominal wage decline, but more common to see prices of goods decline. Rapid technological change in the 1980s led to sharp declines in the prices of computers and calculators, for example.

Did You Know?   Real wages often decline when annual increases in wages don't match annual increases in prices. Average hourly earnings, adjusted for inflation, were lower in the 1980s than in the 1970s. Although inflation rates were higher in the first half of the decade, average hourly earnings were on an increasing trend from 1981 through 1986. They have declined every year since, even as consumer price increases have abated.

In addition to behavioral dissimilarities in inflation attributable to product differences such as goods versus services, the rates vary because of using nonidentical measurement processes. The Consumer Price Index and the Producer Price Index are *fixed weight* measures of inflation, meaning that the same basket of goods is analyzed each month. The GDP implicit deflator is a *variable weight* measure of inflation, which means that the basket of goods and services being priced depends on what was produced during a particular quarter.

WHY IS INFLATION BAD?

We all agree that inflation is bad, but why? In fact, inflation doesn't hurt everyone. So it's a wonder that everyone feels it is such an evil even though it is easy to see how inflation hurts the public in general. Rising prices reduce purchasing power. For instance, when gasoline prices rise by 5 cents a gallon, a weekly fill-up of 12 gallons of gas means that you are 60 cents poorer—not a great deal, but it can mean the cost of a candy bar or a soft drink at lunch. People on fixed incomes are hurt more by inflation than individuals whose wages rise with inflation. If your salary increases 5 percent and consumer prices rise 5 percent a year, then you are neither better nor worse off. But a rise in consumer prices will hurt those individuals whose incomes don't increase at all, or anyone whose wage increase is smaller than the gain in consumer prices.

Inflation creates instability in the economy and distorts economic decisions. Debtors should love inflation. Consumers who borrow to buy a house and students who take out loans to finance their education are able to repay their loans in dollars whose value is lower than at the time of borrowing. Moreover, as their wages increase with inflation, their monthly loan payments become less onerous. Congress should love inflation. It pushes people up into higher tax brackets and increases tax revenues without imposing new tax laws that would be unfavorable with constituents. (Tax reform efforts in the 1980s indexed some exemptions to inflation, reducing the tax bite.) Creditors are key losers in times of unexpected inflation as those who borrowed money return it in its reduced value. Company pensions are not adjusted for inflation although Social Security payments are adjusted annually by the yearly rise in the Consumer Price Index.

In periods of rapidly accelerating inflation, consumers and businesses may buy items they don't really need to avoid future price increases. Under different circumstances, funds might be put to better use. Holders of bonds are big losers as bond prices decline sharply when interest rates are rising. Such increases in rates occur to partly compensate lenders. Those who hold real property, such as real estate, are winners in an inflationary environment. Collectors of gold, silver, and antiques might also benefit.

Did You Know? Inflation can be good. Economist A. Gary Shilling explains, "Inflation bails out almost anything: paying someone too much for something, buying a building or a piece of equipment you don't need."[1] This view explains how the banking system may have been saved by the inflation of the 1970s and early 1980s. Loan officers made poor decisions on real estate loans but were saved by appreciating property values coming from inflation. However, as inflation moderated significantly in the second half of the 1980s, real estate was no longer increasing in value. *Unexpected* low inflation rates hurt creditors, too.

Some people argue that it is only unexpected inflation that causes problems, not anticipated inflation rates. After all, if we knew that we had to live with inflation, then we could take it into account when conducting transactions. Wages could be indexed (as many already are); interest rates could be indexed (similar to adjustable rate loans). The tax reform actions of the mid-1980s indexed tax brackets so that consumers would not automatically be shifted to a higher tax bracket when their salaries were merely keeping up with inflation. However, indexing economic transactions embeds inflation even more deeply into the system. If wages are indexed to inflation, producers may be tempted to raise their product prices even higher to cover increased wage costs (which are three-quarters of business costs).

If inflation is caused by "too much money chasing too few goods," the only thing we have to do is prevent the spread of "too much" money. That happens to be the job of the Federal Reserve System, which keeps track of the money supply in the financial system. When the Fed adds money (or reserves) to the banking system, it is said to be easing monetary policy. The easing allows interest rates to decline, thereby promoting economic growth through the interest-sensitive sectors. For instance, lower mortgage rates spur home sales. When the Fed takes money out of the banking system (drains reserves), it is said to be tightening monetary policy. The more restrictive monetary policy raises interest rates, thereby hindering economic growth through interest-sensitive sectors—higher mortgage rates curtail housing construction.

Congress instituted the Federal Reserve System in 1913 to handle several tasks. In addition to sustaining the stability of the banking system, it was commissioned to maintain price stability and promote economic growth. Since inflation is a monetary phenomenon, only the Federal Reserve can prevent it. The primary goal of the Federal Reserve Board is to uphold a balancing act between "reasonable" economic growth and low or no inflation. According to their speeches and testimony, Federal Reserve officials currently on the Board of Governors are striving for zero inflation.

> The Fed must make an assessment of what kind of policy will lead to the best growth of employment and the best growth of output . . . Price stability is the best way to get there.[2]
>
> Wayne Angell, Fed Governor
> Miami Meeting of the American
> Institute of Banking, Oct. 2, 1992

The best way the Fed can contribute to its goal of maximum sustained economic growth over time is to fulfill its unique role to foster price level stability. If the Fed fails to do that, there is no other institutional way to keep inflation in check.[3]

> Edward Kelley
> Fed Governor
> Statement to reporters following an
> address to the Financial Analysts of
> New Orleans, Oct. 14, 1992

The inflation indicators described in this chapter are as abundant as the indicators of consumer spending discussed in Chapter 3. Some of the high-frequency indicators favored by financial market participants are not necessarily worthwhile indicators for individual investors who don't have the data at their fingertips every minute of the day. The monthly and quarterly indicators of inflation are all reasonable to follow, although some may have more bugs than others on a month-to-month basis. On the whole, inflation is important to financial market participants and government policy-making officials, or else so many indicators wouldn't be published.

HIGH-FREQUENCY INDICATORS —COMMODITY PRICES

In anticipating inflationary pressures, oil and food prices are closely scrutinized key commodities. Oil, as a source of energy or a natural resource in the production of goods, is a key component of economic activity used in manufacturing, and it is an important product used by consumers as well. Food is an indispensable item in every person's budget.

Crude Oil Prices

Crude oil is traded at the New York Mercantile Exchange (NYMEX). Both spot and futures prices of crude oil are determined in the market. The spot price reflects the current value of the commodity, whereas the futures price reflects the price at some point in the future such as three or six months hence. Thus, if the spot price of (Texas) crude oil is $20.00

per barrel, you can purchase Texas crude today for $20.00 per barrel. But if the futures price of crude oil is $21.00 per barrel, you can purchase Texas crude today at the price of $21.00 per barrel for delivery three or six months hence.

Market Reaction   Financial market participants in the fixed-income, equity, and foreign exchange markets, often look at the futures price of crude oil as an indicator of inflation. As a group, traders react to actual economic and political events as well as rumors of these events. While traders in the financial markets are reacting to crude oil futures prices, commodity traders are making prices in the futures and spot markets. Furthermore, commodity traders can be as reactionary as stock, bond, or foreign exchange traders. Thus, rumors that Saudi Arabia will sharply curtail oil production will cause commodity traders to push up the price of oil in the spot and futures market.

Financial market traders will react negatively to the change in crude oil prices, and bond prices, stock prices, and the value of the dollar will all decline. A few minutes later, commodity traders may learn that the rumor was false and push prices back down. Bond prices, stock prices, and the value of the dollar will shoot back up. In the meantime, millions of dollars will have switched hands in the financial and commodity markets, creating quite a few winners and losers.

Food Prices

Food prices are also commodity prices that are closely monitored by financial market participants. Although no equivalent of OPEC intervenes in any of the crop or livestock markets, food is nonetheless affected by supply factors—largely natural disasters or bountiful harvests. Literally speaking, supply shocks can come and go with the tides. The most famous food price hike came on the heels of *El Niño* in 1973, which killed the anchovies off the coast of Peru, among other things (see box, "El Niño"). Over the course of several years, price fluctuations are smoothed out by droughts and bumper crops. Food price changes, like changes in the price of oil, tend to affect *relative* prices, rather than the price level. A historical series of the consumer price index shows that food prices don't tend to accelerate sharply during droughts if the overall economy is experiencing only modest inflation. However, when consumer prices of all other goods and services accelerate sharply, droughts or natural disasters among agricultural commodities lead food prices to spike as well.

Watch Out For: Oil is an important commodity in the U.S. economy. Changing oil prices might indicate changing prices in other commodities. Because supply-and-demand considerations cause oil futures prices to change frequently. Getting caught up in hourly price changes is not entirely useful in terms of long-term inflationary expectations.

Economic theory tells us that interaction of supply and demand determines the prices of all goods and services. Because of OPEC (Organization of Petroleum Exporting Countries), however, supply plays a greater role than demand in the determination of oil prices. For more than 20 years, OPEC has controlled prices by turning the oil spigot off and on. Although changes in oil prices affect the *pattern* of inflation, they should not affect the *underlying rate* of inflation unless the oil price change is sustained for an extended period. In that case, it would be factored in all stages of production and consumption behavior. A short-term increase in the price of oil is most likely to affect a change in *relative prices,* not the *price level.* Only the Federal Reserve can create inflation through excessive growth in the stock of money. When the Federal Reserve does not ratify an increase in oil prices with a rise in monetary reserves, prices of other goods or services will have to decline. Thus, oil price increases alone can't cause inflation; they can only cause higher gasoline and fuel oil prices.

Financial market participants realize that only the Fed can ultimately control inflation. Nonetheless, they constantly monitor changes in oil prices as a precursor of inflationary pressures in the economy. Small changes in the spot or futures price are not likely to affect players in the fixed-income, stock, or foreign exchange markets. But large changes will certainly impact the markets. All markets will move down when oil prices spurt up; all markets will move up when oil prices drop.

Traders certainly must track changes in oil prices because someone is bound to react to them. But it is worth noting whether changes are coming from rumors or actual events. Moreover, the changes will not be automatically reflected in other inflation indicators such as the Consumer Price Index or the Producer Price Index. Even when price increases or decreases in the spot market are sustained and translated in those indexes, a few months will probably elapse since crude oil is not a processed commodity (which it needs to be for inclusion in the indexes).

Typical investors will find that major movements in the spot or futures price of crude oil are more meaningful than hourly price changes. Checking the nightly closing price will keep you adequately informed. If you decide to track crude oil prices on a daily basis, logging the daily close will allow you to monitor longer term trends. Figure 7.1 illustrates how variations within the month could be large (note October 1992), but smaller from one month to the next (note September and October).

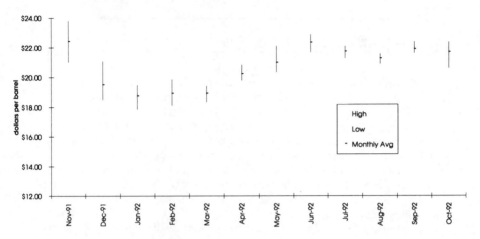

Figure 7.1   This chart depicts the average monthly level of crude oil prices, along with the highs and lows for the month. Notice that the variation is wider in some months than in others. (*Source: Market News Service, Inc.*)

El Niño

Now commonly called *El Niño,* this warming of surface waters of the Pacific Ocean off South America was originally dubbed *Corriente del Niño* by Peruvian fishermen in the late 1800s. Translated directly, it means "Current of the Christ Child." In 1892, scientist Camilo Carillo was referring to the unseasonably warm weather at Christmastime that ruined fishing in the Port of Paita (Peru). Although the term might have been coined then, similar warming conditions were found in ship captains' logs one hundred years earlier.

In 1992, weather phenomena across the globe were blamed on El Niño: draught in southern Africa, blizzards in Greece, and the warmest U.S. winter in nearly a century. How is this relevant to the U.S. economy? Strange weather patterns in the spring of 1992 threatened the corn and soybean crops in Illinois, part of the major grain growing region in the United States. A reduction in crops leads to higher food prices.

How seriously should the market participant take El Niño? In 1983, its last major occurrence, U.S. fishermen netted 22 million pounds of anchovies, down from 103 million pounds in the previous year.

CRB Futures Price Index

The Commodity Research Bureau (CRB) publishes an index that reflects the prices of 27 commodities, several of which are grains or other agricultural products. The CRB Futures Price Index is traded on the New York Futures Exchange (NYFE) and is divided into eight subindexes:

1. *Grains.* Barley, corn, oats, rye, soybean meal, CBT (Chicago Board of Trade) wheat, and Minneapolis wheat.
2. *Livestock and Meats.* Cattle, hogs, pork bellies.
3. *Precious Metals.* Gold, platinum, silver.
4. *Industrials.* Cotton, copper, crude oil, lumber, silver, platinum.
5. *Oilseeds.* Flaxseed, soybean, rapeseed.
6. *Softs (imported).* Coffee, cocoa, and sugar.
7. *Energy.* Crude oil and heating oil.
8. *Miscellaneous.* Orange juice, potatoes, and soybean oil.

The three commodities that are in more than one subindex (crude oil, platinum, and silver) are only counted once when calculating the total index. The CRB Futures Price Index is designed so that changes in any one commodity price will not cause extraordinary changes in the whole.

One problem with the index is the heavy weight given to agricultural products—the seven grains and the three oilseeds, along with the miscellaneous category of orange juice, potatoes, and soybean oil. Moreover, two of the precious metals serve double duty by also reflecting industrial commodities (silver and platinum).

Research shows that the CRB Futures Price Index does not predict month-to-month changes in either the Consumer Price Index or the Producer Price Index. However, the CRB Index tends to move in the same direction as the PPI or CPI over the course of the year, in the same way that all inflation indicators move in the same general direction. Figure 7.2 shows that changes in magnitude and direction are not correlated monthly.

Did You Know? The CRB Index may be a better indicator of bond yields than inflation. Nancy Lazar, an economist for ISI Group, a New York investment firm, has found a high correlation between the CRB Index and bond yields. Her analysis shows that the CRB Index and bond yields have moved in the same direction 82 percent of the time over the past 30 years.[4]

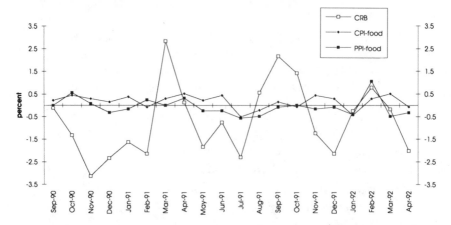

Figure 7.2 The Consumer Research Bureau Index posts larger monthly changes relative to food price gains in the Producer Price Index and the Consumer Price Index. The three series move in tandem only part of the time. (*Source: Market News Service,* Bureau of Labor Statistics, Department of Labor.)

Market Reaction Just like spot and futures prices of crude oil, the CRB Index is closely monitored by financial market participants as a precursor of inflation. Another resemblance to crude oil futures is that the market for this series is fluid and there is no set time of day for market reaction: It is continuous. Going along with the premise that accelerating inflation is unfavorable, a sudden sharp increase in the CRB Index will cause bond prices to fall (and yields to rise), stock prices to fall, and the value of the dollar to fall in the foreign exchange market. A drop in the index will cause the reverse reaction: Interest rates will fall (bond prices will rise); stock prices and the dollar will rise.

Watch Out For: Keep track of the various subcomponents of the CRB Index. Although it was designed so that no one commodity will cause significant changes to the total index, single components can cause it to move. Moreover, the grain category is heavily weighted. If grain traders are worried about droughts, all the grains will be affected and increases in these could add significantly to the index.

On the whole, it is not cost-efficient to look at hourly changes in the CRB Index. If you want to monitor this index, (although it is not necessary given all the other monthly indicators of inflation), keeping a log of the daily closing price will allow you to consider the long-term trend rather than short-term aberrations.

MONTHLY INDICATORS

Index of Prices Received by Farmers

The Department of Agriculture releases the Index of Prices Received by Farmers, more commonly known as the "Ag Price Index," at the end of the month for the current month, but it only reflects price changes through the middle of that month. The index is not adjusted for seasonal variation.

The Index of Prices Received by Farmers comprises crops (44.2 percent) and livestock and products (55.8 percent). For the most part, the price changes are based on average prices for all grades and qualities at the point of sale (such as the local market) about the middle of the month. All the prices are then revised in the following month when averages are calculated for the entire month for some of the commodities.

The index is based on prices of 44 commodities that account for more than 90 percent of the total value from marketings of all farm commodities in the years 1971–1973 (it has not been updated in 20 years). The price data are obtained by personal interview, mail, and telephone follow-up on a voluntary basis from buyers of farm products.

The weights of crops and livestock are determined on average quantities sold during 1971–1973. The index is based to the year 1977. Table 7.1 lists the weights of commodities for the major categories.

Is the Ag Price Index related to other inflation indicators? Although it is related to food price changes in the Producer Price Index and the Consumer Price Index, it can vary significantly over time. First, the Ag Price Index is not adjusted for seasonal variations. The food components in both the Consumer Price Index and the Producer Price Index are seasonally adjusted. Second, the Ag Price Index measures prices at the first point of sale and is based on average prices for all grades. The Producer Price Indexes and the Consumer Price Index typically adjust for quality and grades. Finally, all the crops and livestock are weighted differently in each of the three series.

Market Reaction   The Ag Price Index is reported late in the afternoon and gets little attention from financial market participants. However, an unexpectedly large rise in the index can spur a drop in bond prices if market psychology is already negative. Conversely, an unexpectedly large drop in the index may lead to a rise in bond prices if market psychology is positive. The foreign exchange and stock markets ignore this index altogether. Commodity market participants may find this series interesting although they are more likely to keep a close watch on the CRB Index, which is available continuously.

Table 7.1   Relative Weights (Percents) for
Prices Received by Farmers

All farm products	100.0
Crops	44.2
Food grains	7.2
Feed grains and hay	12.1
Cotton	2.9
Tobacco	2.4
Oil-bearing crops	9.2
Fruit	4.1
Commercial vegetables	4.1
Potatoes and beans	1.8
Livestock and Products	55.8
Meat animals	37.2
Dairy products	11.1
Poultry and eggs	7.5

Source: Department of Agriculture.

Producer Price Indexes

The Producer Price Indexes (PPI) (there are three) are reported the second week of the month for the previous month by the Bureau of Labor Statistics (BLS) of the Labor Department. These figures are seasonally adjusted. All the Producer Price Indexes are fixed weight measures of inflation, and monthly percentage changes are reported as a matter of course. The figures are sometimes annualized, or compared on a year-to-year basis.

Watch Out For: Look at the trend in the Ag Price Index, not a one-month change. Because this series is not seasonally adjusted, you should look at year-to-year changes rather than month-to-month changes. Generally speaking, the index should decline or post small increases during periods of harvest, and larger increases during off seasons. On a more technical note: The way the index is reported makes monthly changes move in increments of 0.7 percentage points. So the index will rise (or fall) 0.7 percent, 1.4 percent, 2.1 percent, and so forth.

The Producer Price Index for Finished Goods is regarded as "the" measure of producer price inflation. Producer prices are measured by stage of processing: The other two indexes reflect prices of intermediate goods and crude materials. The Producer Price Index for Finished Goods gets all the attention and is considered a leading indicator of consumer price inflation. Actually, each index might be viewed as a leading indicator for the next stage of production. Thus, the Producer Price Index for Crude Materials could portend price changes in the Producer Price Index for Intermediate Goods, which subsequently could indicate price changes in the Producer Price Index for Finished Goods.

Although these various measures of inflation show overall correlation, it is important to know which specific goods are actually priced and how they are weighted. For example, the Producer Price Index for Finished Goods is heavily weighted toward consumer goods (77 percent) rather than capital equipment (23 percent). Therefore, it might be more worthwhile to look at subcomponents of the intermediate goods index to forecast subcomponents of the finished goods index. It certainly would not make sense to use prices of construction supplies to indicate the direction of apparel prices.

These indexes are calculated with 2,800 commodities and 10,000 quotations to represent the movement of prices of all commodities in the manufacturing, agriculture, forestry, fishing, mining, gas and electricity, and public utilities sectors. The universe includes all goods that are domestically produced or imported, for sales in commercial transactions in primary markets in the United States.

Finished goods are commodities that will not undergo further processing and are ready for sale to the ultimate user (either consumer or business firm). They are further divided into three categories: (1) capital equipment, (2) consumer goods less foods, and (3) consumer foods. Capital equipment includes civilian aircraft, automobiles and trucks, farm equipment, and machine tools. Consumer goods include gasoline and fuel oil, apparel, tobacco products, cars, and furniture. Consumer foods include unprocessed foods such as eggs and fresh vegetables, as well as processed foods such as bakery products and meats.

Because economists like to exclude unstable components from economic series, it has become common practice to look at the Producer Price Index excluding food and energy prices which is considered a proxy for the core rate of inflation. In this manner, we can assess the underlying trend in producer prices without having to worry about aberrations in food and energy prices. From one month to the next, it is reasonable to ignore a sharp rise in food or energy prices because they could easily be reversed in the subsequent month. Over a period of six months or a year, however, it is important to consider food and energy prices because they are a major consumer expense.

Intermediate materials, supplies, and components are commodities that have been processed but require further processing before they become finished goods. Examples are flour, cotton yarns, steel mill products, and motor vehicle parts.

This index tends to be slightly more volatile than the finished goods index, so it is better to look at the pattern of growth than at a one-month change. Broadly speaking, changes in this index predict price changes in the finished goods index.

Crude materials for further processing include products that have not been manufactured or fabricated but will be processed before becoming finished goods. Crude foods and feeds include items such as grains and livestock. Examples of crude nonfood materials include natural gas, crude petroleum, and raw cotton.

Because this index includes items that are largely affected by supply—oil and food—monthly price fluctuations can be highly erratic. This index will predict price changes in the other two, over the long term, not from one month to the next.

Price data are generally collected monthly, primarily by mail questionnaire. Respondents are asked to provide net prices reflecting applicable discounts. Although the Bureau of Labor Statistics attempts to base the producer price indexes on actual transactions prices, list or book prices are used when transaction prices are unavailable. For the most part, prices are obtained directly from producing companies on a voluntary and confidential basis, but some prices are taken from trade publications. Since January 1967, prices generally have been reported for the Tuesday of the week containing the thirteenth day of the month.

The Bureau of Labor Statistics attempts to price commodities that are identical in quality. Adjustments are made for quality differences. For example, when new model year cars are introduced with additional features, the BLS estimates the price adjustments of the new features. Producer Price Indexes are designed to measure real price changes—those changes not due to quality adjustments, quantity, or terms of sales. However, quality adjustments are difficult to fully capture.

Are the Producer Price Indexes related to other inflation indicators? Some economists tend to extrapolate PPI changes to the Consumer Price Index on a month-to-month basis. That is not a good idea, even conceptually. Even though the Producer Price Index for Finished Goods is heavily weighted toward consumer goods rather than capital equipment, the PPI weights are extremely different from those weights used in the

Consumer Price Index. Also, the Producer Price Index for Finished Goods doesn't incorporate prices of services, as does the Consumer Price Index. Finally, seasonal adjustment patterns differ between the two series.

Table 7.2 shows the major components of the Producer Price Index for Finished Goods along with their relative importance as of December 1991. (Minor variations in weights are made annually in the PPI based on the total shipment values of those goods for the year. Benchmark revisions, which would incorporate major structural changes are made infrequently—typically every 10 years or so.)

Market Reaction Financial market participants pounce on the Producer Price Indexes figures when they are reported. The fixed-income market will obviously prefer to see low inflation over high inflation. Thus, the larger the monthly rise in the PPI, the more negative the impact on the bond and money markets. High inflation leads to high interest rates. Low inflation points to declining interest rates.

The equity and foreign exchange markets will also view accelerating inflation negatively. Stock prices may decline and the value of the dollar will probably drop when producer price increases are large and accelerating.

Table 7.2   Producer Price Index—Finished Goods (weights (percents), December 1991)

Capital Equipment	24.749
Passenger cars	7.759*
Trucks	4.740*
Civilian aircraft	4.108
Consumer Goods less Foods	53.336
Nondurable goods	36.030
Electric power	6.301
Residential gas	2.285
Gasoline	3.606
Fuel oil	0.572
Apparel	4.555
Tobacco	2.854
Durable goods	17.306
Consumer Foods	21.915
Meats, poultry, and fish	5.669

* A portion of this category is included in consumer goods.

Source: Monthly Labor Review, March 1993, Bureau of Labor Statistics, Department of Labor.

Here, financial market participants will often look at the Producer
Price Index for Finished Goods excluding food and energy prices as
well as the total PPI in determining the rate of inflation. Increases in
food and energy prices are often discounted because they can be transitory. Large spurts in these components are less likely to cause negative market reactions than increases in the core rate.

Consumer Price Index

The Consumer Price Index (CPI), which is compiled monthly by the
Bureau of Labor Statistics, measures price changes for a fixed basket of
goods and services purchased by all urban consumers and wage
earners. Unlike the Producer Price Indexes, which only price data
around the middle of the month, the CPI captures price changes in the
beginning, middle, and end of the month. These figures are reported
three weeks after the end of the month. The Consumer Price Index is
seasonally adjusted and is based to the years 1982–1984 = 100. There

Watch Out For: First, look at the core rate in the Producer Price
Index for Finished Goods, excluding food and
energy prices. Second, beware of special factors
that can cause the PPI to rise or fall sharply. For example, tobacco prices
tend to spurt several times a year putting upward pressure on the PPI. As
shown in Table 7.2, tobacco has a fairly hefty weight in the index. Car
prices also tend to pick up in the fall when auto manufacturers introduce
new model year cars. Apart from food, energy, apparel, tobacco, and automobiles, none of the other categories have large enough weights to sin-
gularly impact the price index.

The current dollar value of shipments for the previous year determines the relative importance of the components of the PPI. Although the
volume of tobacco products has declined over the years, prices have risen
sharply. As a consequence, the current dollar value of tobacco shipments
has risen, causing tobacco products to gain a greater share of the PPI. As
a result, financial market participants will often discount increases in
the PPI that are due to tobacco products.

With respect to the intermediate and crude materials indexes, keep
track of their long-term trend. Both of these series also have an energy
and food component that will overshadow the underlying rate. Long-
term trends reveal more about inflationary pressures than one-month
aberrations.

are two versions of the CPI: for all urban consumers (CPI-U), and for wage earners and clerical workers (CPI-W). The CPI-W has a longer history and tends to be used for labor contracts. The differences between the two series are usually minor from month to month.

The weights currently attributed to categories in the Consumer Price Index were determined by the 1982–1984 Consumer Expenditure Survey. Seven major expenditures groups—food and beverages, housing, apparel and upkeep, transportation, medical care, entertainment, and other goods and services—are divided into 69 expenditure classes and these are divided into 184 item strata. These are disaggregated further still into lower level categories called entry-level items. You can imagine the detail used in determining the Consumer Price Index. For example, we can take the major expenditure group "Food and Beverages"; divide it into "Food for Home Consumption"; look at "Bread Consumption"; and break that down further into "White Bread" or "Wheat Bread." The Bureau of Labor Statistics then makes sure that white bread or wheat bread is priced consistently from that point forward. Otherwise, if survey takers indiscriminately priced wheat bread in some months and white bread in others, we would not be pricing the same basket of goods.

Although the major weights of the expenditure categories are not generally changed from year to year, changes in the more detailed entry-level items do get changed causing minor variations in relative importance every year. Major overhauls are done roughly every 10 years.

Prices are collected by agents from a probability sample of about 21,000 retail stores and other outlets in 91 urban areas. These outlets include department stores, independent stores, specialty shops, and public utilities that have been selected to represent the population. Prices are also collected from physicians and dentists, hospitals, beauty parlors, repairpeople, and service contractors. Rental rates are collected from about 40,000 renters and 20,000 homeowners. Goods and services are adjusted for quality differences in the CPI, as they are in the PPI. In fact, the Bureau of Labor Statistics is constantly striving to improve the CPI. In recent years, several articles in the *Monthly Labor Review* have described improvements in the medical care, used car, and shelter components of the CPI, with respect to quality adjustments in the index.

Prices are usually gathered by personal interview, but sometimes are collected by mail. Food prices are gathered monthly in all areas. Most other items are priced monthly in the five largest urban areas, and bimonthly in other areas.

The national index is calculated by combining the area totals with weights based on 1980 population of all urban consumers. About half the weight is carried by the 23 largest areas. (Roughly one-quarter of the weight is carried by the five largest urban areas.) In addition to the national index, separate indexes are calculated for 28 of the 91 areas. There are monthly indexes for the five largest areas and bimonthly indexes for the remaining 23 areas. This means that the Consumer Price Index for all urban consumers covers about 80 percent of the noninstitutional population.

The Consumer Price Index is often dubbed the "cost-of-living" index. It is used to compute annual increases in many contracts—including salary negotiations and rental agreements. Despite these uses, the CPI is not a true cost-of-living index because it doesn't include changes in federal, state, and local income taxes. Also, it measures the same basket of goods regardless of changing prices. A true cost-of-living index would allow consumers to substitute goods that were less expensive but equally satisfying. In addition, new items either aren't included or haven't increased their weight in the index even though consumer expenditures have increased on these goods. These include such items as videocassette recorders, smoke detectors, personal computers, compact disc players, and compact discs.

In the same way that people think of the Consumer Price Index as a cost-of-living measure, they often use the metropolitan and regional indexes to compare price levels among regions. That's not appropriate because it doesn't give you the information you want. The different indexes only represent varying price changes from month to month relative to a base year. There is no guarantee that the cost of living was equivalent in all regions during that base year. The base period could have been different in each of the urban areas, which is not reflected in the index. The cost-of-living concept would need to account for the varying state income taxes. Local area taxes, such as sales taxes, are included in the Consumer Price Index, however. Excise taxes, such as those on cigarettes and alcoholic beverages are also included.

The Bureau of Labor Statistics considers these factors while experimenting with new measures. A 1989 *Monthly Labor Review* article describes the current research in cost-of-living indexes. The three indexes take into account substitution effects when prices change; expenditures of various demographic groups; and income-based versus expenditure-based indexes. Each of these three series would move the CPI closer to a true "cost-of-living" measure.

On another note, the homeownership component of the Consumer Price Index gets a lot of attention because it is heavily weighted. In the past, home prices and mortgage rates were directly incorporated to estimate changes in housing costs. Since 1983, the homeownership component has been calculated as a rental equivalent. Homeowners are asked to estimate how much rent they would have to pay if they were renting their home instead of owning it. The Bureau of Labor Statistics prices housing units in areas where actual rental units are abundant to corroborate these estimates. Therefore, the investment cost of the home is not incorporated in the Consumer Price Index. In switching from the house price/mortgage rate rule to the rental equivalent, the CPI now reflects a flow-of-services concept in this component. As result, the run-up in home prices and mortgage rates of the early 1980s was incorporated into the index. However, the subsequent drop in mortgage rates was not. In addition, it took a lot longer for the drop in the value of housing across the country in the late 1980s to be reflected in the CPI as a rental equivalent than if home prices had been included. Both factors caused the Consumer Price Index to be overstated in the second half of the 1980s and the early 1990s.

The weights for the main components of the Consumer Price Index are detailed in Table 7.3. These will show why it is inappropriate to utilize monthly changes in the Producer Price Indexes to predict monthly changes in the CPI. As shown in Table 7.3, the share of services in the Consumer Price Index stands at 55 percent, whereas the share of goods stands at 45 percent. Thus, roughly 75 percent of the Producer Price Index for Finished Goods correlates with less than half of the Consumer Price Index.

As a general rule, monthly changes in the Consumer Price Index tend to be more stable than monthly changes in the Producer Price Index for finished goods because the CPI is heavily weighted toward services. Prices of services tend to be sticky, although even inflation in the service industry can moderate given enough sluggish economic activity. Food and energy prices at the consumer level can be just as volatile as at the producer level. Consequently, economists point to the Consumer Price Index excluding food and energy as another proxy for the core rate of inflation, but this is only relevant on a monthly basis when special factors include transitory movements. It is more appropriate to include food and energy prices in the CPI when analyzing annual inflation rates. After all, consumers can't purge food and energy spending just because prices have increased. First Chicago money market trader Greg Mills once told me that if we excluded all the categories from the CPI, we would have no inflation! I think he was reflecting his annoyance (with great wit) at economists who used "special factors" as a constant excuse to explain away inflationary pressures every month. He's

Table 7.3   Consumer Price Index
(weights (percents), December 1992)

Food and beverages	17.396
Food at home	9.780
Food away from home	5.997
Alcoholic beverages	1.620
Housing	41.404
Shelter	27.880
Renters' costs	7.993
Homeowners' costs	19.683
Maintenance and repairs	0.204
Fuel and other utilities	7.280
Household furnishings and operations	6.243
Apparel and upkeep	6.005
Transportation	17.012
Private transportation	15.484
New vehicles	5.001
Used cars	1.184
Motor fuel	3.268
Maintenance and repairs	1.527
Other private transportation	4.504
Public transportation	1.528
Medical care	6.931
Entertainment	4.350
Other goods and services	6.902
Tobacco	1.748
Personal care	1.187
Personal and educational expenses	3.968
All items	100.000
Excluding food and energy	76.929
Commodities	44.095
Services	55.905

Source: Bureau of Labor Statistics, Department of Labor.

right, of course. We economists can go to extremes at times in trying to explain things away.

Market Reaction   Financial market participants anxiously await the Consumer Price Index because it propels much activity in the marketplace. The fixed income, equity, and foreign exchange markets all react adversely to sharp increases in inflation. Interest rates will rise; stock prices will fall; and the value of the dollar will decline in the foreign

Watch Out For: Look at the core rate of inflation, measured by the Consumer Price Index excluding food and energy prices, just as you did with the Producer Price Indexes. Once again, you should be watching for special factors that could cause unusual spurts or dips in the monthly index. Tobacco prices could contribute to consumer price increases, but not to the same degree they affect producer prices. The weights for tobacco products are smaller in the CPI. Education costs will spurt in the Consumer Price Index, usually during the fall months, but increases are smoothed out over the year. Apparel prices will cause spikes in the fall and spring when new lines are introduced for the seasons. A one- or two-month spurt in apparel prices will usually be followed by declines in subsequent months, although the magnitude of the declines depends on the strength of retail sales. Medical care seems to be the one component that contributes strongly to price increases month after month.

Long-term trends are usually more important than monthly blips. Keep an eye on the rate of inflation for the most recent three months, six months, and year. Look at the total CPI as well as the index excluding food and energy prices. The only time to ignore an increase in food and energy prices totally is when you are certain prices will reverse in coming months. Food and energy prices make up about 25 percent of consumer expenditures. It would be foolish to ignore big price changes in those categories because they could potentially have important ramifications with respect to inflation, economic activity, and Federal Reserve policy.

The following cautionary note will remind you of the adage, "Statistics don't lie, but people do." When the December CPI is reported in January, the Bureau of Labor Statistics also publishes the annual inflation rate. The BLS calculates the annual inflation rate by averaging the monthly price indexes to get an annual average of the CPI. They then take the percentage change from the previous year's average of the monthly indexes. Table 7.4 shows that, depending on the pattern of inflation, the annual average change in consumer prices may be vastly different from the yearly change in consumer prices as calculated by the percentage change from December to December. The December-to-December percentage change more accurately reflects the inflation rate over the course of the year. Government administration officials, however, tend to cite the measure that shows a lower rate of inflation (which is not surprising). Beware of politicians! The Bureau of Labor Statistics is an apolitical agency and always reports both measures with equal attention.

Table 7.4   Annual Changes in the
Consumer Price Index

	Dec. to Dec.	Annual Avg.
1980	**12.5**	13.5
1981	**8.9**	10.3
1982	**3.8**	6.2
1983	3.8	**3.2**
1984	**3.9**	4.3
1985	3.8	**3.6**
1986	**1.1**	1.9
1987	4.4	**3.6**
1988	4.4	**4.1**
1989	**4.6**	4.8
1990	6.1	**5.4**
1991	**3.1**	4.2
1992	**2.9**	3.0

Source: These data are from Commerce and Labor Department publications.

exchange market because the rise in interest rates is due to price increases, not economic expansion. Market participants, in a similar
fashion to their approach with the Producer Price Indexes, discount
increases in food and energy prices to some degree. A sharp increase
in the Consumer Price Index excluding food and energy prices will
bring about a more negative reaction than an increase in the total CPI.

QUARTERLY INDICATOR

GDP Deflators

The GDP deflators are comprehensive measures of inflation because
they encompass changes in prices in all sectors of the economy: consumer products, capital goods, the foreign sector, and government. Although all indicators of inflation move in the same direction over time,
there is no strict correlation between the GDP deflators, the Consumer
Price Index, and the Producer Price Indexes on a quarter-to-quarter basis. The Bureau of Economic Analysis releases the GDP deflators together with gross domestic product and national income about four

weeks after the end of the quarter. The figures are seasonally adjusted and annualized.

There are actually three GDP deflators: the implicit deflator, the fixed weight deflator, and the chain-price index. Until the late 1980s, the implicit deflator was the primary focus of attention. Since 1989, the Commerce Department has promoted the fixed weight index instead. The implicit deflator measures changes in prices as well as changes in the composition of output. Some goods are less expensive than other goods, so depending on the combination of goods and services produced in any given quarter, *regardless of the price changes*, the implicit price deflator can rise or fall. This makes the implicit price deflator a *variable* basket of goods. It is rare to see an outright decline in the implicit GDP deflator, but its rate of increase varies significantly from one quarter to the next.

The fixed weight deflator works on the same principle as the consumer and producer price indexes since it measures prices for a composition of GDP chosen in a certain time-period. Currently, 1987 weights are used. Consequently, the fixed weight deflator only reflects changes in prices.

The chain-price index combines the variable and fixed weight baskets. For any given quarter, it shows the basket of goods of the previous quarter. Over time, however, the basket of goods is changing. Admittedly, this has questionable relevance to the inflation picture and gets little attention, if any.

In principle, the GDP fixed-weight deflator and the implicit price deflator should show little variance from the consumer and producer price indexes since the Bureau of Economic Analysis uses several subcomponents of the Consumer Price Index and the Producer Price Indexes to deflate components of GDP. For example, the CPI for new cars is used to deflate the auto component of personal consumption expenditures. These indexes are then identical. In fact, the deflators (implicit and fixed weight) for personal consumption expenditures are quite similar to the CPI, and the variations mainly reflect differences in weights.

Typically, the rate of inflation measured by the GDP deflator is lower than that measured by the Consumer Price Index because prices of capital goods, which are in GDP but not in the CPI, are less expensive than consumer goods. Over time, the measures move in the same direction. When the Consumer Price Index and the Producer Price Index show a more moderate rate of inflation, so do the GDP deflators. Figure 7.3 shows the implicit price deflator compared with the Consumer

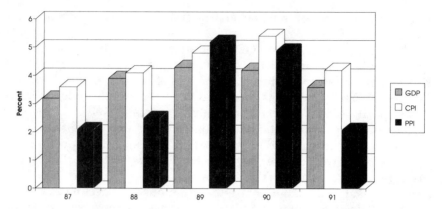

Figure 7.3 The general trend in inflation is similar in these three measures of inflation, but the three series never have the exact inflation rate for a particular year. *(Source: Economic Report of the President, 1992.)*

Price Index for all urban consumers and the Producer Price Index for Finished Goods.

Market Reaction   Financial market participants eagerly await the GDP deflators. In the past few years, more attention has focused on the fixed weight deflator than on the implicit price deflator. An acceleration in the deflator is unfavorable news to all markets. Stock prices will decline, bond prices will fall (yields will rise), and the value of the dollar will also decrease. A moderation in the inflation measures will lead to the opposite effect. Stock prices, bond prices, and the foreign exchange value of the dollar will increase.

WAGE INFLATION

In looking at commodity prices, the Producer Price Indexes, the Consumer Price Index, or the GDP deflators, we are looking at prices paid for the purchases of goods and services. There is another side to the inflation picture. Instead of looking at product prices, we can look at the major cost of doing business—labor. Wages are a form of prices and therefore are another indicator of inflation. When wages rise without corresponding increases in productivity, the cost to producers increases, and the prices consumers pay will have to rise as well.

Watch Out For: The fixed weight GDP deflator is more meaningful than the implicit price deflator. The implicit price deflator reflects changes in the composition of GDP as well as changes in prices. Although less frequent reports, such as these quarterly deflators, might have less volatility than more frequent reports (such as the monthly indicators), both the implicit and fixed weight GDP deflators can have quirks from time to time as do the PPI and the CPI. For example, government pay raises typically occur in the first quarter, boosting the deflator in the government sector and possibly the deflator overall. Seasonal adjustment factors can't be utilized to account for the annual pay raise because the magnitude of increase is not stable from year to year. Also, changes in commodity prices get reflected in CCC inventories, which tend to move sharply (either up or down) from time to time. Usually, you can apply "the rule of reverse sign": If the federal nondefense price deflator rises sharply in one quarter, it will probably fall as much in the subsequent quarter.

Finally, changes in oil prices or the prices of other imported goods have major impacts on the deflator, and these are not always intuitive or reasonable. Mostly, they indicate an accounting problem that you can solve by looking at the price deflator over a two- or three-quarter period. When import prices rise sharply, the GDP deflator will moderate substantially because goods and services not produced in the United States are subtracted from GDP. When prices rise, a greater dollar value of imports is subtracted from GDP. Higher import prices should really be reflected in the higher prices paid by consumers and businesses, but sometimes a lag occurs between the prices importers pay and the prices consumers pay. Thus, a quarter with high import prices (and a small rise in the GDP deflator) is likely to be followed by a quarter with stable import prices (and a large rise in the GDP deflator). Changing import prices come not only from changes in the prices of goods and services but also from movements in the exchange value of the dollar.

As always, monitoring a trend is preferable to taking the figures at face value. Increases in the GDP deflator (either the fixed weight or the implicit) will tend to be lower than price changes measured by the CPI because capital goods (investment spending) tend to be less expensive than consumer goods. Thus, declines in prices of investment-type goods will offset some of the gains in consumer goods. (The declines in investment goods are mainly due to the technology-induced price decline of computers.)

The following sections describe three measures of wage inflation that are readily available and easy to understand. These are monitored by financial market participants and federal government policy makers including the Federal Reserve. Incidentally, the media generally allot little coverage to these indicators. Your best bet is to scour the financial press. Local city newspaper coverage is likely to be minimal or buried for these series relative to other economic indicators.

MONTHLY INDICATOR

Average Hourly Earnings

Average hourly earnings are released one week after the end of the month with the employment situation by the Bureau of Labor Statistics. These monthly payroll figures from the Establishment Survey are reported before deductions for taxes, social insurance, and fringe benefits. They include pay for overtime, holidays, vacation, and sick leave but *exclude* retroactive pay or bonuses unless they are earned and paid regularly each pay period. The figures are seasonally adjusted.

Average hourly earnings for workers in private industry are derived by dividing total nonfarm payrolls by total hours reported for each industry except government employees. The hourly earnings figures reflect changes in basic hourly rates as well as increases in premium pay because of overtime hours worked. For example, if employees worked a 40-hour workweek, no premium would be paid for overtime, but if they worked 42 hours in a given week, they'd be paid time and a half for the extra 2 hours. However, the true hourly wage rate would remain unchanged. The calculated figure for average hourly earnings is misleading because hourly wages did not increase on the whole. Changes in the number of employees in low-paid work versus high-paid work also affect the hourly earnings figures. This is like our variable versus fixed basket problem. Suppose manufacturers hire skilled machinists one month, and substitute them with apprentice machinists the next month. The month in which the skilled workers were hired will show a larger gain in hourly earnings than the month in which the apprentices were hired.

Average hourly (and weekly) earnings are available for mining, construction, manufacturing (through the two-digit standard industry classifications), transportation and public utilities, wholesale trade, retail trade, finance, insurance and real estate, and services. Seasonally adjusted figures are available for all the aforementioned categories except the two-digit SIC classifications in the manufacturing sector. The Bureau of Labor Statistics even estimates average hourly earnings for manufacturing excluding overtime by assuming that the overtime hours are paid at time and a half. In addition, the Bureau of Labor Statistics estimates total private average hourly earnings in constant (1982) dollars by deflating the current dollar figure by the Consumer Price Index for Urban Wage Earners and Clerical Workers (CPI-W).

Because of the inconsistency in the series from changes in employment or overtime, you should not place a lot of weight on average hourly earnings; they do not represent labor costs to the employer. But just as other measures of inflation tend to move in tandem, so do the measures of wage inflation. This is the only monthly indicator of wage inflation, so it is a good proxy for other measures that are calculated quarterly but are adjusted for occupation or industry shifts and overtime pay.

Watch Out For: You must never take the one-month change in hourly earnings at face value. The mix effect due to employment or overtime changes makes this series erratic even though it is seasonally adjusted. It is conventional to look at year-over-year changes in hourly earnings to reduce the month-to-month volatility. Nonetheless, the trend in this series has greater significance because even the year-to-year changes are volatile, as seen in Figure 7.4.

If the monthly rise in average hourly earnings is particularly large, you might check whether overtime hours increased in the manufacturing sector. Finally, this series is frequently revised. Always check the revisions to the previous months' figures. An initial gain of 0.6 percent in one month, which would be worrisome in terms of signaling inflationary pressures, could easily be halved two months later.

Keep reminding yourself that you are focusing on the long term. Though you should not discount entirely one month blips in average hourly earnings, don't worry about them too much. Look at a three-month moving average of the monthly changes in this series in addition to the year-over-year change. For example, the BLS reported an initial rise of 0.7 percent in average hourly earnings in August 1992 and, one month later, reported a drop of 0.2 percent for September hourly earnings. Incidentally, overtime hours in the manufacturing sector declined 5.4 percent between August and September.

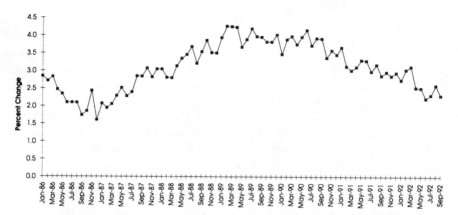

Figure 7.4 Average hourly earnings are so volatile from month to month that even the year-to-year change is jumpy. Most series show smoother patterns on a year-over-year basis. (*Source:* Bureau of Labor Statistics, Department of Labor.)

Market Reaction   Despite its volatility, financial market participants pounce on the average hourly earnings data: It is the first inflation news for the month. A spurt in hourly wages in negative for all the markets—stock, fixed-income, and foreign exchange—because it signals inflationary pressures.

QUARTERLY INDICATORS

Employment Cost Index

The Employment Cost Index (ECI), which is released quarterly by the Bureau of Labor Statistics, measures the rate of change in total employment compensation including changes in wages and salaries as well as changes in employers' costs for benefits. The Employment Cost Index measures the change in the cost of labor free from the influence of shifts among occupations and industries, which is a problem with the average hourly earnings data that are available monthly. The survey is conducted quarterly for the pay period including the twelfth day of the four months: March, June, September, and December. Data is released on the fourth Tuesday in the month following the survey.

The Employment Cost Index covers wage and benefit data in all establishments and occupations in the private nonfarm and public sectors. On the wage and salary side, it is not affected by changes in the labor force since it looks at costs of employing a fixed set of labor inputs. (It is similar to the Consumer Price Index and the Producer Price Indexes in that it is a fixed weight index.) However, the benefit cost component is not fixed. It provides the change in the cost of benefits for a fixed labor force. They are not reflecting changing prices for the same basket of benefits. Consequently, the benefit cost index will change if the price of benefits changes (higher pay for holidays), or if there are changes in benefits (an additional holiday).

Each quarter, straight-time average hourly wage and salary rates, and benefits data are collected from a probability sample of about 23,000 occupations with 4,400 sample establishments in private industry. About 6,000 occupations with 1,000 sample establishments are surveyed for state and local governments.

Wages and salaries are defined as the hourly straight-time wage rate. (If workers are not paid on an hourly basis, it is the straight-time earnings divided by the corresponding hours.) Straight-time wages and salaries are total earnings before payroll deductions. They exclude premiums for overtime, shift differentials, and nonproduction bonuses in lieu of wage increases. Production bonuses, incentive earnings, commission payments, and cost-of-living adjustments are included in straight-time wage and salary rates.

Benefits covered by the Employment Cost Index are numerous. They include paid leave (vacations, holidays, sick leave); supplemental pay (for overtime and shift differentials, and nonproduction bonuses); insurance benefits (life, health, sickness, and accident); retirement and savings benefits (pension, savings, and thrift plans); legally required benefits (social security, railroad retirement and supplemental retirement, federal and state unemployment insurance, workers' compensation, and other legally required benefits); and other benefits such as severance pay and supplemental unemployment plans.

The geographic coverage of the index includes all states and the District of Columbia. Statistics are published for metropolitan areas as well as the total U.S. average. The Employment Cost Index is similar to the Consumer Price Index in that it allows for regional differences. The Producer Price indexes, as you will remember, do not account for regional differences in prices.

Until December 1990, the Bureau of Labor Statistics did not adjust the Employment Cost Index for seasonal variation. As of the December report (released in January 1991), the figures are available on a seasonally adjusted as well as an unadjusted basis. The seasonally adjusted data are more useful in identifying trends since they eliminate the effect of normal patterns that occur at the same time and in about the same magnitude every year.

In calculating the percentage change in quarterly data, figures are typically annualized for easier comparisons. That is not the case with the Employment Cost Index, as seen in Table 7.5. Although the wage and benefit cost trends are evident, financial market participants and economists are not accustomed to looking at quarterly rates. It will be more useful either to multiply the quarterly increase in the Employment Cost Index times four, or to look at the year-over-year change.

The wages and salaries portion of the ECI is somewhat correlated to the average hourly earnings figures released monthly with the employment release. However, the average hourly earnings figures can be skewed by changes in the composition of occupations or industries, whereas the ECI adjusts for that. Moreover, seasonal adjustment factors may be different in the two reports.

The Labor Department, which designed and conducts the survey, cautions users to the limitations of this index. The Employment Cost Index is not a measure of change in the total cost of employing labor. For example, it does not estimate training costs. Also, it does not report retroactive pay. The index does not cover all employers and employees in the United States, although it does cover nearly all workers in the civilian nonfarm economy. For example, it doesn't cover the self-employed.

Market Reaction   Financial market participants react to the Employment Cost Index as they would to any other inflation measure. Because it is a quarterly release, and a more stable series than most, the market impact is muted. The reaction to any economic indicator depends on

Table 7.5   Percentage Changes in the Employment Cost Index for Civilian Workers

	Three Months Ended (seasonally adjusted)						12 Months Ended (NSA)
	Jun 91	Sep 91	Dec 91	Mar 92	Jun 92	Sep 92	Sep 92
Compensation Costs	1.3	0.8	0.9	0.9	0.8	0.7	3.5
Wages and salaries	0.9	0.6	0.9	0.7	0.6	0.4	2.7
Benefit costs	1.5	1.6	1.2	1.3	1.1	1.5	5.2

Source: Bureau of Labor Statistics, Department of Labor.

current financial market sentiment. However, market sentiment is a more important factor in figures that are released less frequently. Market participants may choose to ignore potentially bad news (an increase in employment costs) when they are in a good mood. In the same vein, they may ignore potentially good news (a deceleration in employment costs) when they are in a bad mood.

Watch Out For: Look at the quarterly pattern of change in the ECI. Even with seasonal adjustment, occasional blips will occur. A jump in employment costs in a stable or rising trend is potentially worrisome and should be considered as such. A jump in costs in a declining trend is more likely to be an aberration. Look at price changes in wages and salaries as well as benefits. Wages and salaries adjust more quickly to cyclical downturns. Benefits include costs for medical care insurance and have been on the upswing for years. Thus, a slower rate of increase is more likely in wages and salaries than in benefits, even after a prolonged and deep recession. As shown in Table 7.5, wage costs rose 2.7 percent in the 12 months ending September 1992. In contrast, benefit costs rose 5.2 percent during the same period.

Productivity and Costs

Productivity and costs are compiled and published by the Bureau of Labor Statistics. These quarterly figures are made available after the Bureau of Economic Analysis releases gross domestic product and national income. Unlike most economic reports that tend to have regular release dates at about the same time each month, the productivity and costs figures are released about every other month either in the first or second week of the month. Productivity and costs are seasonally adjusted and percentage changes are calculated at annualized rates.

Productivity and cost figures are available for four categories: business, nonfarm business, manufacturing, and nonfinancial corporations. The manufacturing sector can be divided further into durable and nondurable goods. The generic title of productivity and costs represents three sets of figures. Productivity is equal to output per hour. Costs represent compensation per hour and unit labor costs. In contrast to the earnings series described previously, productivity and cost data represent true business costs.

Productivity describes the relationship between output and the amount of labor time incurred in its production. Simply put, it is the ratio of output to hours worked. (Figure 7.5 depicts annual trends in this series.) Although the output produced per hour depends on many factors such as capital investment, changes in technology, capacity utilization, managerial skills, and the characteristics of the work force, these influences are not distinguished in the productivity index. To arrive at the output per hour measure, the Bureau of Labor Statistics needs to calculate labor input and output in the business sector. The primary source of hours and employment data is the monthly Establishment Survey used for the employment situation. The weekly hours data are adjusted to the "hours at work" definition using the BLS Hours at Work Survey, conducted for this purpose. The Household Survey provides data for the farm sector; and the national income accounts are used for government enterprises, proprietors, unpaid family workers, and paid employees of private households. Business output is equal to real gross domestic product (in 1987 dollars) less general government, output of nonprofit institutions, output of paid employees of private households, rental value of owner-occupied dwellings, and the statistical discrepancy in computing the national income and product accounts. Labor inputs that correspond to these categories are also excluded. Business output was 78 percent of gross domestic product in 1991 whereas nonfarm business output was 77 percent of GDP.

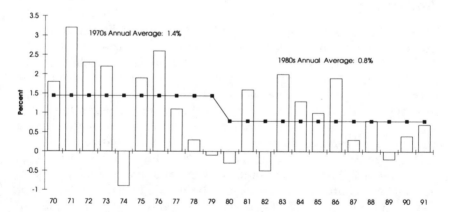

Figure 7.5 Productivity varies over the business cycle; it appears to change in the long run as well judging from the downward shift in productivity gains from the 1970s to the 1980s. (*Source:* Bureau of Labor Statistics, Department of Labor.)

Total manufacturing measures are calculated by adding together the series in the nondurable and durable goods sectors. Durable goods manufacturing includes primary metals; fabricated metal products; industrial machinery and equipment; electronic and other electric equipment; transportation equipment; instruments; lumber and products; furniture and fixtures; stone, clay, and glass products; and miscellaneous manufacturers. Nondurable goods industries include textile mill products, apparel products, paper and allied products, leather and products, printing and publishing, chemicals and products, petroleum products, rubber and plastic products, food, and tobacco products. Manufacturing accounted for 19 percent of GDP in 1991, down from about 22 percent in 1990.

Nonfinancial corporate output equals business output less unincorporated business; the output of corporations engaged in banking; finance, stock, and commodity trading; and credit and insurance agencies. This sector accounted for roughly 55 percent of gross domestic product in 1991.

Compensation per hour is calculated with data from the national income accounts adjusted by the Bureau of Labor Statistics to include an estimate of the value of the wages, salaries, and supplements attributed to proprietors' hours. Compensation includes wages and salaries (including shift differentials and overtime), payments in kind, commissions, supplements, and employer contributions to employee benefit plans and taxes. Weekly hours include all hours for which an employee was in pay status, including paid leave. Compensation costs are available in a current and real dollar index. The current dollar figures are adjusted by the Consumer Price Index to arrive at the inflation-adjusted data.

Finally, *unit labor costs* are calculated by dividing compensation per hour by output per hour. Unit labor costs reflect the true cost of business per worker. Unit labor costs increase if compensation per hour rises without an offsetting gain in output per hour. This suggests that productivity is an important element in the wage–price relationship. As long as productivity increases, wages could rise without putting upward pressure on unit labor costs and inflation. In Figure 7.6, the gap between unit labor costs (ulc) and compensation (comp) represents productivity gains. During recession years, productivity typically declines as producers limit worker layoffs more than they curtail production. Both Figures 7.5 and 7.6 show that productivity was positive during the recession years of 1990–1991, but fell in 1989. This reveals a greater number of job cuts during the recession in 1990, a trend that continued even when a meager recovery began in 1991.

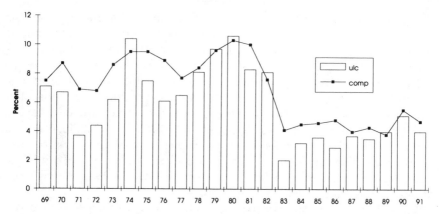

Figure 7.6   The annual growth rate in unit labor costs moderated during the 1980s. Compensation of workers generally outpaced labor costs, except for recession years. (*Source:* Bureau of Labor Statistics, Department of Labor.)

Watch Out For: It is important to understand the normal, cyclical behavior of productivity. Productivity tends to decline during economic downturns when businesses are slow to lay off workers even though they have already curtailed production. When the economy begins to recover, productivity increases because producers initially raise production without rehiring workers.

Productivity and costs figures come from a variety of sources—national income and production accounts, industrial production from the Federal Reserve, employment surveys. As a result, revisions in any of the source data can lead to revisions in productivity, compensation, and unit labor costs. The major source of revisions comes from frequent changes in the national income accounts and the employment data.

Use the productivity and unit labor cost figures to get a better indication of the long-term implications of the inflationary environment. As long as unit labor costs stay low and productivity increases are healthy, prospects for accelerating inflation are small. Since labor costs constitute three quarters of total business costs, product prices won't have to be raised if unit labor costs remain moderate.

Market Reaction   Financial market participants seem less enthusiastic about quarterly statistics than monthly ones. Perhaps that's because the monthly data are more familiar. Nonetheless, they realize that increases in productivity are good for the economy and the inflation environment. Increases in compensation and unit labor costs bode poorly for inflation prospects. Inflation is negative for all markets—fixed-income, equity, and foreign exchange—so they would all move in the same direction. Nevertheless, market reaction tends to be muted with this release, although traders might use it as an excuse to confirm current positive or negative market sentiment. You'll just never know in advance whether these particular figures will be exciting or ho-hum.

Key Points

- Inflation tends to be bad news for everyone. Stock prices, bond prices, and the value of the dollar will decline with accelerating inflation.
- A lower rate of inflation will cause bond prices to rally and stock prices and the value of the dollar to rise.
- Inflation indicators abound. Longer term trends tell you more about inflationary pressures than daily blips in oil prices or the CRB index.
- Most indicators of inflation move in the same direction, though they may not move by the same magnitude. Because some of the indicators (CPI, PPI) are used in the construction of other indicators (GDP deflators), that is not surprising.
- Increasing productivity is the key to holding down inflation: Higher productivity lowers producers' costs but allows wages to rise.
- Table 7.6 summarizes the inflation indicators, their approximate dates of release and source agencies.

Table 7.6   Indicators of Inflation

Month	Approximate Day	Indicator	Data for	Source Agency
Jan	Daily	Crude Oil Prices	Current day	NYMEX
	Daily	CRB Index	Current day	NYFE
	1 to 10	Average hourly earnings	Dec	Bureau of Labor Statistics
	9 to 14	PPI	Dec	Bureau of Labor Statistics
	10 to 19	CPI	Dec	Bureau of Labor Statistics
	27 to 28	Employment Cost Index	Q4	Bureau of Labor Statistics
	22 to 30	GDP Deflators	Q4	Bureau of Economic Analysis
	28 to 31	Ag Prices	mid Jan	U.S. Department of Agriculture
Feb	Daily	Crude Oil Prices	Current day	NYMEX
	Daily	CRB Index	Current day	NYFE
	1 to 10	Average hourly earnings	Jan	Bureau of Labor Statistics
	3 to 11	Productivity and Costs	Q4	Bureau of Labor Statistics
	9 to 14	PPI	Jan	Bureau of Labor Statistics
	10 to 19	CPI	Jan	Bureau of Labor Statistics
	22 to 30	GDP Deflators	Q4	Bureau of Economic Analysis
	28 to 31	Ag Prices	mid Feb	U.S. Department of Agriculture
Mar	Daily	Crude Oil Prices	Current day	NYMEX
	Daily	CRB Index	Current day	NYFE
	1 to 10	Average hourly earnings	Feb	Bureau of Labor Statistics
	3 to 11	Productivity and Costs	Q4	Bureau of Labor Statistics

Table 7.6 ***(Continued)***

Approximate				
Month	Day	Indicator	Data for	Source Agency
Mar	9 to 14	PPI	Feb	Bureau of Labor Statistics
	10 to 19	CPI	Feb	Bureau of Labor Statistics
	22 to 30	GDP Deflators	Q4	Bureau of Economic Analysis
	28 to 31	Ag Prices	mid Mar	U.S. Department of Agriculture
Apr	Daily	Crude Oil Prices	Current day	NYMEX
	Daily	CRB Index	Current day	NYFE
	1 to 10	Average hourly earnings	Mar	Bureau of Labor Statistics
	9 to 14	PPI	Mar	Bureau of Labor Statistics
	10 to 19	CPI	Mar	Bureau of Labor Statistics
	27 to 28	Employment Cost Index	Q1	Bureau of Labor Statistics
	22 to 30	GDP Deflators	Q1	Bureau of Economic Analysis
	28 to 31	Ag Prices	mid Apr	U.S. Department of Agriculture
May	Daily	Crude Oil Prices	Current day	NYMEX
	Daily	CRB Index	Current day	NYFE
	1 to 10	Average hourly earnings	Apr	Bureau of Labor Statistics
	3 to 11	Productivity and Costs	Q1	Bureau of Labor Statistics
	9 to 14	PPI	Apr	Bureau of Labor Statistics
	10 to 19	CPI	Apr	Bureau of Labor Statistics
	22 to 30	GDP Deflators	Q1	Bureau of Economic Analysis

Table 7.6   (Continued)

| Approximate | | | | |
Month	Day	Indicator	Data for	Source Agency
May	28 to 31	Ag Prices	mid May	U.S. Department of Agriculture
June	Daily	Crude Oil Prices	Current day	NYMEX
	Daily	CRB Index	Current day	NYFE
	1 to 10	Average hourly earnings	May	Bureau of Labor Statistics
	3 to 11	Productivity and Costs	Q1	Bureau of Labor Statistics
	9 to 14	PPI	May	Bureau of Labor Statistics
	10 to 19	CPI	May	Bureau of Labor Statistics
	22 to 30	GDP Deflators	Q1	Bureau of Economic Analysis
	28 to 31	Ag Prices	mid June	U.S. Department of Agriculture
July	Daily	Crude Oil Prices	Current day	NYMEX
	Daily	CRB Index	Current day	NYFE
	1 to 10	Average hourly earnings	June	Bureau of Labor Statistics
	9 to 14	PPI	June	Bureau of Labor Statistics
	10 to 19	CPI	June	Bureau of Labor Statistics
	27 to 28	Employment Cost Index	Q2	Bureau of Labor Statistics
	22 to 30	GDP Deflators	Q2	Bureau of Economic Analysis
	28 to 31	Ag Prices	mid July	U.S. Department of Agriculture
Aug	Daily	Crude Oil Prices	Current day	NYMEX
	Daily	CRB Index	Current day	NYFE
	1 to 10	Average hourly earnings	July	Bureau of Labor Statistics

Table 7.6   *(Continued)*

Approximate				
Month	Day	Indicator	Data for	Source Agency
Aug	3 to 11	Productivity and Costs	Q2	Bureau of Labor Statistics
	9 to 14	PPI	July	Bureau of Labor Statistics
	10 to 19	CPI	July	Bureau of Labor Statistics
	22 to 30	GDP Deflators	Q2	Bureau of Economic Analysis
	28 to 31	Ag Prices	mid Aug	U.S. Department of Agriculture
Sep	Daily	Crude Oil Prices	Current day	NYMEX
	Daily	CRB Index	Current day	NYFE
	1 to 10	Average hourly earnings	Aug	Bureau of Labor Statistics
	3 to 11	Productivity and Costs	Q2	Bureau of Labor Statistics
	9 to 14	PPI	Aug	Bureau of Labor Statistics
	10 to 19	CPI	Aug	Bureau of Labor Statistics
	22 to 30	GDP Deflators	Q2	Bureau of Economic Analysis
	28 to 31	Ag Prices	mid Sep	U.S. Department of Agriculture
Oct	Daily	Crude Oil Prices	Current day	NYMEX
	Daily	CRB Index	Current day	NYFE
	1 to 10	Average hourly earnings	Sep	Bureau of Labor Statistics
	9 to 14	PPI	Sep	Bureau of Labor Statistics
	10 to 19	CPI	Sep	Bureau of Labor Statistics
	27 to 28	Employment Cost Index	Q3	Bureau of Labor Statistics
	22 to 30	GDP Deflators	Q3	Bureau of Economic Analysis

Table 7.6 *(Continued)*

Approximate Month	Day	Indicator	Data for	Source Agency
Oct	28 to 31	Ag Prices	mid Oct	U.S. Department of Agriculture
Nov	Daily	Crude Oil Prices	Current day	NYMEX
	Daily	CRB Index	Current day	NYFE
	1 to 10	Average hourly earnings	Oct	Bureau of Labor Statistics
	3 to 11	Productivity and Costs	Q3	Bureau of Labor Statistics
	9 to 14	PPI	Oct	Bureau of Labor Statistics
	10 to 19	CPI	Oct	Bureau of Labor Statistics
	22 to 30	GDP Deflators	Q3	Bureau of Economic Analysis
	28 to 31	Ag Prices	mid Nov	U.S. Department of Agriculture
Dec	Daily	Crude Oil Prices	Current day	NYMEX
	Daily	CRB Index	Current day	NYFE
	1 to 10	Average hourly earnings	Nov	Bureau of Labor Statistics
	3 to 11	Productivity and Costs	Q3	Bureau of Labor Statistics
	9 to 14	PPI	Nov	Bureau of Labor Statistics
	10 to 19	CPI	Nov	Bureau of Labor Statistics
	22 to 30	GDP Deflators	Q3	Bureau of Economic Analysis
	28 to 31	Ag Prices	mid Dec	U.S. Department of Agriculture

CHAPTER 8

Other Measures
of Production

Featured Indicators	Initial Claims for Unemployment Insurance
	Unemployment Rate
	Nonfarm Payrolls
	Average Workweek
	Index of Help Wanted Advertising
	Index of Industrial Production
	Capacity Utilization Rate
	Purchasing Managers Index (NAPM)
	Business Outlook Survey of the Philadelphia Fed
	Index of Leading Indicators

Many of the economic indicators discussed in other chapters describe spending: retail sales, manufacturing shipments, the merchandise trade balance. These fit on the product side of the national income and product accounts. Other indicators directly assist in establishing the direction of the sector such as personal income and consumer sentiment, which determine personal consumption expenditures. Many of the indicators are used in the actual computation of GDP (retail sales), or national income (personal income). Still, gross domestic product is a measure of production, not sales, and its major drawback is a quarterly release schedule.

This chapter describes other indicators, including some for production, that are not all-encompassing but are reported monthly and on a more timely basis. Financial market participants, federal government policymakers, and the media closely monitor these series.

HIGH-FREQUENCY INDICATOR

Initial Claims for Unemployment Insurance

Initial claims for unemployment insurance are reported weekly. Every Thursday, the Employment and Training Division of the Labor Department reports initial jobless claims with a one-week lag. The data represent actual claims filed and come from state unemployment agencies in contrast to the monthly employment report, which is derived from a survey. This is an important distinction. Many people believe that the nation's unemployment rate is based on the number of people collecting jobless benefits, but that is not so. These two separate indicators are only related in a theoretical, not a statistical sense.

The unemployment insurance programs cover all 50 states plus the District of Columbia, Puerto Rico, and the Virgin Islands. Although the claims are seasonally adjusted, weekly data are highly erratic so it is unwise to emphatically declare a new trend with one week's data. The figures could be especially misleading during holiday periods. Standard seasonal adjustment procedures typically use five years of past data to calculate the appropriate seasonal adjustment. However, since holidays don't always occur in the same week each year, the adjustment process is flawed. The best way around this problem is to look at a four-week moving average of the series. (See Figure 8.1.)

Over the long run, initial unemployment claims are closely related to the monthly employment statistics released by the Bureau of Labor Statistics division of the Labor Department. Often, market participants base their expectations of the employment situation on jobless claims, and many economists use initial claims to forecast nonfarm payroll employment. The success rate is mediocre. Because the figures come from two different sources, there are any number of reasons for the monthly differences between jobless claims and the employment situation, including different seasonal adjustment factors, different samples, or other statistical quirks.

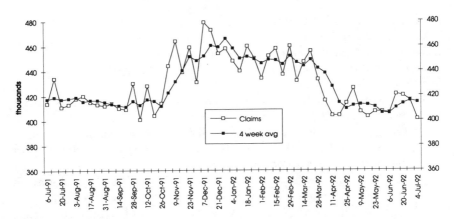

Figure 8.1 The four-week moving average of initial jobless claims reflects the trend more easily than the actual weekly fluctuations. (*Source: Market News Service, Inc.*, Department of Labor.)

The Employment and Training Division also releases continuing benefits. These figures are released at the same time as new jobless claims, but with a three-week instead of a one-week lag. As the number of persons collecting continuing benefits increases, it points to a soft labor market where jobs are hard to find. A drop in continuing benefits suggests that employment prospects are on the mend. Analysts use new jobless claims to predict changes in employment as measured by nonfarm payrolls. Actually, initial jobless claims do somewhat better in predicting the unemployment rate (although even then the correlation is not tremendously high). Continuing jobless benefits are better predictors of monthly payroll changes, although again, the correlation is not tremendously high.

Market Reaction   As previously mentioned, financial market participants like frequent data. The more frequent the indicator, the more ammunition traders have when reacting to economic conditions. Otherwise, they must respond to forecasts and rumors. Given the choice, real data are preferable to rumors and predictions, even though the data will probably be revised many times over. Weekly jobless claims became a favorite with market participants when the economy first fell into recession in 1990 and the report anxiously awaited every week as the nascent recovery began in 1991. As long as doubts linger about job prospects and the unemployment rate remains uncomfortably high, jobless claims will continue to be a weekly favorite among traders. Market participants have a "flavor of the month" mentality. At one time or other, each of the various statistics has had greater stature than others. To paraphrase Andy Warhol, we all have 15 minutes of fame.

Participants in the fixed-income market view a rise in jobless claims favorably, because it points to a deteriorating labor market. A worsening economic environment coupled with a lack of inflationary pressure means interest rates will decline through the market mechanism or with the help of Federal Reserve easing.

Professionals in the foreign exchange market will sell the dollar on this news because a languishing economy means low interest rates. As long as the U.S. investment return is less than that of foreign countries, then the demand for dollars will drop weakening the U.S. currency.

Stock prices will likely fall with a rise in jobless claims. Although declining interest rates are good for the stock market, a weak economy bodes poorly for corporate profits, the life blood of improving stock prices.

Watch Out For: Check for holidays in the reporting week. For example, Presidents' Day in February, is a federal holiday for government workers (and bankers). Claims offices will not be open as a result, and so workers at the state unemployment office will only have four days in which to process claims during that week rather than the normal five. A shortened workweek could cause a decline of roughly 20,000 in new claims on a base of about 350,000. The week following a holiday will usually post a larger than normal rise in claims to compensate for the holiday in the previous week.

October marks the beginning of several holidays throughout the fall and winter season. Claims tend to be extremely erratic until the end of February, so never take a week's number at face value. It is much safer to check the four-week moving average of this series throughout the entire year. Figure 8.2 illustrates the higher volatility of initial jobless claims during this period.

Do not fall into the trap of assuming that a decline in the number of reported initial jobless claims automatically means an increase in nonfarm payrolls. Jobless claims are the direct result of layoffs. Just because fewer persons were laid off, it doesn't mean employers increased hiring.

Always look at the trend rather than at a one-week figure even if you're looking at the four-week moving average of jobless claims. In an environment of rising claims, you're likely to see falling interest rates, especially as the economy heads for recession. On the other hand, when jobless claims are in a downward mode, recovery may be at hand and rates will start increasing soon. Claims are a good lead indicator of economic activity, although the lead time could be several months. Initial unemployment insurance claims are one of the 11 series in the Index of Leading Indicators.

In periods of prolonged recession or high unemployment rates, the federal government can declare a state of emergency in the labor market allowing workers who have run out of benefits without finding a job to file for extended—or emergency—benefits. Those unemployed workers eligible for extended benefits would refile under the new program, and the figures are reported separately by the agency. For example, on September 24, 1992, the Labor Department reported that 414,000 (seasonally adjusted) unemployed workers filed for unemployment insurance for the first time in the week ended September 12. At the same time, 17,612 unemployed workers filed under the emergency benefit program. (The emergency benefits figures are not seasonally adjusted.) Benefits for unemployment insurance vary by state. In Illinois, for example, workers are eligible for 26 weeks of unemployment compensation under the regular program.

On September 24, 1992, the Labor Department also reported that 3.2 million unemployed workers were receiving regular (continuing) benefits, whereas an additional 1.3 million unemployed persons were receiving emergency benefits in the week ended September 5. (Continuing benefits are reported with a three-week lag, while initial claims are reported with a one-week lag.)

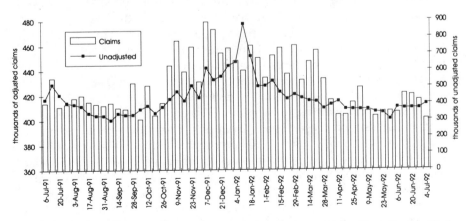

Figure 8.2 This chart shows how important it is to seasonally adjust initial jobless claims: The unadjusted figures varied from 300,000 to 900,000 during the year. Despite the seasonal adjustment process, claims remain volatile from one week to the next. (*Source: Market News Service, Inc.,* Department of Labor.)

MONTHLY INDICATORS

The Employment Situation

The Bureau of Labor Statistics (BLS), a division of the Labor Department, issues an employment report each month, just one week after the end of the month. Several indicators are part of this report; each is used for different analysis. Financial market participants love this report because it is so timely. Economists also love its timeliness but appreciate its rich detail of information even more.

Unemployment Rate

One of the most common economic indicators, possibly second only to inflation, is the *civilian unemployment rate*. The unemployment rate rises during cyclical downturns and falls during periods of rapid economic growth. The nation's jobless rate comes from a survey of 60,000 households conducted by the Commerce Department's Bureau of the Census but is analyzed by the Bureau of Labor Statistics. Respondents are interviewed by telephone about their own employment status and the status of everyone in their household over the age of 16 years, for the Sunday-to-Saturday calendar week that includes the twelfth of the month.

If the respondents were working in the week including the twelfth, they are counted as employed and in the labor force. Workers don't have to be paid for work to be counted as employed if they worked at least 15 hours (per week) in a family-operated business. The self-employed and farm workers are included in this survey as well. Respondents are asked more than whether they are employed. The interviewer asks individuals who were not employed during the relevant week whether they were actively seeking employment in the previous four weeks; were waiting to report to work to a new job within 30 days; or were waiting to be recalled to a job from which they were laid off. If one of these three situations hold, the worker is unemployed, but still a member of the labor force. Individuals are not in the labor force if they classify themselves as "engaged in own home housework," "in school," "unable to work" (because of long-term physical or mental disability), "retired," and "other." The last category provides the famed classification of "discouraged workers," that is, workers who think they cannot find a job because of labor market conditions or personal factors such as age, education, or training. Workers who are in a labor dispute (on strike) as well as workers who are on unpaid leave for illness, bad weather, or personal reasons, are counted as employed and in the labor force.

Once we know the number of people who are employed along with the number of people who are unemployed, we can calculate the unemployment rate. The labor force is the sum of employed plus unemployed individuals. The unemployment rate is equal to the number of unemployed persons divided by the total number of persons in the labor force.

$$\frac{\text{Unemployed}}{\text{Employed} + \text{Unemployed}} = \text{Unemployment Rate}$$

Either the numerator (number of unemployed) or the denominator (number in the labor force) can cause changes in the unemployment rate. The unemployment rate will increase whenever the labor force increases (barring an equal rise in the number of employed persons) and whenever the number of unemployed persons increases (barring any change in the labor force). Conversely, either a drop in the labor force, or a decline in the number of unemployed persons, will cause the jobless rate to decrease.

A person must be in the labor force before he or she can become employed (unless the job seeker is lucky enough to find employment on the first day of searching). Whenever people first start looking for a job, the labor force increases, by definition. Someone may enter the work force and find a job within a month. In that case, the labor force will increase by one, but so will employment. Thus, employment and the labor force could increase by similar amounts. Consequently, a rise in the labor force does not always lead to a greater number of unemployed persons.

The unemployment rate is considered a lagging indicator of economic activity. During a recession, many people will drop out of the labor force (and possibly become discouraged workers, or attend school, or engage in own home housework) because they think they won't be able to find a job. If individuals are not in the labor force, they can't be counted as unemployed. As a result, the unemployment rate may be understated during a recession. In the early stages of a recovery, labor force growth accelerates because more people reenter the labor force believing it will now be easier to find a job. Thus, they start looking for work, but it may still take several weeks (or months) to find a job. In the meantime, they are counted as unemployed (and in the labor force), whereas they had not been counted before.

Table 8.1   Labor Force Statistics: Summary Table
(thousands)

	Jan 92	Feb 92	Mar 92	Apr 92
Total				
Civilian Noninstitutional Population	190,759	190,884	191,022	191,168
Civilian labor force	126,028	126,185	126,548	126,743
Labor force participation rate	66.1	66.1	66.2	66.3
Employed	117,036	116,962	117,264	117,515
Employment to population ratio	61.4	61.3	61.4	61.5
Unemployed	8,992	9,223	9,284	9,228
Unemployment rate (%)	7.1	7.3	7.3	7.3
Men, 20 Years and Over				
Civilian Noninstitutional Population	84,464	84,549	84,549	84,671
Civilian labor force	65,121	65,161	65,436	65,572
Labor force participation rate	77.1	77.1	77.4	77.4
Employed	60,664	60,606	60,843	61,033
Employment to population ratio	71.8	71.7	72.0	72.1
Unemployed	4,457	4,555	4,593	4,539
Unemployment rate (%)	6.8	7.0	7.0	6.9
Women, 20 Years and Over				
Civilian Noninstitutional Population	93,125	93,208	93,256	93,320
Civilian labor force	54,143	54,239	54,458	54,534
Labor force participation rate	58.1	58.2	58.4	58.4
Employed	50,889	50,925	51,114	51,136
Employment to population ratio	54.6	54.6	54.8	54.8
Unemployed	3,254	3,314	3,344	3,398
Unemployment rate (%)	6.0	6.1	6.1	6.2
Both Sexes, 16 to 19 Years				
Civilian Noninstitutional Population	13,169	13,127	13,176	13,177
Civilian labor force	6,764	6,785	6,654	6,637
Labor force participation rate	51.4	51.7	50.5	50.4
Employed	5,483	5,431	5,307	5,346
Employment to population ratio	41.6	41.4	40.3	40.6
Unemployed	1,281	1,354	1,347	1,291
Unemployment rate (%)	18.9	20.0	20.2	19.5

Source: Monthly Labor Review, U.S. Department of Labor, Bureau of Labor Statistics, March 1993.

	May 92	June 92	July 92	Aug 92	Sep 92	Oct 92	Nov 92	Dec 92
	191,307	191,455	191,622	191,790	191,947	192,131	192,316	192,509
	127,039	127,298	127,350	127,404	127,274	127,066	127,365	127,591
	66.4	66.5	66.5	66.4	66.3	66.1	66.2	66.3
	117,580	117,510	117,722	117,780	117,724	117,687	118,064	118,311
	61.5	61.4	61.4	61.4	61.3	61.3	61.4	61.5
	9,459	9,788	9,628	9,624	9,550	9,379	9,301	9,280
	7.4	7.7	7.6	7.6	7.5	7.4	7.3	7.3
	84,755	84,842	84,944	85,010	85,075	85,159	85,259	85,369
	65,844	65,813	65,782	65,857	65,805	65,811	65,740	65,785
	77.7	77.6	77.4	77.5	77.3	77.3	77.1	77.1
	61,087	61,027	61,070	61,104	61,125	61,088	61,206	61,326
	72.1	71.9	71.9	71.9	71.8	71.7	71.8	71.8
	4,757	4,786	4,712	4,753	4,680	4,723	4,534	4,459
	7.2	7.3	7.2	7.2	7.1	7.2	6.9	6.8
	93,416	93,479	93,562	93,635	93,703	93,771	93,849	93,960
	54,468	54,682	54,834	54,773	54,611	54,578	54,832	55,010
	58.3	58.5	58.6	58.5	58.3	58.2	58.4	58.5
	51,104	51,233	51,307	51,247	51,141	51,182	51,435	51,494
	54.7	54.8	54.8	54.7	54.6	54.6	54.8	54.8
	3,364	3,449	3,527	3,526	3,470	3,396	3,397	3,516
	6.2	6.3	6.4	6.4	6.4	6.2	6.2	6.4
	13,136	13,134	13,116	13,145	13,369	13,200	13,208	13,181
	6,727	6,803	6,734	6,774	6,858	6,677	6,793	6,796
	51.2	51.8	51.3	51.5	5.2	50.6	51.4	51.6
	5,389	5,250	5,345	5,429	5,458	5,417	5,423	5,491
	41.0	40.0	40.8	41.3	4.2	41.0	41.1	41.7
	1,338	1,553	1,389	1,345	1,400	1,260	1,370	1,305
	19.9	22.8	20.6	19.9	20.4	18.9	20.2	19.2

In attempting to measure the unemployment rate, the Bureau of Labor Statistics compiles a slew of statistics derived from the telephone survey of households (whose official name is the Current Population Survey, or CPS). Table 8.1 shows the civilian labor force and civilian employment for men and women over the age of 16. The employment detail is phenomenal, but it isn't necessary to distinguish unemployment rates of detailed age groups by gender or race in order to understand the macroeconomy. It is important, however, to distinguish between the employment behavior of adult men (aged 20 or more), adult women, and teens (16- to 19-year-olds). Their employment and labor force behavior tend to vary from month to month, which is relevant for seasonal adjustment purposes. Many adult women leave the labor force in June when the school year ends and reenter it in September when school starts again, so they can be on the same schedule as their children. The seasonal behavior of women in the labor force is more muted today than it was in the 1950s and 1960s, but the pattern remains, nonetheless. In the opposite flow, teens largely enter the labor force at the end of the school year but leave it again at the start of the new school year. The seasonal adjustment mechanism can also take this factor in stride.

The cyclical behavior of employment among adult men, women, and teens can also diverge. Historically, men have suffered greater increases in unemployment than women during recessions due to their greater numbers in manufacturing and construction industries, which are more prone to layoff than service industries. During expansions, the jobless rate of adult women has tended to be higher than that of adult men. The gap in unemployment rates between men and women narrowed significantly during the 1980s so that the unemployment rates of both groups are now more similar during expansions and recessions.

Did You Know?   In the 1970s, the unemployment rate of adult men was 1.5 percentage points lower, on average, than the jobless rate of adult women. In the 1980s, the differential narrowed to less than 0.1 percentage point. Women had lower unemployment rates in 1982 and 1983. This pattern has continued into the 1990s with adult women posting lower unemployment rates than adult men, perhaps reflecting the effects of the 1990–1991 recession.

In addition to employment and labor force statistics of men and women by age, sex, and race, the household survey also includes employment by industry, part-time versus full-time employment; unemployment by type of loss (resignation versus layoff); and unemployment rates by duration. Unemployment rates for the 11 largest states are also available monthly. These statistics all serve to decipher the state of the U.S. labor market on a monthly basis.

Finally, the level of discouraged workers is available on a quarterly basis. Discouraged workers always exist, in good times and in bad. The level of such workers is relatively high even during economic expansions when labor markets are tight and jobs are relatively easy to find, as Figure 8.3 shows. Because the number of discouraged workers increases sharply during recessions, it is more meaningful to analyze changes in the number of discouraged workers over the business cycle, rather than actual levels.

Market Reaction The seemingly perverse behavior of fixed-income market participants holds for the unemployment rate. A rising unemployment rate is associated with a weak or contracting economy and declining interest rates. Bond prices rally on the news. Conversely, a decreasing unemployment rate is associated with an expanding economy and potentially rising interest rates. Bond prices will fall. Professionals in the equity and foreign exchange markets will appear more rational

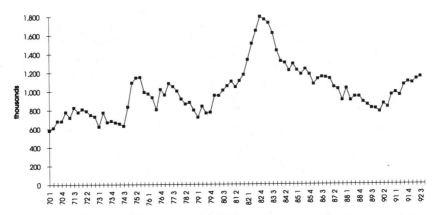

Figure 8.3 The level of discouraged workers is high even in the best of times. (*Source:* Bureau of Labor Statistics, Department of Labor.)

to the casual observer: Stock prices and the foreign exchange value of the dollar rise when the unemployment rate falls.

Nonfarm Payrolls

The unemployment rate and its slew of data are derived from a survey of households. Another set of statistics comes from a survey of about 350,000 establishments, officially known as the Current Employment Statistics Survey. The main figures from this survey are payrolls of nonagricultural business establishments. Since this survey simply asks respondents to provide the number of workers currently on their payrolls, double counting occurs when individuals hold more than one job. For instance, several years ago, I was employed full time at a bank and taught part time in the evening at two different universities for a few months. Consequently, I was counted on three payrolls even though only one of my jobs was full-time employment. When I quit one of the university positions and went off its payroll, it appeared as a drop in employment. Table 8.2 lists the goods and services industries that make up the payroll data.

Watch Out For: Temporary aberrations could move the unemployment rate in either direction. Moreover, based on BLS analysis, the civilian unemployment rate must change by at least 0.2 percentage points before it can be considered statistically significant. Nevertheless, a 0.1 percentage point gain for six consecutive months that cumulatively increases the jobless rate by 0.6 percentage points is certainly significant even though the jobless rate did not increase by the requisite of 0.2 points in any particular month.

Major aberrations can occur in the unemployment rate during the summer months when teens end their school year and are job hunting. This pattern is well known and fully expected by seasonal adjustment factors. The only problem is that teens don't enter the labor force in the same numbers each May and June. Furthermore, fewer and fewer 16- to 19-year-olds entered the labor force in each year of the 1980s as that demographic age group has shrunk.

Fewer-than-expected teens entering the workforce in May and June can cause the total labor force to shrink on a seasonally adjusted basis and lead to a drop in the unemployment rate. In August or September, when these student workers go back to school, the unemployment rate will rise again. Consequently, view movements in the unemployment rate during the summer months with a skeptical eye.

The components that make up the unemployment rate are significant. A rise in the jobless rate due to a decrease in employment is worse news for the economy than a rise in the unemployment rate due to a greater number of persons entering the labor force. Labor force growth accelerates when individuals believe the job outlook is improved; it moderates significantly during recessions when job prospects appear poor. Although many economists tend to credit this phenomenon to discouraged workers, that theory does not explain all labor force behavior. Such behavior changes over the business cycle because different people have various alternatives for the use of their time. When the economy is in recession and wages are lower, the cost of unemployment declines and other options such as going to school or raising a family become more desirable. On the flip side, a business cycle expansion accompanied by rising wages makes it more costly to stay at home and raise children, attend school, or consider other options.

The unemployment rate is a lagging indicator of economic activity, so do not be unduly concerned about increases in the jobless rate when other economic indicators show a more positive economic picture. Although economists accept the unemployment rate as a lagging indicator, a rising jobless rate can still be disconcerting. To a much greater degree than other economic indicators, the unemployment rate along with the inflation rate, can have political ramifications because it affects consumers directly. As a result, the Federal Reserve Board keeps a close watch on the unemployment rate. If it rises too rapidly or too steeply, the Fed could be under pressure by the Administration to ease monetary policy (lower interest rates) in an effort to boost economic activity, thus causing a decline in the jobless rate. A good case in point: The unemployment rate rose to 7.8 percent in June 1992 during the most mild and most doubted recovery in history. Within an hour of the BLS report, the Federal Reserve cut the discount rate 50 basis points to 3 percent, bringing this rate to its lowest level since 1963.

The Fed and many economic analysts also look at other data such as the employment-to-population ratio, which tends to be more stable than the jobless rate from month to month. This ratio shows that a major share of the U.S. population are now employed despite the 1990–1991 recession followed by a lackluster recovery in 1992. The series has risen fairly steadily during the postwar period, although the employment-to-population ratio tends to decline during periods of recession. As a result, the employment-to-population ratio peaked at 63 percent in 1989 and subsequently dipped to 61.6 percent in 1991 and 1992. Yet, this ratio was higher than it was after the 1981–1982 recession and equal to the level reached in 1987.

Table 8.2   Employees on Nonfarm Payrolls
(thousands, seasonally adjusted)

	Jan 92	Feb 92	Mar 92	Apr 92
Total	108,100	108,142	108,200	108,377
Total Private	89,643	89,681	89,693	89,835
Goods-Producing	23,527	23,525	23,532	23,530
Mining	657	653	651	646
Construction	4,587	4,582	4,603	4,605
Manufacturing	18,283	18,290	18,278	18,279
Durable Goods	10,422	10,430	10,417	10,409
Lumber and wood	680	686	689	688
Furniture and fixtures	466	464	465	467
Stone, clay and glass	517	517	518	520
Primary metals	711	710	710	708
Fabricated metal products	1,344	1,342	1,342	1,341
Industrial machinery and equipment	1,954	1,950	1,948	1,949
Electronic and electrical equipment	1,570	1,564	1,560	1,557
Transportation	1,850	1,872	1,863	1,859
Instruments	963	959	956	952
Miscellaneous manufacturing	367	366	366	368
Nondurable Goods	7,861	7,860	7,861	7,870
Food and products	1,672	1,671	1,671	1,677
Tobacco products	50	50	49	50
Textile mill products	678	681	682	682
Apparel and other products	1,024	1,025	1,025	1,023
Paper and allied products	687	686	687	689
Printing and publishing	1,524	1,519	1,519	1,521
Chemicals and allied products	1,073	1,073	1,071	1,072
Petroleum and coal products	158	158	157	157
Rubber and plastics	871	874	877	876
Leather and products	124	123	123	123
Service Producing	84,573	84,617	84,668	84,847
Transportation and public utilities	5,746	5,753	5,754	5,746
Wholesale trade	6,010	6,003	5,997	5,993
Retail trade	19,118	19,143	19,092	19,177
Finance, insurance and real estate	6,665	6,673	6,675	6,682
Services	28,577	28,584	28,643	28,707
Government	18,457	18,461	18,507	18,542

Source: Monthly Labor Review, U.S. Department of Labor, Bureau of Labor Statistics, March 1993.

May 92	June 92	July 92	Aug 92	Sep 92	Oct 92	Nov 92	Dec 92
108,496	108,423	108,594	108,485	108,197	108,571	108,646	108,736
89,950	89,885	89,988	89,803	89,547	89,948	89,961	90,036
23,548	23,470	23,459	23,362	22,996	23,270	23,280	23,261
641	634	633	626	620	623	622	619
4,632	4,600	4,584	4,591	4,574	4,601	4,590	4,581
18,275	18,236	18,242	18,145	17,802	18,046	18,068	18,061
10,398	10,371	10,347	10,298	10,271	10,231	10,247	10,240
687	684	683	682	683	689	695	697
467	469	470	465	461	461	461	462
522	521	521	520	520	518	518	519
707	706	702	701	699	695	695	693
1,343	1,338	1,335	1,334	1,330	1,323	1,323	1,323
1,959	1,954	1,947	1,941	1,943	1,935	1,935	1,934
1,554	1,549	1,545	1,536	1,538	1,534	1,537	1,536
1,842	1,836	1,829	1,816	1,797	1,782	1,790	1,788
949	946	943	938	935	930	927	921
368	368	372	365	365	364	366	367
7,877	7,865	7,895	7,847	7,531	7,815	7,821	7,821
1,678	1,671	1,685	1,672	1,661	1,661	1,664	1,664
49	49	49	51	50	49	47	49
679	680	682	675	677	672	675	677
1,026	1,023	1,034	1,013	1,007	1,004	1,006	1,004
691	689	689	687	392	688	688	686
1,522	1,520	1,522	1,521	1,523	1,520	1,518	1,518
1,073	1,073	1,070	1,072	1,069	1,069	1,069	1,068
156	155	154	153	152	152	152	151
880	883	884	880	877	877	880	882
123	122	126	123	123	123	122	122
84,948	84,953	85,135	85,123	85,201	85,301	85,366	85,475
5,745	5,745	5,742	5,729	5,738	5,731	5,732	5,740
5,993	5,988	5,972	5,964	5,957	5,969	5,976	5,968
19,150	19,156	19,184	19,106	19,122	19,146	19,116	19,159
6,681	6,672	6,660	6,661	6,669	6,680	6,669	6,677
28,833	28,854	28,971	28,981	29,065	29,152	29,188	29,231
18,546	18,538	18,606	18,682	18,650	18,623	18,685	18,700

Business establishments are asked to give their employment statistics for the pay period that includes the twelfth of the month, although this doesn't necessarily correspond to the calendar week referenced in the household survey since companies have different pay schedules, such as weekly or biweekly, for their workers. In contrast to the household survey, which covers self-employed workers, nonfarm payrolls do not. Furthermore, workers involved in labor disputes (on strike) during the relevant week are not included in the figures either. Similarly, individuals on layoff are not on payrolls even if the layoff period is only a week.

Nonfarm payrolls and household employment have minor differences making it impossible for them to move in tandem or by the same magnitude from month to month. It isn't unusual to see increases in nonfarm payrolls and decreases in household employment in the same month, and vice versa. Over the long run, changes in nonfarm payrolls mirror changes in household employment. In the mid to late 1980s, a widening gap developed between household employment and nonfarm payroll employment. After the 1992 benchmark revisions, the gap was revealed to be even larger than initially estimated. Labor Department economists, who have studied this discrepancy between the two surveys, still find it hard to explain. Differences in definition between the two surveys provide a potential reason for this gap. Farm workers and the self-employed are included in household employment but are excluded from payroll employment. Since the number of farmers didn't increase during the late 1980s, an increase in farm workers would not be a viable solution to this puzzle. The other possibility is that the number of self-employed workers rose. Anecdotal evidence suggests that the number of consultants and small businesses are on the rise as corporations try to curtail overhead costs. These individuals would be counted as employed by the household data although not by the establishment data. Further studies need to be conducted to find statistical evidence to prove this or similar theories.

In the past, nonfarm payroll employment was considered to be a better indicator of current economic conditions than household employment, but this series has deteriorated over the past few years as the structure of the economy has changed. Small businesses aren't usually featured in the establishment survey. If the U.S. economy is shifting toward small businesses, the establishment survey would not entirely catch these employment gains.

Market Reaction Players in the fixed income market favor small increases or outright declines in nonfarm payrolls because they signal economic weakness. Economic weakness usually portends lower interest rates through decreased market demand for loans or Federal Reserve easing. For example, the Federal Reserve eased on September 4, 1992, by lowering the equilibrium federal funds rate by 25 basis points to 3 percent, on the heels of another report of mediocre nonfarm payrolls for the month.

Did You Know? Components of the establishment survey are good predictors of personal income, which is released three weeks after the employment situation. The monthly percentage changes in average hourly earnings, the private average workweek, and private (excluding government workers) nonfarm payrolls give you a good estimate of the monthly percentage change in private wages and salaries (nearly 50 percent of total personal income).

Conversely, robust increases in nonfarm payrolls could indicate a healthy economy and portend higher interest rates as credit demands pick up or the Federal Reserve tightens to prevent inflationary pressures. The potential for higher interest rates makes foreign exchange market participants eager for robust gains in nonfarm payrolls as they will push up the value of the dollar. Participants in the equity market also will favor healthy employment gains because a strong economy means healthy corporate profits, which is a boon for stock prices.

Did You Know? Special factors affecting employment statistics can be numerous in any single month. Economist Joan Schneider of Continental Bank in Chicago cited several special factors for the September employment situation in her September 25, 1992, newsletter, *Projections.* She warned that nonfarm payroll employment would have a downward bias in September due to the "winding down of a special federally funded summer job program which added about 150,000 youth to payrolls in July and August." Also, she cited a potential rise in the civilian unemployment rate from the jump in teen unemployment.

In addition, Ms. Schneider cited temporary strike activity as a problem: GM workers were returning to work, but some teachers were just beginning their labor dispute. Other issues in the September report included a shortened workweek due to the inclusion of Labor Day in the employment survey week, and the labor market impact of Hurricane Andrew.

Ms. Schneider concluded, "Many of these developments will influence the employment statistics on a temporary basis, but their impact in any one or two months can be substantial and is hard to isolate. Thus, statistics in recent and forthcoming employment reports should be evaluated with care."

Just a few days before the release of the September employment report, Labor Department officials, Bill Goodman and George Wakiji, in an interview with *Market News Service, Inc.*, mentioned the same special factors that had been described by the Continental Bank economist.[1]

Watch Out For: There are many pitfalls to guard against when analyzing nonfarm payrolls. First, labor strikes affect the pattern of growth of nonfarm payrolls. If workers are on strike during the relevant pay period (including the twelfth of the month), the rise in nonfarm payrolls will be understated. When workers return to their jobs, nonfarm payroll employment increases will be overstated. The telephone workers' strike in 1983 caused a 411,000 plunge in total nonfarm payrolls in August and a subsequent spurt of 733,000 workers in September when the labor dispute ended. Economic analysts discussed the effects of the telephone workers' strike in advance, so that the initial plunge in payrolls didn't cause financial market participants to anticipate an economic downturn and the subsequent burst didn't lead them to anticipate an economic expansion with inflationary pressures.

Discounting changes in payrolls because of known strikes may work against you, too. In 1989, Eastern Airlines workers went on strike. Unfortunately, they never returned to work because Eastern went bankrupt. Thus, an initial job loss of roughly 25,000 workers that was glossed over because it was due to a labor dispute turned into a permanent job loss without market realization. Because the Bureau of Labor Statistics is well aware of the impact that changes in the employment situation have on the financial market, it typically headlines especially large labor disputes or other special factors in reports. This practice quickly alerts financial market participants and the media to potential aberrations.

The changing nature of the economy will induce temporary quirks in the seasonal adjustment process for the monthly figures. For example, just as retail sales have a strong seasonal component and tend to increase sharply in November and December, so does retail trade employment.

Then when retail sales slough off in January and February, retail trade workers will be laid off.

In the mid to late 1980s, retailers began to hire fewer workers before the holiday season because retail sales growth moderated. Since seasonal adjustment factors were expecting larger gains in employment, this hiring policy had the effect of depressing seasonally adjusted retail trade employment in November and December. Fewer workers were actually hired so this was appropriate.

The problem became apparent in January and February when the seasonal adjustment factors expected heavy layoffs (which never occurred). If retailers didn't hire the workers to begin with, they certainly couldn't fire them. As a result, January and February retail trade employment was blown up and the January rise in nonfarm payrolls was substantially overstated (by 100,000 thousand workers or more). This problem occurred for several years until the seasonal adjustment factors could take into account the smaller amount of seasonal hiring and firing.

Although the seasonal adjustment process may be "cleaned up" now, I would continue to monitor the retail trade situation. Who knows, employment could shoot up in the 1990s and the reverse problem would occur (strong seasonally adjusted increases in November and December, but large seasonally adjusted declines in January and February).

Seasonal problems are not limited to retail trade. Construction employment also has a strong seasonal component that could be thrown out of whack by unusual weather patterns. For example, exceptionally warm weather during the winter months could artificially boost construction employment between December and April. Unusually rainy weather during the spring and summer could understate employment then.

Apart from checking nonfarm payrolls for special factors, see if gains or declines in nonfarm payrolls are consistent across the board or are concentrated in a certain sector. For example, a broadly based rise in payroll employment shows better labor market conditions than a rise concentrated in just one sector. In the early 1980s, the service sector continuously posted robust gains in each month. Recovering from the 1981–1982 recession, a rapidly rising service sector seemed to hide the fact that manufacturing employment gains were modest.

Also, distinguish between increases in private nonfarm payrolls versus increases in government payrolls. Government payroll employment has quirks of its own such as temporarily hired census workers once every decade. In 1990, the Bureau of the Census added more than 100,000 workers per month, on average, to government payrolls from March to May. The bulk of these workers came off the payrolls between July and September, again averaging changes of more than 100,000 per month— this time in reverse.

Average Workweek

The establishment survey, just like the household survey, provides a complete set of statistics. In addition to nonfarm payrolls, the establishment survey includes average weekly hours of production workers on nonfarm payrolls by industry; average hourly and weekly earnings of production or nonsupervisory workers on private nonfarm payrolls by industry (discussed in Chapter 7 as an indicator of inflation); and indexes of aggregate weekly hours of production of nonsupervisory workers on private nonfarm payrolls by industry.

Financial market participants have caught on to two of the three sets of indicators. Private average weekly hours, otherwise known as the average workweek, is a leading indicator of employment. Businesses tend to adjust total hours worked by increasing or decreasing the workweek before hiring someone new or laying someone off. The average workweek in manufacturing is actually one of the components of the Index of Leading Indicators. This is a leading indicator of economic activity because producers tend to increase the number of hours worked before hiring new workers during a business upturn, or decrease the number of hours worked before laying off people during a downturn. The factory workweek also includes changes due to overtime hours. Since employment data are reported two weeks before production data (for the same month), the number of hours worked per week in manufacturing along with the number of workers on manufacturing payrolls is a good predictor of industrial production for the current month.

Market Reaction   The financial market's fascination with the average workweek is a new phenomenon: Participants only began to pay attention to these figures in 1991. Fixed-income market players see a rise in the workweek as a potential for future employment gains and therefore a healthy economy. By itself, it would point to rising interest rates. Conversely, a decline in the average workweek potentially suggests economic weakness and declines in employment (and interest rates). Bond market participants would favor the bad economic news and consequently lower interest rates. Foreign exchange market players would prefer good economic news in order to have the exchange value of the dollar rise on higher interest rates.

Index of Help Wanted Advertising

The Conference Board releases its Index of Help Wanted Advertising monthly about four weeks after the end of the month. That means May

Watch Out For: Changes in the average workweek are common on a month-to-month basis. Thus, you should never take one-month changes at face value. Always look at the trend or pattern of growth. For instance, the average workweek fell to 34.3 hours in September 1992, from 35.6 hours in the previous month. As Continental Bank economist Joan Schneider had warned in her weekly commentary, the decline was due to a shortened workweek because of the Labor Day holiday.

Because the employment situation is so rich with information and the financial markets scrutinize so many of the statistics in the report, I have described each of the indicators individually and in detail. Real life is not so straightforward. The employment situation is reported all at once: the unemployment rate, nonfarm payrolls, the average workweek, hourly earnings. Not all indicators will always move in the same direction telling the same story about the economy and potential consequences for interest rates, stock prices, and the foreign exchange value of the dollar. For example, the unemployment rate could rise at the same time that nonfarm payrolls increase and the workweek declines. In point of fact, the civilian unemployment rate fell in September 1992 (good economic news); nonfarm payrolls fell 57,000 during the month (bad economic news); the average workweek fell (bad economic news); and average hourly earnings declined (good economic news).

What did the financial markets make of that? On the whole, they viewed the economy as sluggish and lackluster but were actually *expecting* larger declines in nonfarm payrolls. Market expectations of the various indicators along with market sentiment are key determinants of behavior after an economic indicator has been released. As it turned out, market participants were somewhat disappointed because the figures were not weak enough to justify immediate Fed easing.

figures would be reported near the end of June. Since this indicator is released about three weeks after the employment situation, it isn't useful to predict changes in the unemployment rate or nonfarm payrolls, but it can be helpful in assessing hiring attitudes at economic turning points.

The national index is a composite of 51 individual indexes for cities across the country. Only one newspaper is surveyed for each city. Thus, for Chicago, either the *Sun-Times* or the *Tribune* help wanted advertising would be surveyed, but not both. Because the cities were chosen for their density of population, the largest urban areas in the country are included in this index, limiting the monthly survey to nonagricultural employment. Moreover, help wanted advertising does not include the self-employed (since they would have to place ads for themselves and then answer them), so on a monthly basis, the index corresponds more closely to the nonfarm payroll series of the Labor Department's establishment survey rather than to household employment, which gives us the unemployment rate.

Raw help wanted advertising data are adjusted for two factors. First, each month is adjusted for the number of weekdays and Sundays. Sunday advertisements tend to be heavier so an extra Sunday in any given month would increase the help wanted index if it weren't considered. Second, like all good economic data, the figures are adjusted for seasonal variation. The 51 city indexes are adjusted for these two factors before each city index is multiplied by its appropriate weight in the national index. These weights are adjusted annually as population and employment shift among regions. The Conference Board also publishes regional indexes using the city indexes to compile them. Of course, the weights are different for each city relative to its region.

The composite help wanted index has a pronounced cyclical pattern. The index rises during expansions as the demand for labor increases with gains in production and falls when the demand for labor declines in a contracting economy. Help wanted advertising decreases since firms are hiring fewer workers. During economic expansions, help wanted advertisements increase not only because new jobs are created, but also because there is greater turnover among the employed, who feel comfortable about changing jobs. During recessions, not only are fewer new jobs created, but workers tend to hold on to their jobs for fear of layoffs that are more likely to affect those with less seniority.

Although the help wanted index is reported late in the month, it has properties of a leading indicator—at least near cyclical peaks. When the economy is approaching its cyclical peak, its rate of growth may slow. As a result, the rate of new hiring may also moderate leading to a decline in help wanted advertising. Thus, the help wanted index begins to decline even when the economy is still growing. Declines in the index could be fairly sharp as slowdowns spread across various industries. In the postwar recessions, declines averaged roughly 40 percent.

The help wanted index has not served as a leading indicator at cyclical troughs. Firms may first recall workers that were laid off before they hire new workers, in which case, they need not advertise. Another factor that can hold down advertising during periods of slack labor demand is the easy accessibility of workers. One week's ad may bring in hundreds of resumes. During tight labor markets, when the economy is near its peak, firms may have to advertise for several weeks to gather enough resumes for proper hiring decisions.

Market Reaction Most economic releases are reported when the financial markets are open. The help wanted index is released after markets have already closed. Usually, the financial press will bury the story in a corner and the local press may not even carry it. As a result, financial market participants don't react to this indicator. Moreover, economists who work with traders may not have much to say about these figures because they can't use them to predict nonfarm payrolls or the unemployment rate for the upcoming month. Although the help wanted index isn't necessarily useful to day traders who react to current news events, the series will have greater significance to those traders who take a longer perspective of the economy. Similarly, the investor or policymaker who takes the long-term perspective will find the help wanted index useful in confirming evidence of labor market trends. The help wanted index will increase with employment during expansionary periods, and decrease with employment during recessions. Figure 8.4 illustrates the inverse relationship between the help wanted index and the civilian unemployment rate.

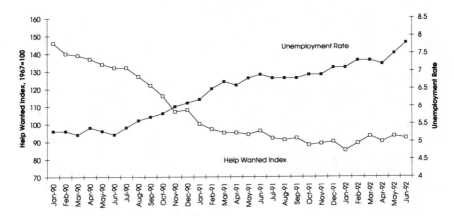

Figure 8.4 Neither the unemployment rate nor the help wanted index fluctuate wildly from month to month. As a result, they are not easily used as predictors of each other. The long-term trend does show a strong (negative) correlation between the two series with the unemployment rate moving upward as the help wanted index trends downward. (*Source:* Data are from Commerce Department publications.)

The Index of Industrial Production

The Federal Reserve Board compiles and publishes the Index of Industrial Production each month. A preliminary estimate is released about two weeks after the end of the month. This index, which covers manufacturing, mining, and utilities, is constructed from 250 individual series and basically accounts for about one-fifth of gross domestic product. The Index of Industrial Production is seasonally adjusted and is reported on a monthly basis. Although this series represents a relatively small portion of GDP, it does account for a large portion of the goods that are cyclically sensitive to the economy, such as consumer durables and business equipment.

The Index of Industrial Production is grouped by products. About 47 percent of the Index covers production of final products including consumer durable and nondurable goods, business equipment, and defense equipment. Final products are generally purchased by consumers, businesses, or government for final use. Intermediate products such as construction and business supplies account for roughly 14 percent of the Index. These products become inputs in nonindustrial sectors: construction, agriculture, and services. Production of materials which covers about 39 percent of the Index, includes such goods as consumer parts, basic metal materials, textile, pulp and paper, and chemical materials, and energy materials. These require further processing within the industrial sector. Table 8.3 shows the relative importance of each category to total industrial production.

Industrial production can also be grouped by industry to cover durable and nondurable goods manufacturing, mining, and utilities. A more detailed look might include lumber and products, fabricated metals, electrical machinery, apparel products, coal mining, and electric utilities. Table 8.4 provides a detailed listing of the classifications.

Although the Federal Reserve Board has actual production figures for some industries (such as auto assemblies and electricity usage), it generally bases its preliminary release on the number of total hours worked in manufacturing using the Labor Department's unadjusted data from the employment situation. Therefore, even though the Fed seasonal adjustment factors are different from the employment seasonal factors, you can predict the initial change in production by calculating the number of total hours worked in manufacturing. (Simply multiply the average factory workweek times the number of employed workers in manufacturing for the current and previous month. Take the percentage change and you will have your forecast.) Figures are

Table 8.3   Industrial Production by Market Group
(1987 = 100)

	1991 Weight	Apr 92	May 92	June 92	July 92	Aug 92	Sep 92
Total Index	100.0	108.1	108.9	108.5	109.2	108.9	108.6
Products	61.4	109.0	109.7	109.1	109.5	109.3	109.1
Final products	47.1	110.6	111.4	110.6	111.0	110.9	110.8
Consumer goods	26.1	110.1	110.8	109.8	110.3	110.1	110.2
Durable construction goods	5.3	107.9	111.1	109.2	108.5	108.8	108.1
Automotive products	2.3	106.5	110.6	108.0	106.4	106.0	106.2
Other	3.1	109.1	111.5	110.2	110.1	111.0	109.6
Nondurable construction goods	21.8	110.7	110.7	110.0	110.8	110.4	110.8
Food and tobacco	9.1	107.6	107.7	107.5	108.5	108.4	108.6
Clothing	2.2	95.3	96.4	95.6	96.7	95.5	95.0
Chemical products	3.8	120.8	121.4	121.9	121.5	121.9	121.3
Paper products	2.9	125.1	124.3	121.7	121.9	121.8	122.3
Energy	2.7	108.9	107.2	104.8	107.4	105.6	108.4
Equipment, Total	21.0	111.3	112.3	111.7	111.9	112.1	111.5
Business equipment	15.8	123.0	124.5	124.2	124.5	125.1	124.7
Defense and space	4.6	84.7	84.2	83.6	82.9	82.2	81.2
Oil and gas	0.5	79.2	79.2	74.6	78.6	75.0	74.3
Manufactured homes	0.1	100.7	100.3	97.1	112.0	106.1	106.3
Intermediate Products	14.2	103.9	104.4	104.4	104.8	104.4	104.0
Construction supplies	5.4	96.5	97.8	97.2	98.0	97.9	96.8
Business supplies	8.8	109.0	109.0	109.4	109.6	108.8	109.0
Materials, Total	38.6	106.8	107.7	107.6	108.9	108.2	107.9
Durable goods	19.4	108.7	110.4	110.2	111.1	111.1	110.4
Nondurable goods	8.9	109.4	109.7	110.4	111.5	109.8	109.8
Energy materials	10.4	101.3	101.3	100.6	102.9	101.5	102.0

Source: Federal Reserve Statistical Release, G.17 (419), October 16, 1992.

revised for three subsequent months as the Federal Reserve gets more complete data. After that, industrial production figures are revised annually or with benchmark revisions that occur less frequently. Data for the annual and benchmark revisions come from various sources: *Census of Manufacturers and Mineral Industries, Annual Survey of Manufacturers,* the *Minerals Yearbook,* and the Department of Energy.

This indicator is procyclical; that is, it rises during economic expansions and falls during recessions. In fact, the Index of Industrial Production is one of the four coincident indicators of economic activity put

Table 8.4   Industrial Production by Industry Groups
(1987 = 100 seasonally adjusted)

	1991 Weight	Apr 92	May 92	June 92	July 92	Aug 92	Sep 92
Total Index	100.0	108.1	108.9	108.5	109.3	108.9	108.6
Manufacturing	84.7	109.0	109.9	109.6	110.1	109.8	109.4
Durable	47.3	107.6	109.1	108.5	109.0	109.0	108.2
Lumber and products	1.8	97.2	97.4	95.4	99.3	98.1	96.6
Furniture and fixtures	1.3	101.1	103.3	100.3	100.8	102.0	100.4
Stone, clay, and glass	2.2	95.6	96.7	96.6	96.5	97.2	97.0
Primary metals	3.1	100.9	102.0	102.1	105.6	104.8	103.1
Fabricated metals	5.0	100.6	102.2	102.2	102.4	101.7	100.3
Nonelectrical machinery	9.9	124.1	126.7	126.4	127.9	128.6	128.9
Electrical machinery	8.9	111.0	112.3	112.2	112.6	113.1	112.7
Transportation equipment	9.0	98.0	99.6	98.2	96.6	96.5	95.3
Instruments	3.6	119.0	119.8	118.5	118.6	118.5	117.7
Miscellaneous	1.4	118.9	118.4	117.8	120.1	118.3	117.9
Nondurable	37.5	110.7	110.9	111.0	111.6	110.9	110.8
Foods	8.9	109.6	109.3	109.0	110.2	110.4	110.5
Tobacco products	1.0	101.0	102.5	103.6	102.7	103.8	103.4
Textile mill products	1.7	106.3	106.8	105.3	107.1	106.3	106.9
Apparel products	2.1	98.0	99.0	98.1	99.3	97.7	96.5
Paper and products	3.5	107.0	105.8	107.3	109.6	106.1	106.5
Printing and publishing	6.7	113.7	113.4	113.0	112.3	112.3	112.2
Chemicals and products	8.9	115.8	117.0	117.5	117.4	117.2	116.7
Petroleum products	1.3	110.3	108.5	108.9	109.1	105.3	107.0
Rubber and plastics	3.1	116.5	117.1	117.3	118.4	117.7	117.9
Leather and products	0.2	84.1	86.2	86.2	87.6	83.3	83.4
Mining	7.5	99.1	99.7	98.0	100.6	99.3	98.1
Metal mining	0.4	154.2	166.4	154.0	164.1	165.7	165.8
Coal	1.2	104.0	107.6	98.6	112.0	107.5	104.3
Oil and gas extraction	5.1	94.2	93.4	93.9	94.0	93.0	92.0
Stone and earth metals	0.7	105.9	108.0	105.6	106.2	107.4	107.8
Utilities	7.8	108.2	107.3	106.7	109.3	108.2	111.0
Electric	6.3	111.0	110.2	109.7	113.0	111.7	115.2
Gas	1.5	97.7	96.6	95.3	95.4	95.5	95.6
Special Aggregates Manufacturing excluding:							
Motor vehicles and parts	80.8	109.6	110.3	110.1	110.8	110.4	110.0
Office and computing machines	81.2	107.2	108.1	107.6	108.1	107.7	107.2

Source: Federal Reserve Statistical Release, G.17 (419), October 16, 1992.

together by the Bureau of Economic Analysis. It is typically used as a proxy for GDP even though it only covers 20 percent of total production in the country. The premise is that services and structures will move in the same direction as the manufacturing sector. However, it also reflects the portion of the economy that has greater peaks during an expansion and deeper troughs during a recession.

Capacity Utilization Rate

The capacity utilization rate, closely linked to the Index of Industrial Production, measures operating capacity of the idle resources in the economy. The Federal Reserve Board releases it at the same time as industrial production, about two weeks after the end of the month. Technically defined, the utilization rate for an industry is equal to an output index divided by a capacity index. Output is measured by the Index of Industrial Production. The capacity measures the attempt to capture "sustainable practical capacity" as indicated by work schedules and the availability of inputs to operate machinery and equipment in place.

Generally, a capacity utilization rate of about 88 percent in the total manufacturing sector signals capacity constraints. At that point, factories are close to full capacity, and inflationary pressures become evident. Capacity constraints arise at an operating rate of 85 percent to 88 percent because it isn't usually efficient for factories to operate at full (100 percent) capacity. Table 8.5 shows that not all factories are operating at the same rate. Some may operate at 110 percent of capacity (working overtime in three shifts, perhaps) whereas others operate at 60 percent. In September 1992, for example, electric utilities were operating at 91.1 percent capacity and gas utilities were operating at 66.4 percent during the same month. This indicates the pace of activity in the various sectors.

Capacity constraints could set in for some companies and not for others. That's why commodity price increases are not uniform across industries. The capacity utilization rate rises during expansions and falls during recessions. A high and rising operating rate signals the need for new investment in plant and equipment, as well as potential inflationary pressures.

Market Reaction A rise in industrial production (and the capacity utilization rate) signals economic growth, whereas a decline in production indicates contraction. Thus, fixed-income market participants view a rise in industrial production (and the capacity utilization rate)

Table 8.5 Capacity Utilization: Manufacturing, Mining, and Utilities (percent of capacity, seasonally adjusted)

	1967–91 Average	Apr 92	May 92	June 92	July 92	Aug 92	Sep 92
Total Index	82.1	78.7	79.1	78.6	79.1	78.7	78.4
Manufacturing	81.4	77.7	78.2	77.8	78.0	77.7	77.2
Durable	79.4	74.6	75.5	75.0	75.2	75.1	74.4
Lumber and products	82.4	77.1	77.2	75.6	78.7	77.7	76.5
Furniture and fixtures	82.5	77.7	79.3	76.8	77.1	77.9	76.6
Stone, clay, and glass	78.2	72.9	73.7	73.6	73.5	74.1	73.9
Primary metals	79.9	78.5	79.5	79.7	82.7	82.2	81.0
Fabricated metals	77.8	75.1	76.2	76.2	76.3	75.7	74.6
Nonelectrical machinery	81.2	75.1	76.4	76.0	76.6	76.8	76.8
Electrical machinery	80.3	74.7	75.3	75.0	75.1	75.2	74.7
Transportation equip.	75.2	70.6	71.7	70.6	69.4	69.2	68.2
Instruments	82.6	74.0	74.3	73.2	73.0	72.7	72.0
Miscellaneous	76.5	80.7	80.1	79.6	80.9	79.6	79.1
Nondurable	83.6	81.8	81.8	81.6	81.9	81.2	81.0
Foods	82.3	79.3	78.9	78.5	79.2	79.2	79.1
Textile mill products	86.0	89.3	89.6	88.2	89.6	88.8	89.2
Apparel products	81.1	74.8	75.5	74.7	75.6	74.2	73.2
Paper and products	89.8	89.3	88.3	89.3	91.1	88.1	88.2
Printing and publishing	86.9	80.2	79.7	79.1	78.4	78.0	77.7
Chemicals and products	79.8	80.4	81.1	81.3	81.1	80.8	80.2
Petroleum products	85.4	90.8	89.3	89.6	89.8	86.6	88.0
Rubber and plastics	83.9	84.9	85.1	84.9	85.5	84.8	84.7
Leather and products	82.1	72.5	74.4	74.4	75.7	72.0	72.0
Mining	87.4	86.3	86.9	85.4	87.6	86.5	85.5
Metal mining	77.1	76.5	82.5	76.3	81.1	81.8	81.8
Coal	87.4	80.0	82.6	72.5	85.6	82.0	79.4
Oil and gas extraction	88.1	90.9	90.2	90.7	90.9	90.0	89.1
Stone and earth metals	84.7	75.1	76.5	74.6	75.0	75.6	75.7
Utilities	86.7	83.4	82.7	82.1	84.1	83.2	85.3
Electric	89.1	88.2	87.5	87.0	89.5	88.4	91.1
Gas	81.9	67.8	67.1	66.2	66.3	66.3	66.4

Source: Federal Reserve Statistical Release, G.17 (419), October 16, 1992.

as a warning of inflationary pressures. This means interest rates will rise. The flip side is that a drop in production (and utilization) portends economic weakness, allowing interest rates to decline as market participants anticipate Federal Reserve accommodation.

Players in the stock and foreign exchange markets favor gains in industrial production and the capacity utilization rate since they portend economic strength. Equity market professionals will look toward

Watch Out For: The Index of Industrial Production and the capacity utilization rate are inextricably linked. It is not necessary to view them as two separate indicators. They always move in the same direction, and they will always tell a similar story. However, they serve a different purpose. Industrial production will signal economic growth. The capacity utilization rate reflects the extent of resources utilization and the point at which inflationary pressures set in. For example, a 1 percent rise in industrial production should not cause fears of inflationary pressures when the operating rate is 78 percent. However, it could indicate inflation will accelerate when the utilization rate is around 85 percent.

Among the economic indicators, economists can always point to quirks in the data or special factors that will force market participants to take note. It is usually more difficult to find quirks in the Index of Industrial Production, which tends to be straightforward: An increase means economic growth; a decrease means weakness. Check to see whether the increase (or decrease) in production is broadly based, or concentrated in one sector. Broadly based gains suggest a more solid foundation for economic growth. Increases in only one or two sectors could suggest some fragility in the economy. For example, strength might be exacerbated by increased production in utilities. Hot summer weather spurs air conditioners and pushes up electricity usage. This is not a sustainable trend, nor is it something on which to base growth. Natural disasters can also play havoc with the figures. Hurricane Andrew, which hit Florida in August 1992, reduced the output of utilities and mining during the month. The drop in the mining industry in Florida certainly will be short-lived as the economy gradually recovers. Whether mining is resumed at its "normal" pace or makes up for lost output is another matter.

increases in corporate earnings whereas foreign exchange professionals will look toward higher interest rates. High interest rates in the United States relative to other countries increase the demand for U.S. securities and therefore U.S. dollars. This suggests an appreciating exchange value of the dollar.

Purchasing Managers Index (NAPM)

The National Association of Purchasing Managers, a private organization, compiles a set of production and inflation data monthly. The most common of the set of indicators is the Purchasing Managers Index, known in the financial markets as the NAPM. The data are reported on the first day of the subsequent month (May figures are reported June 1), making this the most timely of all monthly indicators—its appearance could predate the employment situation by as much as a week. The figures are available on a seasonally adjusted basis (as well as unadjusted). Unlike most other economic data, these figures are never revised from month to month. Every year, however, new seasonal adjustment factors are computed by the Commerce Department causing minor variations in the pattern of the NAPM from month to month for the previous few years.

The NAPM is a composite index of five series: (1) new orders, (2) production, (3) supplier deliveries (also known as vendor performance), (4) inventories, and (5) employment. The indexes for prices, new export orders, and import orders are not included in the composite but are available separately, as shown in Table 8.6. The National Association of Purchasing Managers sends out a questionnaire once a month to 250 geographically diversified companies that are representative of the industry in their contribution to gross domestic product.

The NAPM indexes are different from most other indexes. Instead of setting a base year equal to 100, and measuring growth from there, the NAPM series are set at a trigger rate of 50 percent. According to the NAPM, an index level of 50 percent or more indicates that the economy as well as the manufacturing sector is expanding; an index level less than 50 percent but greater than 44 percent suggests that the manufacturing sector has stopped growing, but the economy is still expanding; a level less than 44 percent signals a recession both in the economy and in the manufacturing sector.

The NAPM get these figures based on answers to rather straightforward questions. Purchasing managers are asked if their business situation is "better," "same," or "worse" than the previous month. Sometimes, the terms "higher" or "faster" are substituted for "better"; sometimes, "slower" is substituted for "worse." In any case, the questionnaire is not asking for actual levels, just a subjective assessment of the company's business prospects. The responses are then tallied: The responses for "same" are cut in half and added to the responses for "higher." This sum is equal to the unadjusted index. Seasonal adjustment factors, which are calculated by the Commerce Department, are applied to yield the seasonally adjusted figures for each individual component. Table 8.7 shows an example using the Imports Index, which is not seasonally adjusted.

The most important factor to keep in mind about the NAPM, or any of the subindexes, is that you can't use them as if they were normal

Table 8.6 U.S. Purchasing Managers' Index Summary

	Jan 92	Feb 92	Mar 92	Apr 92	May 92	June 92	July 92	Aug 92	Sep 92
Purchasing Managers' Index	47.4	52.4	54.1	51.3	56.3	52.8	54.2	53.7	49.0
New orders index	50.3	57.5	62.4	56.7	61.0	58.3	59.8	59.8	49.6
Production index	50.6	58.6	60.1	56.6	62.9	56.4	57.6	56.4	52.6
Supplier deliveries	48.0	48.7	49.5	47.4	49.9	50.6	52.3	50.7	51.9
Inventories	43.3	43.1	43.8	42.4	49.2	43.6	48.6	46.4	41.2
Employment	40.5	44.5	42.8	43.9	49.1	46.1	45.8	47.2	45.2
Prices	43.4	45.7	46.6	49.6	56.2	55.6	58.2	57.5	52.1
New export orders	51.3	55.9	52.9	52.3	56.9	51.9	54.6	53.7	56.6
Import orders (NSA)*	46.5	48.0	51.0	53.0	53.0	49.5	49.5	48.5	45.5

* NSA = Not seasonally adjusted.

Source: Several publications from the National Association of Purchasing Managers.

Table 8.7   Imports Index
(not seasonally adjusted)

	Lower	Higher	Same			Index
Jan 92	16	(	9 + (.5* 75)	)	=	46.5
Feb 92	18	(	14 + (.5* 68)	)	=	48.0
Mar 92	8	(	10 + (.5* 82)	)	=	51.0
Apr 92	11	(	17 + (.5* 72)	)	=	53.0
May 92	8	(	14 + (.5* 78)	)	=	53.0
June 92	14	(	13 + (.5* 73)	)	=	49.5
July 92	13	(	12 + (.5* 75)	)	=	49.5
Aug 92	14	(	11 + (.5* 75)	)	=	48.5
Sep 92	17	(	8 + (.5* 75)	)	=	45.5

numbers. For example, the NAPM stood at 47.4 in January (1992), 52.4 in February, 54.1 in March, 51.3 in April. This pattern signifies that the manufacturing sector continued to contract in January, but the economy was growing (the Index stood between 44 and 50). In February, March, and April of the same year, both the manufacturing sector and the economy were expanding because the Index surpassed 50. However, the rise in March does not necessarily mean that conditions were 3.2 percent better than in February, nor does it mean that the April pace was 5.2 percent worse than in March. For the most part, you have to view the figures in the context of trends above or below 50 for growth or contraction. The farther the index is away from 50 percent, the stronger the economy when the index value is more than 50, and the weaker the economy when the index value is less than 50.

The rationale for incorporating the five components in the NAPM is fairly straightforward. New orders are a leading indicator of economic activity. Manufacturers' orders lead to increases in production. Production reflects the current state of affairs and is a coincident indicator of the economy. As output expands, producers hire additional workers to meet the increased demands. Employment is also a coincident indicator. Inventories are typically a lagging indicator of economic activity. Inventory buildups usually continue into a cyclical downturn as manufacturers are not sure whether the decline in demand is temporary or permanent. Inventories may continue to decline early in a recovery as producers unload stocks that were built up during the recession. Supplier deliveries, also known as vendor performance, work in much the same way as unfilled orders. When producers slow down their deliveries, it means they are busy and can't fill all the orders quickly. Slower deliveries mean rapid economic growth. In contrast, faster deliveries suggest a moderating economy. When orders can be filled rapidly, it means producers aren't as busy. Vendor performance is included in the Commerce Department's Index of Leading Indicators.

Market Reaction   Financial market participants have anxiously anticipated the NAPM ever since Federal Reserve Chairman Alan Greenspan once claimed that he placed great emphasis on this report. As usual, equity and foreign exchange market players look forward to healthy figures, whereas the fixed income market professionals prefer weakness. As the NAPM moves in an upward direction, portending economic strength, bond market participants will anticipate inflationary pressures or the end of a favorable environment for Federal Reserve easing conditions. Conversely, a declining trend in the NAPM will lead to a bond market rally.

Business Outlook Survey of the Philadelphia Fed

The Business Outlook Survey is compiled and published monthly by the Economic Research Division of the Federal Reserve Bank of Philadelphia. Financial market participants and economists know it as the *Philadelphia Fed Survey*. It is reported on the third Thursday of the month for the current month. For example, data for September 1992 were released on September 17, 1992. Figures are seasonally adjusted.

The Federal Reserve Bank of Philadelphia began to conduct monthly surveys of manufacturers in May 1968 to monitor business conditions in its district. The Business Outlook Survey (BOS) was based on the premise that surveying businesses about recent activity is one of the least costly methods of gathering economic data. Recent activity is available before other indicators reported by the government or private agencies. The tradeoff is that most other economic data is quantitative whereas this survey is qualitative. Therefore, it is helpful in indicating "where we are and whither we are tending" in the Philadelphia Fed region as well as the country.

This survey is limited to manufacturing firms with plants in the area that employ at least 350 workers. It covers durable and nondurable industries. About 100 of the 550 eligible establishments agreed to participate in the monthly survey. Each month, the managers of the plants receive the survey questionnaire in the mail. On average, the response rate is just better than 50 percent each month. The sample is periodically revised to

Watch Out For: Changes in the NAPM cannot be read like ordinary numbers. Anything above 50 signals economic growth as well as a robust manufacturing sector. It is not surprising to see the index move up and down from one month to the next. The magnitude of increase in the NAPM is not as relevant as the trend—is the NAPM showing upward or downward momentum?

If the index begins to move downward (even when the level remains above 50), it could be signaling the beginning of an economic downturn, or at least moderating economic activity. When the economy is in recession and the index increases from 39 to 41, the economy is still very weak. However, if the NAPM begins to move upward, it could be signaling a recovery.

You may want to monitor the components separately. Which part of the index is showing more strength: production, new orders, employment? A broadly based rise in the composite index is more favorable for a sustainable recovery. However, only the new orders and supplier deliveries series are leading indicators. Employment and production are coincident indicators of the economy, and inventories are somewhat lagging. So don't be alarmed in the early stages of recovery if only parts of the index are moving upward.

The Price Index is not part of the composite and must be monitored separately. Inflation is a lagging indicator in that increases in the Consumer Price Index tend to moderate further even into the first year of recovery. Conversely, the CPI may continue to accelerate in the early stages of recession. Yet, prices of sensitive materials that are used in the early stages of production are leading indicators of the economy. Thus, the Purchasing Managers' Price Index should start rising early in the recovery.

It is also useful to monitor the New Export Orders Index. This series was not seasonally adjusted until early 1992. The foreign sector has been an important factor in the U.S. economy since the 1980s. Rising export orders contribute to domestic production but can also compete for our resources and thus exacerbate inflationary pressures during an expansion.

A final word of caution: The NAPM's timeliness and lack of frequent revision make it a respectable indicator of the economy. However, it is only one of the several economic indicators available. Put it in perspective. Consider its movements in combination with durable goods orders, the Index of Industrial Production, and the employment situation. It is not the final word on the economy. I'm sure Mr. Greenspan would agree.

The NAPM Family

The National Association of Purchasing Managers has published its indexes for years. In fact, one component—supplier deliveries, also known as vendor performance—had always been a component of the Index of Leading Indicators. As with most series, the NAPM had its fans. But around the end of 1987, the tide turned when newly appointed Federal Reserve Chairman Alan Greenspan stated that he closely monitored this monthly indicator, causing financial market participants to monitor the NAPM. The new indicator became popular because people were worried about a potential recession on the heels of the October 1987 stock market crash. As it happened, no recession developed and the economy grew at a healthy pace.

The NAPM, however, did not go away; financial market participants continued to favor it as a major market indicator. (Never underestimate the words of a Federal Reserve Chairman.) No one ever accused the financial markets of doing anything half-heartedly. Once the NAPM had become a major fixture, it spawned purchasing managers indexes from cities all over the United States. Again, these had always been calculated, but no one in the financial markets had ever known (or cared) about them before. These days, Chicago, Milwaukee, and Detroit regularly publish purchasing managers reports of their own.

The Purchasing Managers Index of Chicago (PMIC) is always reported the day before the national index is released. The distribution of purchasing agents in Chicago is similar to the national distribution, so the PMIC gets much attention. Many economists and traders base their expectations of the national index on the PMIC's direction of movement. Although it's a reasonable assumption, statistical analysis shows the correlation to be loose, at best (see Table 8.8).

I once jokingly told the traders I worked with that I would use the Milwaukee index to forecast the Chicago index, which I would then use to forecast the national index. They weren't terribly amused. The Milwaukee index sometimes comes out about a day before the Chicago index. Statistically speaking, there is no good reason that the Milwaukee index should be a good predictor of the Chicago or national index. The Detroit Index usually is reported after the Chicago index, and sometimes even after the national index, although generally near the first day of the month. The Detroit Index is heavily weighted toward the auto industry, so it doesn't necessarily move in the same direction as the Chicago, Milwaukee, or national indexes from month to month.

Table 8.8 Purchasing Managers Index

	NAPM	Chicago	Milwaukee	Detroit
Jan 92	47.4	49.2	NA	37.1
Feb 92	52.4	48.0	NA	53.1
Mar 92	54.1	51.1	NA	54.5
Apr 92	51.3	54.3	55.0	57.8
May 92	56.3	54.7	58.0	56.2
June 92	52.8	55.7	57.0	57.1
July 92	54.2	59.2	51.0	56.6
Aug 92	53.7	58.4	50.0	51.0
Sep 92	49.0	59.6	61.0	52.0

include new participants who were not previously eligible and remove firms that no longer meet participation requirements. The sample size remains roughly 100, although the 1992 revision update may reveal a somewhat larger number.

The questionnaire includes two sets of questions on 10 measures of business activity: employment, working hours, general activity, new orders, order backlogs, shipments, inventories, delivery times, prices paid, and prices received. The first set of questions regards current conditions; they are either "up," "down," or "unchanged" from the previous month (for each measure). The survey participants are also asked about their expectations for six months in the future. Again, they must respond with "higher," "lower," or "about the same." The expectations section also asks about capital spending plans.

To track economic conditions easily, a diffusion index, which is calculated for each measure, determines the diversity of the components of some aggregate indicator. The premise behind the BOS diffusion index is similar to the NAPM diffusion index, but the calculation is a bit different. The BOS measures the diversity of responses to each question by subtracting the percentage of respondents reporting a decrease from the percentage of respondents reporting an increase. When all the respondents report an increase from the previous month, the index can post a maximum value of +100. Conversely, when all the respondents report a decrease in an indicator, the index would post a minimum value of −100. Usually, the index value will be somewhere between these two extremes. The degree of agreement in responses (on either end of the spectrum), reflects the degree to which manufacturing firms are participating in the expansion or recession. Table 8.9 lists the components.

Table 8.9 Business Outlook Survey: Philadelphia Fed (seasonally adjusted)

	July vs. June				June vs. May			
	Down (%)	Unchanged (%)	Up (%)	Diffusion Index	Down (%)	Unchanged (%)	Up (%)	Diffusion Index
General Business Conditions	4.8	62.1	31.8	27.0	21.0	43.9	31.9	10.9
Company Indicators								
New orders	10.0	59.3	30.8	20.8	18.6	50.4	30.6	11.9
Shipments	13.8	57.3	28.9	15.0	13.2	50.9	33.5	20.3
Unfilled orders	15.4	72.3	12.3	-3.0	24.4	60.1	11.1	-13.3
Delivery time	7.4	82.0	10.6	3.1	8.2	81.2	7.9	-0.4
Inventories	19.0	49.4	31.6	12.6	24.6	48.2	26.8	2.2
Prices paid	4.2	77.9	17.2	12.9	1.3	85.9	12.1	10.9
Prices received	13.6	73.7	12.7	-0.9	6.2	83.8	10.0	3.7
Number of employees	15.8	67.4	16.4	0.7	16.0	60.5	23.5	7.6
Average workweek	14.0	68.6	15.4	1.4	19.6	62.7	17.7	-1.9

Source: Philadelphia Fed Survey Table: July Conditions, *Market News Service, Inc.*, July 19, 1992.

The expectations portion of the questionnaire is calculated in the same fashion. The BOS subtracts the percentage of respondents expecting lower activity from the percentage of respondents expecting a higher pace of activity. The diffusion index for each measure has a maximum value of +100 and a minimum of −100.

In the beginning of a business downturn, all firms will not show declining activity at the same time. Nor will all firms post growth at the same time when the economy begins to recover. As the economy enters a new phase of economic activity, responses are likely to be diverse and the diffusion index will probably fall somewhere between +100 and −100. As the economy grows robustly or declines sharply, the diffusion index will tend toward one of the extremes showing less diversity among manufacturing industries.

Financial market participants like to use the BOS, alias the Philadelphia Fed Survey, as a predictor of the NAPM diffusion index. Is that appropriate? This diffusion index is designed to work as a leading indicator. The BOS has in fact signaled four of the five recessions since 1968. It failed to signal the 1981–1982 recession, but it has not given any false signals. The general activity index had turned down more than 12 months before the recession began in August 1990. According to Timothy Schiller, an economist at the Federal Reserve Bank of Philadelphia, the signal for the 1990–1991 recession was considered an early lead.[2] Studies done by the Economic Research Department of the Philadelphia Fed show that the general activity index works well as a predictor of regional and national economic activity. However, not all the specific components, such as the average workweek and new orders, are good predictors of their official government counterparts (from the Labor Department and the Census Bureau).

The Economic Research Department cautions users in their correlation of the BOS with other regional or national indicators. First, the timing of the BOS is different from most statistics. Official statistics are usually collected in the middle of each month. In contrast, the BOS takes place from about the 20th of one month to the 5th of the following month, so it reflects data for both the current month and the previous month. For example, the Bureau of Labor Statistics surveys employment for the week including the twelfth. In July 1992, the twelfth falls on a Sunday, so the survey period includes the week of July 12 to July 18. The BOS for August would include the collection period of July 20 to August 5. Because of this late employment survey week, the figures would be comparable. Thus, you would compare July employment with the August BOS. In June 1992, the twelfth fell on a Friday and the survey week began on Sunday June 7 and ran to Saturday June 13. In this early employment survey, the BOS for June, which covers May 20 to June 5, might be more comparable. This time, you would compare employment and the BOS for the same month—June. Therefore, you need to look at either same months or off-months to check correlations between series.

Another essential distinction when comparing the BOS with official statistics is that it is better to look at the change in the indicator rather than at the level. The BOS index represents qualitative data, not quantitative data, so if the BOS diffusion index posts a decline for a couple of months, you might expect either an outright decline in industrial production, or a decline in the *rate of change* in industrial production. (See Figure 8.5.)

Market Reaction   Any indicator that is timely is well received by financial participants who use the Philadelphia Fed Survey as a precursor of the NAPM. Although it is a diffusion index, it is not read in the same way as the NAPM, so they are not directly comparable. Financial market participants may react to its movements but more cautiously relative to other economic indicators. This series is more difficult to read as an index. However, market participants will take into account

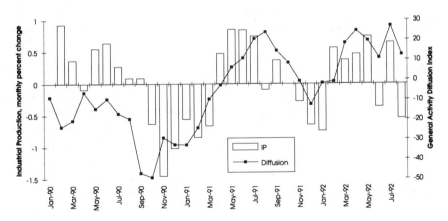

Figure 8.5   This chart depicts the strong correlation between the Philadelphia Fed Index of general activity and monthly changes in the Index of Industrial Production. Trends don't always predict exact monthly changes very well, however. (*Source:* Data are from Commerce Department publications and Federal Reserve Bank of Philadelphia.)

the analysis suggested by the Philadelphia Fed. If the analysis shows that activity has deteriorated, the bond market will rally and interest rates will decline. Stock and foreign exchange market professionals don't pay too much attention to this series.

Watch Out For: First look at the index level of the Philadelphia Fed Survey. An index on either extreme, +100 to −100, shows the magnitude of disparity. The closer the index is to the positive high end, the more robust the activity; and the closer the index is to the negative low end, the more lackluster the activity. Next, look at the direction of change. Is the diffusion index becoming more positive, less positive, more negative, less negative? As the index becomes less negative and more positive, it points toward improving economic conditions. In contrast, as the index becomes less positive and more negative, it reflects deteriorating economic conditions.

You may also want to look at the separate measures such as employment, workweek, new and unfilled orders, shipments, inventories, vendor performance, and prices paid and received. The BOS is a reasonable economic indicator if you use it cautiously. There are, however, many economic indicators each month, and you certainly don't have to react to all of them. If you are looking for confirming evidence for a particular viewpoint, the Business Outlook Survey is useful. But take care when relying on this survey to support new trends.

Index of Leading Indicators

The Index of Leading Indicators is a measure of the *direction* of economic activity. This index is a composite of 11 series chosen for their timeliness, consistency, and forecasting ability. The index is seasonally adjusted, with an index set to 1982 = 100. The Bureau of Economic Analysis (BEA) releases the index about four or five weeks after the end of the month. In conjunction with the Index of Leading Indicators, the BEA also releases the Index of Coincident Indicators and the Index of Lagging Indicators. During the 1980s, they did not receive as much attention as the leading index, but since the 1990–1991 recession, financial market participants and economists have started to look a bit more closely at these series as well. (See Figure 8.6.)

The Bureau of Economic Analysis, with the help of the Columbia Business Cycle Research Center, did a major overhaul of this index in

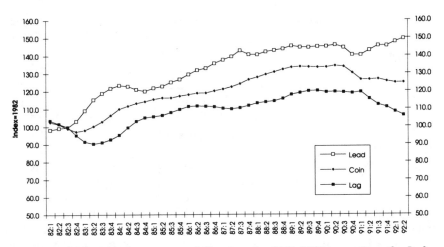

Figure 8.6 During the recovery following the 1981-1982 recession, the Index of Leading Indicators increased decidedly as did the Index of Coincident Indicators. In the recovery following the 1990-1991 recession, the Index of Leading Indicators inched up more slowly, and the Index of Coincident Indicators is virtually flat. (*Source:* Data are from Commerce Department publications.)

January 1989, dropping some series, adding others. The premise behind the major revision was that the structure of the U.S. economy had changed in the postwar period shifting to more production of services than goods. It has been argued that the Index of Leading Indicators was designed to signal the direction of the manufacturing sector more than anything else. As part of the 1989 overhaul, consideration was given to lead indicators for the service sector and the consumer. Nevertheless, most series in the index remain wedded to the manufacturing sector. A major concession comes from the consumer expectations variable. The 11 indicators that now make up the index are the average workweek in manufacturing, initial unemployment insurance claims (excluding claims for Puerto Rico and the Virgin Islands), vendor performance, stock prices (measured by the S&P 500), real money supply (measured by the M2 component and adjusted for inflation), sensitive (raw materials) prices, housing permits, new orders for consumer durables, contracts and orders for plant and equipment, real (inflation-adjusted) unfilled orders, and consumer expectations. In the ten postwar recessions, the Index of Leading Indicators signaled the trough of the recessions by three months, on average. A rough rule of thumb is that three consecutive declines in this index portend a recession; likewise, three straight increases in the leading indicators portend a recovery.

Many analysts claim that the magnitude of change in this index will reveal the depth of the upcoming recession or the magnitude of increase during a recovery. This is not true. The Index of Leading Indicators was designed simply to signal direction of economic activity, nothing more.

This indicator gets much attention in the local press although financial market participants don't pay as much attention to it. Financial market participants have learned that it reveals no new information when it is reported four to five weeks after the end of the month. The majority of the 11 indicators have already been released by the time this index is calculated. Moreover, it has been revised several times in the postwar period after it failed to identify a turning point correctly, although in retrospect it always looks good. In general, less attention should be given to the magnitude of changes in the Index of Leading Indicators as predictors of economic growth rates.

The Index of Coincident Indicators includes four series: the Index of Industrial Production; personal income less transfer payments in 1987 dollars; nonfarm payroll employment; and manufacturing and trade sales in 1982 dollars. The premise behind the Index of Coincident Indictors is that these will move exactly in line with the economy. When the economy is growing, this index will be rising; when the economy is declining, this index will decrease also.

The Index of Lagging Indicators incorporates seven indicators: the average duration of employment (in weeks); the ratio of inventories to sales (manufacturing and trade); the change in the index of labor cost per unit of output in manufacturing; the average prime rate charged

---

Watch Out For: Determine whether increase or decreases in the index are broadly based. Otherwise, it will be difficult to get a good reading. In addition, just look at the direction of change. Don't worry about the magnitude of increases or decreases. Only worry about this index at turning points in the economy.

by banks; commercial and industrial loans outstanding (in 1982 dollars); the ratio of consumer installment credit to personal income; and the change in the consumer price index for services (at an annualized rate). The premise behind this index is that certain sectors of the economy lag the business cycle. Thus, the lagging index would continue to post declines as the economy was beginning to expand and would continue to increase after the economy had already fallen into recession.

Market Reaction   Although financial market participants don't usually react strongly to this series, market players grab any piece of information that will prove their point when market sentiment is either particularly negative or positive. For example, in the early stages of recovery, bond traders may still have doubts about the economy. If the leading index posts a solid gain, the traders will feel that the recovery is more likely assured and interest rate increases are around the corner. As the economy heads toward recession, bond traders will use a decline in the leading indicators index to confirm that interest rates are headed downward.

Key Points

- Production indicators that show signs of strength for the economy will cause bond prices to fall (yields to rise) and stock prices and the value of the dollar to increase.
- Production indicators that portend weakness for the economy will cause bond prices to rise (yields to fall) and stock prices and the value of the dollar to decline.
- Most indicators are useful as long as observers or financial market participants don't overreact at their release.
- Never take one month's data at face value. Look at the trend of the series, especially when blips occur.
- The Employment Situation is rich with information and is released on a timely basis. If you were to choose only one indicator to watch regularly, this should be it.
- Table 8.10 summarizes the production indicators, their approximate dates of release, and the source agencies.

Table 8.10   Indicators of Production

Month	Approximate Day	Indicator	Data for	Source Agency
Jan	1 to 3	NAPM	Dec	National Assoc. of Purchasing Management
	Every Thurs	Initial unemployment claims	Wk end Sat (1 week lag)	Employment and Training Division, BLS
	Every Thurs	Continuing benefits	Wk end Sat (3 week lag)	Employment and Training Division, BLS
	1 to 10	Unemployment rate	Dec	Bureau of Labor Statistics
	1 to 10	Nonfarm payrolls	Dec	Bureau of Labor Statistics
	1 to 10	Average workweek	Dec	Bureau of Labor Statistics
	14 to 17	Index of Industrial Production	Dec	Federal Reserve Board
	14 to 17	Capacity utilization rate	Dec	Federal Reserve Board
	Third Thurs	Philadelphia Fed Survey	Jan	Federal Reserve Bank of Philadelphia
	29 to 4	Index of Leading Indicators	Dec	Commerce Department
	Last week	Help Wanted Index	Dec	Conference Board
Feb	1 to 3	NAPM	Jan	National Assoc. of Purchasing Management
	Every Thurs	Initial unemployment claims	Wk end Sat (1 week lag)	Employment and Training Division, BLS
	Every Thurs	Continuing benefits	Wk end Sat (3 week lag)	Employment and Training Division, BLS
	1 to 10	Unemployment rate	Jan	Bureau of Labor Statistics
	1 to 10	Nonfarm payrolls	Jan	Bureau of Labor Statistics
	1 to 10	Average workweek	Jan	Bureau of Labor Statistics
	14 to 17	Index of Industrial Production	Jan	Federal Reserve Board
	14 to 17	Capacity utilization rate	Jan	Federal Reserve Board

Table 8.10 *(Continued)*

Approximate				
Month	Day	Indicator	Data for	Source Agency
Feb	Third Thurs	Philadelphia Fed Survey	Feb	Federal Reserve Bank of Philadelphia
	29 to 4	Index of Leading Indicators	Jan	Commerce Department
	Last week	Help Wanted Index	Jan	Conference Board
Mar	1 to 3	NAPM	Feb	National Assoc. of Purchasing Management
	Every Thurs	Initial unemployment claims	Wk end Sat (1 week lag)	Employment and Training Division, BLS
	Every Thurs	Continuing benefits	Wk end Sat (3 week lag)	Employment and Training Division, BLS
	1 to 10	Unemployment rate	Feb	Bureau of Labor Statistics
	1 to 10	Nonfarm payrolls	Feb	Bureau of Labor Statistics
	1 to 10	Average workweek	Feb	Bureau of Labor Statistics
	14 to 17	Index of Industrial Production	Feb	Federal Reserve Board
	14 to 17	Capacity utilization rate	Feb	Federal Reserve Board
	Third Thurs	Philadelphia Fed Survey	Mar	Federal Reserve Bank of Philadelphia
	29 to 4	Index of Leading Indicators	Feb	Commerce Department
	Last week	Help Wanted Index	Feb	Conference Board
Apr	1 to 3	NAPM	Mar	National Assoc. of Purchasing Management
	Every Thurs	Initial unemployment claims	Wk end Sat (1 week lag)	Employment and Training Division, BLS
	Every Thurs	Continuing benefits	Wk end Sat (3 week lag)	Employment and Training Division, BLS
	1 to 10	Unemployment rate	Mar	Bureau of Labor Statistics
	1 to 10	Nonfarm payrolls	Mar	Bureau of Labor Statistics

Table 8.10 *(Continued)*

Month	Day	Indicator	Data for	Source Agency
	Approximate			
Apr	1 to 10	Average workweek	Mar	Bureau of Labor Statistics
	14 to 17	Index of Industrial Production	Mar	Federal Reserve Board
	14 to 17	Capacity utilization rate	Mar	Federal Reserve Board
	Third Thurs	Philadelphia Fed Survey	Apr	Federal Reserve Bank of Philadelphia
	29 to 4	Index of Leading Indicators	Mar	Commerce Department
	Last week	Help Wanted Index	Mar	Conference Board
May	1 to 3	NAPM	Apr	National Assoc. of Purchasing Management
	Every Thurs	Initial unemployment claims	Wk end Sat (1 week lag)	Employment and Training Division, BLS
	Every Thurs	Continuing benefits	Wk end Sat (3 week lag)	Employment and Training Division, BLS
	1 to 10	Unemployment rate	Apr	Bureau of Labor Statistics
	1 to 10	Nonfarm payrolls	Apr	Bureau of Labor Statistics
	1 to 10	Average workweek	Apr	Bureau of Labor Statistics
	14 to 17	Index of Industrial Production	Apr	Federal Reserve Board
	14 to 17	Capacity utilization rate	Apr	Federal Reserve Board
	Third Thurs	Philadelphia Fed Survey	May	Federal Reserve Bank of Philadelphia
	29 to 4	Index of Leading Indicators	Apr	Commerce Department
	Last week	Help Wanted Index	Apr	Conference Board
June	1 to 3	NAPM	May	National Assoc. of Purchasing Management
	Every Thurs	Initial unemployment claims	Wk end Sat (1 week lag)	Employment and Training Division, BLS

Table 8.10 *(Continued)*

Month	Approximate Day	Indicator	Data for	Source Agency
June	Every Thurs	Continuing benefits	Wk end Sat (3 week lag)	Employment and Training Division, BLS
	1 to 10	Unemployment rate	May	Bureau of Labor Statistics
	1 to 10	Nonfarm payrolls	May	Bureau of Labor Statistics
	1 to 10	Average workweek	May	Bureau of Labor Statistics
	14 to 17	Index of Industrial Production	May	Federal Reserve Board
	14 to 17	Capacity utilization rate	May	Federal Reserve Board
	Third Thurs	Philadelphia Fed Survey	June	Federal Reserve Bank of Philadelphia
	29 to 4	Index of Leading Indicators	May	Commerce Department
	Last week	Help Wanted Index	May	Conference Board
July	1 to 3	NAPM	June	National Assoc. of Purchasing Management
	Every Thurs	Initial unemployment claims	Wk end Sat (1 week lag)	Employment and Training Division, BLS
	Every Thurs	Continuing benefits	Wk end Sat (3 week lag)	Employment and Training Division, BLS
	1 to 10	Unemployment rate	June	Bureau of Labor Statistics
	1 to 10	Nonfarm payrolls	June	Bureau of Labor Statistics
	1 to 10	Average workweek	June	Bureau of Labor Statistics
	14 to 17	Index of Industrial Production	June	Federal Reserve Board
	14 to 17	Capacity utilization rate	June	Federal Reserve Board
	Third Thurs	Philadelphia Fed Survey	July	Federal Reserve Bank of Philadelphia
	29 to 4	Index of Leading Indicators	June	Commerce Department
	Last week	Help Wanted Index	June	Conference Board

Table 8.10 *(Continued)*

Month	Approximate Day	Indicator	Data for	Source Agency
Aug	1 to 3	NAPM	July	National Assoc. of Purchasing Management
	Every Thurs	Initial unemploy-ment claims	Wk end Sat (1 week lag)	Employment and Training Division, BLS
	Every Thurs	Continuing benefits	Wk end Sat (3 week lag)	Employment and Training Division, BLS
	1 to 10	Unemployment rate	July	Bureau of Labor Statistics
	1 to 10	Nonfarm payrolls	July	Bureau of Labor Statistics
	1 to 10	Average workweek	July	Bureau of Labor Statistics
	14 to 17	Index of Industrial Production	July	Federal Reserve Board
	14 to 17	Capacity utilization rate	July	Federal Reserve Board
	Third Thurs	Philadelphia Fed Survey	Aug	Federal Reserve Bank of Philadelphia
	29 to 4	Index of Leading Indicators	July	Commerce Department
	Last week	Help Wanted Index	July	Conference Board
Sep	1 to 3	NAPM	Aug	National Assoc. of Purchasing Management
	Every Thurs	Initial unemployment claims	Wk end Sat (1 week lag)	Employment and Training Division, BLS
	Every Thurs	Continuing benefits	Wk end Sat (3 week lag)	Employment and Training Division, BLS
	1 to 10	Unemployment rate	Aug	Bureau of Labor Statistics
	1 to 10	Nonfarm payrolls	Aug	Bureau of Labor Statistics
	1 to 10	Average workweek	Aug	Bureau of Labor Statistics
	14 to 17	Index of Industrial Production	Aug	Federal Reserve Board
	14 to 17	Capacity utilization rate	Aug	Federal Reserve Board

Table 8.10 (Continued)

Approximate		Indicator	Data for	Source Agency
Month	Day			
Sep	Third Thurs	Philadelphia Fed Survey	Sep	Federal Reserve Bank of Philadelphia
	29 to 4	Index of Leading Indicators	Aug	Commerce Department
	Last week	Help Wanted Index	Aug	Conference Board
Oct	1 to 3	NAPM	Sep	National Assoc. of Purchasing Management
	Every Thurs	Initial unemployment claims	Wk end Sat (1 week lag)	Employment and Training Division, BLS
	Every Thurs	Continuing benefits	Wk end Sat (3 week lag)	Employment and Training Division, BLS
	1 to 10	Unemployment rate	Sep	Bureau of Labor Statistics
	1 to 10	Nonfarm payrolls	Sep	Bureau of Labor Statistics
	1 to 10	Average workweek	Sep	Bureau of Labor Statistics
	14 to 17	Index of Industrial Production	Sep	Federal Reserve Board
	14 to 17	Capacity utilization rate	Sep	Federal Reserve Board
	Third Thurs	Philadelphia Fed Survey	Oct	Federal Reserve Bank of Philadelphia
	29 to 4	Index of Leading Indicators	Sep	Commerce Department
	Last week	Help Wanted Index	Sep	Conference Board
Nov	1 to 3	NAPM	Oct	National Assoc. of Purchasing Management
	Every Thurs	Initial unemployment claims	Wk end Sat (1 week lag)	Employment and Training Division, BLS
	Every Thurs	Continuing benefits	Wk end Sat (3 week lag)	Employment and Training Division, BLS
	1 to 10	Unemployment rate	Oct	Bureau of Labor Statistics
	1 to 10	Nonfarm payrolls	Oct	Bureau of Labor Statistics

Table 8.10   *(Continued)*

Month	Approximate Day	Indicator	Data for	Source Agency
Nov	1 to 10	Average workweek	Oct	Bureau of Labor Statistics
	14 to 17	Index of Industrial Production	Oct	Federal Reserve Board
	14 to 17	Capacity utilization rate	Oct	Federal Reserve Board
	Third Thurs	Philadelphia Fed Survey	Nov	Federal Reserve Bank of Philadelphia
	29 to 4	Index of Leading Indicators	Oct	Commerce Department
	Last week	Help Wanted Index	Oct	Conference Board
Dec	1 to 3	NAPM	Nov	National Assoc. of Purchasing Management
	Every Thurs	Initial unemployment claims	Wk end Sat (1 week lag)	Employment and Training Division, BLS
	Every Thurs	Continuing benefits	Wk end Sat (3 week lag)	Employment and Training Division, BLS
	1 to 10	Unemployment rate	Nov	Bureau of Labor Statistics
	1 to 10	Nonfarm payrolls	Nov	Bureau of Labor Statistics
	1 to 10	Average workweek	Nov	Bureau of Labor Statistics
	14 to 17	Index of Industrial Production	Nov	Federal Reserve Board
	14 to 17	Capacity utilization rate	Nov	Federal Reserve Board
	Third Thurs	Philadelphia Fed Survey	Nov	Federal Reserve Bank of Philadelphia
	29 to 4	Index of Leading Indicators	Nov	Commerce Department
	Last week	Help Wanted Index	Nov	Conference Board

CHAPTER 9

Sources of Information

An undergraduate degree in economics may teach you many things, but it doesn't always guarantee practical knowledge of data. I was not aware of the main sources of economic statistics published by the government until my first graduate course in macroeconomics at the University of Illinois at Chicago when Professor Richard Kosobud spent a couple of hours describing data sources and data-gathering techniques. At the time, my fellow students and I did not show much interest in this information—we were more concerned with sophisticated economic theories. A year later, in my first months on the job as a forecasting economist, the knowledge of data sources proved to be almost more valuable than my understanding of economic theory.

The sources you are likely to use really depend on your needs. If timeliness is important to you, then the Commerce Department's Economic Bulletin Board will keep you abreast of the news. If analysis of long-term trends is more relevant for your personal and professional needs, then the annual *Economic Report of the President* will be your bible. The following pages are not intended to be all-inclusive, but should give you a start at finding the data that you will use regularly.

Several government publications give a strong dose of data with a smaller dose of analysis. The best monthly publication is the *Survey of Current Business*, published by the Commerce Department. It regularly features stories on the national income accounts, regional growth rates, capital formation, and foreign investment. It also contains a section that reports all the monthly and quarterly economic indicators. This publication is quite reasonable in price and should be part of your library if you are seriously interested in following the economy. A few years ago, the *Business Conditions Digest*, another

Commerce Department publication, was folded into the *Survey* making it almost like two publications for the price of one. In 1993, the annual subscription for second-class postage was $29. (U.S. Government Printing Office, 710 N. Capitol Street, NW, Washington, DC 20401; Telephone: (202) 512-0132; Fax: (202) 512-1355.)

The *Federal Reserve Bulletin* includes all statistics published by the Federal Reserve Board including interest rates, installment loan data, financial institution data, currency rates, and industrial production figures among others. The monthly bulletin also includes analytical articles, and topics vary every month. This is another inexpensive source of information—the annual subscription fee was $25 in 1993. (Board of Governors of the Federal Reserve System, Publication Services, MS138, Washington, DC 20551; Telephone: (202) 452-3244.)

If you are primarily interested in the labor market and inflation news, the Labor Department publishes two fine monthly journals: the *Monthly Labor Review* and *Employment and Earnings*. These publications tend to be specific in nature, however, dealing solely with inflation and labor issues. The annual subscription fees for these two reports are $25 and $31, respectively. The *Monthly Labor Review* is primarily known for its research and survey articles although some statistical series are also published; *Employment and Earnings* primarily features detailed statistics regularly released by the Labor Department. (U.S. Government Printing Office, 710 N. Capitol Street, NW, Washington, DC 20401.)

The National Association of Home Builders publishes *Housing Market Statistics*. The data are primarily focused on the housing industry, but many monthly indicators are included. At $105 per year for nonmembers, this publication is somewhat more expensive than the government reports, but it is worth the money if you are specifically interested in the housing market. Another advantage is its timeliness, arriving long before the *Survey of Current Business*. (National Association of Home Builders, 1201 Fifteenth Street, NW, Washington, DC 20005-2800; Telephone: (202) 822-0245.)

For computer aficionados and those individuals who need instant economic reports, the Commerce Department operates the Economic Bulletin Board (EBB). All monthly and quarterly economic indicators are available in full news-release form at the time of the published release. The only delay occurs when you try to dial in at the exact time of release since the whole world wants the information at that time. But the data are certainly available to users within a few hours of release. In addition to on-line usage fees, the Commerce Department charges an annual fee of $35 for the service. The on-line costs depend on the time of day that you log on. If you can wait until late afternoon or early evening for the data, your on-line costs are reduced by two-thirds. Although the EBB is operated by the Commerce Department, news releases from other statistical agencies, such as the Fed, are also included. (U.S. Department of Commerce, Office of Business Analysis, HCHB Room 4885, Washington, DC 20230; Telephone: (202) 377-1986.)

If you need the economic reports relatively quickly but can wait for one day, you will find them in the *Daily Report for Executives*, a daily publication on national issues, which is published by the Bureau of National Affairs. Articles are informative and analytical. The news releases of the monthly and quarterly economic indicators are reported in their entirety. This daily journal is quite expensive relative to the others, with an annual subscription fee of $5,117. (This annual subscription fee compares favorably with a news wire service, which also costs in the thousands.) (Bureau of National Affairs; Telephone: (202) 452-4200)

The individual news releases also can be obtained from the government agencies that produce them on a monthly basis. Commerce Department publications generally will cost a small fee. The Labor Department publications are free. These releases will be sent to you with approximately a two- or three-week delay. Thus, timeliness is an issue here.

The *Economic Report of the President,* an annual publication combining analysis and historical data, is released every February by the President's Council of Economic Advisors. The analysis portion describes different issues every year that are researched by the Council of Economic Advisors. This group of economists is first-rate and the analysis is also. The second half of the book reports annual economic data, in some cases going back to 1929. It includes nonfinancial indicators such as employment statistics, personal income, and GDP as well as financial statistics such as interest rates, foreign exchange rates, and federal budget figures. This is another must for the economic library, especially since it cost only $16 in 1993. (U.S. Government Printing Office, 710 N. Capitol Street, NW, Washington, DC 20401; Telephone: (202) 512-0132; Fax: (202) 512-1355.)

The private sector provides other sources for data and forecasts, but these tend to be more expensive. The two best-known companies are DRI/McGraw-Hill and the WEFA Group. They provide thousands of economic statistical series of U.S. and international indicators through the computer in the same manner as the Economic Bulletin Board.

Although DRI/McGraw-Hill and the WEFA Group are the largest providers of data and economic analysis, they are by no means the only ones, and some of the smaller providers are likely to be less expensive. In the National Association of Business Economists' trade journal, *Business Economics,* you will find advertisements for Citicorp Database Services, FERI Corp., and Haver Analytics, Inc. I don't have recommendations for any particular service. They are probably equally good and the best deal for you will depend on your specific needs.

The advantage to computer on-line service over the hard-copy publications is the ease in getting up-to-date and fully revised data. If you resort to the government publications, it is usually difficult to get more than one year's worth of data from a single source although the government does occasionally produce publications with historical data. For example, in 1992, the Department of Commerce published *Business Statistics, 1963–91.* This publication, which includes the series that are available in the *Survey of Current Business,* cost $20 in 1992. (U.S. Government Printing Office, 710 N. Capitol Street, NW, Washington, DC 20401; Telephone: (202) 512-0132; Fax: (202) 512-1355.)

Depending on your needs, you can call the statistical agencies directly if you need data or analysis of a particular release. I have always found analysts at the Commerce Department, the Labor Department, and the Board of Governors to be very helpful.

Many bank and brokerage economists have information at their fingertips, and are willing to answer your questions (as long as they are short questions). Many business economists write newsletters that they send free of charge. Two words of caution: First, companies are rationalizing all departments, especially staff departments. That means fewer economists are working for banks and brokerage houses than ever before. Their time is rationed, and they may not always be available to help you. Second, economists and banks at investment houses may have to follow a "point of view" based on company policy. Not all are free to speak their mind.

Endnotes

Chapter 1. Cycles, Markets, and Participants

1. Telephone interview with Geoffrey Moore, October 27, 1992.
2. Geoffrey Moore, *Business Cycles, Inflation and Forecasting*, NBER Studies in Business Cycles, no. 24, 2nd ed. (Cambridge, MA: Ballinger, 1983), 189–196.
3. Ibid., 196–201.
4. Ibid., 196–201.
5. Ibid., 196–201.

Chapter 2. Gross Domestic Product

1. Alan Murray, "The Outlook: Investment Credits: A Temporary Answer," *The Wall Street Journal*, December 30, 1991, A1.
2. Joseph Wakefield, "Federal Farm Programs for 1986–90," *Survey of Current Business*, Bureau of Economic Analysis, U.S. Department of Commerce, April 1986, 31–35.
3. Richard D. C. Trainer, "Oui, Non ou Peut-etre," *Financial Market Commentary*, September 18, 1992.
4. Carol Carson, "Replacing GDP: The Updated System of National Economic Accounts," *Business Economics*, July 1992, 44–48.

Chapter 3. The Consumer Sector

1. Joseph B. White, "GM Plans to Sell Part of Its Stake in National Car," *The Wall Street Journal*, November 18, 1992, A3.
2. Telephone interview with Diane Swonk, Senior Regional Economist, First Chicago Corporation, August 21, 1992. Ms. Swonk also analyzes the auto industry for the bank.

3. Constance Mitchell, "For Bond Traders, Johnson Redbook Has Caught Fire as Retail Indicator," *The Wall Street Journal*, July 10, 1992, A2.

4. Dan Weir, "Analysts Debate Accuracy, Uses of Johnson Redbook U.S. Retail Data," *Knight Ridder News Services*, June 1, 1992.

5. Ibid.

6. Mitchell, A2.

7. David W. Wilcox, "The Construction of U.S. Consumption Data: Some Facts and Their Implications for Empirical Work," *American Economic Review*, September 1992, 922–941.

8. Robert B. Avery, Gregory E. Elliehousen, and Arthur B. Kennickell, "Changes in Consumer Installment Debt: Evidence from the 1983 and 1986 Surveys of Consumer Finances," *Federal Reserve Bulletin*, October 1987, 761–778.

9. Robert D. Hershey, "It All Started with Hemlines," *New York Times*, October 8, 1992, C1.

10. Richard T. Curtin, "Index Calculations," Ann Arbor: Survey Research Center, University of Michigan, 1992.

11. Richard T. Curtin, "The Consumer as a Macroeconomic Forecaster: Accuracy of Consumer Attitudes and Expectations," Ann Arbor: Survey Research Center, University of Michigan, 1992.

12. Fabien Linden, "The Measure of Consumer Confidence," *Across the Board* (Conference Board Magazine), XVI, no. 4, (April 1979), 77.

13. Ibid., 77.

14. Ibid., 78.

Chapter 4. Investment Spending

1. Jon Hurdle, "US to Include Rebuilding in New Housing Starts Definition," *Market News Service, Inc.*, September 25, 1992.

2. Ibid.

3. Gerald H. Anderson and John J. Erceg, "How Credible Are Capital Spending Surveys as Forecasts?" *Economic Commentary*, December 1, 1990, Cleveland, OH: Federal Reserve Bank of Cleveland.

Chapter 5. The Foreign Sector

1. "Business Bulletin: A Special Report on Trends," *The Wall Street Journal*, October 1, 1992, A1.

Chapter 7. Inflation

1. Mike Dorning, "Decline May Show Inflation More as Friend Than Foe," *Chicago Tribune*, March 1, 1992, Section 7, page 1.

2. "Angell: Goal of Fed Should Be 'Sound Money,' Price Stability," *Market News Service, Inc.,* October 2, 1992.

3. "Fed's Kelley: Sufficient Liquidity Exists for Strong Recovery," *Market News Service, Inc.,* October 14, 1992.

4. Anita Raghavan, "CRB Futures Index Gets Surprisingly High Marks as Barometer for Forecasting Inflation and Rates," *The Wall Street Journal,* October 12, 1992, C1.

Chapter 8. Other Measures of Production

1. Jon Hurdle, "Labor Official: Special Factors May Cloud Sept. U.S. Jobs Report," *Market News Service, Inc.,* September 30, 1992.

2. Telephone interview with economist Timothy Schiller, an economist at the Federal Reserve Bank of Philadelphia who regularly analyzes the Business Outlook Survey data. (July 1992)

Bibliography

Anderson, Gerald H., and Erceg, John J. "How Credible Are Capital Spending Surveys as Forecasts?" *Economic Commentary*, December 1, 1990. Cleveland, OH: Federal Reserve Bank of Cleveland.

"Angell: Goal of Fed Should be 'Sound Money,' Price Stability." *Market News Service, Inc.*, October 2, 1992.

Avery, Robert B., Elliehausen, Gregory E., and Kennickell, Arthur B. "Changes in Consumer Installment Debt: Evidence from the 1983 and 1986 Surveys of Consumer Finances." *Federal Reserve Bulletin* 73, no. 10 (October 1987) pp. 761–778.

Barron, William G. "Statement before the Joint Economic Committee." U.S. Congress, October 2, 1992.

Bell, John, and Crone, Theodore. "Charting the Course of the Economy: What Can Local Manufacturers Tell Us?" *Business Review,* July–August 1986. Philadelphia: Federal Reserve Bank of Philadelphia, pp. 3–16.

Berenson, Stephen A., and Henderson, Steven W. "Quality Adjustments for Structural Changes in the CPI Housing Sample." *Monthly Labor Review,* November 1990, pp. 40–42.

Bodie, Zvi, Kane, Alex, and Marcus, Alan J. *Essentials of Investment.* Homewood, IL: Irwin, 1992.

Burns, Roger, Briggs, Harry, and Thomas, William. "Effect of Updated Weights on Producer Price Indexes." *Monthly Labor Review,* March 1993, pp. 36–48.

"Business Bulletin: A Special Report on Trends in Finance and Industry." *The Wall Street Journal*, October 1, 1992, p. A1.

Carson, Carol. "Replacing GDP: The Updated System of National Economic Accounts." *Business Economics*, July 1992, pp. 44–48.

Carson, Carol, and Honsa, Jeanette. "The United Nations System of National Accounts: An Introduction." *Survey of Current Business.* Bureau of Economic Analysis, Department of Commerce, June 1990, pp. 20–30.

Case, Karl E., and Fair, Ray C. *Principles of Economics.* Englewood Cliffs, NJ: Prentice-Hall, 1992.

Chiswick, Barry. "A Review of 'Counting the Labor Force,' the Report of the National Commission on Employment and Unemployment Statistics." *Contemporary Economic Problems* (William Fellner, Ed.). Washington, DC: American Enterprise Institute, 1980.

Clark, Lindley H. "The Outlook: Market Still Points to a Slow Recovery." *The Wall Street Journal,* February 10, 1992, p. A1.

"CRB Index Futures: A Whole New World of Opportunities." New York: New York Futures Exchange, 1986.

Curtin, Richard T. "Surveys of Consumers." Ann Arbor: Survey Research Center, University of Michigan, 1992.

Curtin, Richard T. "The Consumer as a Macroeconomic Forecaster: Accuracy of Consumer Attitudes and Expectations." Ann Arbor: Survey Research Center, University of Michigan, 1992.

Curtin, Richard T. "Index Calculations." Ann Arbor: Survey Research Center, University of Michigan, 1992.

Department of Commerce, the Council of Economic Advisors, and the Source Agencies. 1980 Supplement to *Economic Indicators,* Historical and Descriptive Background, Prepared for the Joint Economic Committee by the Office of Federal Statistical Policy and Standards. Washington, DC: GPO, 1980.

Dorning, Mike. "Decline May Show Inflation More as Friend Than Foe." *Chicago Tribune,* March 1, 1992. Section 7, p. 1.

Economic Report of the President. Washington, DC: U.S. Government Printing Office, 1992.

"Employment Cost Index." *BLS Handbook of Methods.* Bulletin 2285, Chapter 8, 1988.

"Employment Cost Index: December 1990." *News.* Bureau of Labor Statistics, Department of Labor, January 29, 1991.

"The Employment Situation: May 1992." *News.* Bureau of Labor Statistics, Department of Labor, June 5, 1992.

"The Employment Situation: September 1992." *News.* Bureau of Labor Statistics, Department of Labor, October 2, 1992.

"Experimental Cost-of-Living Indexes: A Summary of Current Research." *Monthly Labor Review,* July 1989, pp. 34–39.

"Fed's Kelley: Sufficient Liquidity Exists for Strong Recovery." *Market News Service, Inc.,* October 14, 1992.

"Firm Cutting Interest Rates on Some '92 and '93 Models." *The Wall Street Journal,* September 25, 1992, p. A2.

Ford, Ina Kay, and Sturm, Philip. "CPI Revision Provides More Accuracy in the Medical Care Services Component," *Monthly Labor Review,* April 1988, pp. 17–26.

Frumkin, Norman. *Guide to Economic Indicators*. New York: M.E. Sharpe, 1990.

The Future of Home Building. Washington, DC: Department of Economics and Housing Policy, National Association of Home Builders, 1992.

Gillingham, Robert, and Lane, Walter. "Changing the Treatment of Shelter Costs for Homeowners in the CPI." *Monthly Labor Review*, February 1985.

Gilpin, Kenneth N. "The Numbers They Love to Hate." *New York Times*, April 17, 1988. Section 3, p. 4.

"Greenspan: Already Out of Recession." *Market News Service, Inc.*, March 3, 1992.

Gunset, George. "Crops Already Parched by Early Drought." *Chicago Tribune*. June 7, 1992. Section 7, p. 1.

Hamel, Harvey R., and Tucker, John T. "Implementing the Levitan Commission's Recommendations to Improve Labor Data." *Monthly Labor Review*, February 1985, pp. 16–24.

Hershey, Robert D. "It All Started with Hemlines." *New York Times*, October 8, 1992, p. C1.

Hurdle, Jon. "Labor Official: Special Factors May Cloud September U.S. Jobs Report." *Market News Service, Inc.*, September 30, 1992.

Hurdle, Jon. "U.S. to Include Rebuilding in New Housing Starts Definition." *Market News Service, Inc.*, September 25, 1992.

"Industrial Production and Capacity Utilization." Federal Reserve Statistical Release, G.17(419), October 16, 1992. Board of Governors of the Federal Reserve System, Washington, DC.

Jablonski, Mary, Kunze, Kurt, and Otto, Phyllis Flohr. "Hours at Work: A New Base for BLS Productivity Statistics." *Monthly Labor Review*, February 1990, pp. 17–24.

Jelalian, Ara. "U.S. International Trade: Fundamentals and Forecasts." *Economic Issue Backgrounder*. Chicago: First National Bank of Chicago, April 1991.

Kellar, Jeffrey H. "New Methodology Reduces Importance of Used Cars in CPI." *Monthly Labor Review*, December 1988, pp. 34–35.

King, Thomas R. "Are You Searching for a Good Excuse? Just Try El Niño." *The Wall Street Journal*, May 22, 1992, p. A1.

Linden, Fabian. "The Measure of Consumer Confidence." *Across the Board*. (Conference Board Magazine) XVI, No. 4 (April 1979), pp. 74–79.

Mason, Charles, and Butler, Clifford. "New Basket of Goods and Services Being Priced in Revised CPI." *Monthly Labor Review*, January 1987, pp. 3–22.

Mennis, Edward A. "Research Notes: A Brief Comment on Profits." *Business Economics*, October 1992, p. 69.

Mitchell, Constance. "For Bond Traders, Johnson Redbook Has Caught Fire as Retail Indicator." *The Wall Street Journal*, July 10, 1992, p. A2.

Moore, Geoffrey. *Business Cycles, Inflation and Forecasting*. NBER Studies in Business Cycles, no. 24 (2nd ed.). Cambridge, MA: Ballinger, 1983.

Murray, Alan. "The Outlook: Investment Credits: A Temporary Answer." *The Wall Street Journal*, December 30, 1991, p. A1.

Preston, Noreen L. *The Help Wanted Index: Technical Description and Behavioral Trends*, New York: Conference Board, 1977.

"Productivity and Costs." *News*. Bureau of Labor Statistics, Department of Labor, January 3, 1992.

"Productivity and Costs." *News*. Bureau of Labor Statistics, Department of Labor, March 10, 1992.

Randolph, William C., Berenson, Stephen A., and Lane, Walter. "Adjusting the CPI Shelter Index to Compensate for Effect of Depreciation." *Monthly Labor Review*, October 1988, pp. 34–36.

Raghavan, Anita. "CRB Futures Index Gets Surprisingly High Marks as Barometer for Forecasting Inflation and Rates." *The Wall Street Journal*, October 12, 1992, p. C1.

Spinozza, Dawn M. "Two Indexes Track Consumer Confidence." *Cross Sections*, Richmond, VA: Federal Reserve Bank of Richmond, Summer 1991.

Stertz, Bradley. "Chrysler, with an Eye on the Japanese, Plans to Discontinue 10 Day Sales Data." *The Wall Street Journal*, December 3, 1990.

Sturm, Fred. "Forecasts." *Perspectives*. Chicago: Fuji Securities, June 12, 1992.

"Study Shows Public Knows Little about the Economy." *United Press International*, September 10, 1992.

Survey of Current Business. U.S. Department of Commerce. Economics and Statistics Administration, Bureau of Economic Analysis, November 1991.

Survey of Current Business. U.S. Department of Commerce. Economics and Statistics Administration. Bureau of Economic Analysis, December 1991.

Survey of Current Business. U.S. Department of Commerce. Economics and Statistics Administration. Bureau of Economic Analysis, July 1992.

Survey of Current Business. U.S. Department of Commerce. Economics and Statistics Administration. Bureau of Economic Analysis, August 1992.

Survey of Current Business. U.S. Department of Commerce. Economics and Statistics Administration. Bureau of Economic Analysis, September 1992.

Swonk, Diane C. "Auto Sales in the 1990s: Can We Afford More Growth?" *TrendWatch* (First National Bank of Chicago). May 1992.

Swonk, Diane C. "The Japanese Invasion: From Imports to Transplants." *TrendWatch*. First National Bank of Chicago. January 1992.

Tainer, Evelina M. "Regional Disparities: Midwest a Winner," *Simply Economics* Vol. 1, no. 8. October 5, 1992.

Tainer, Evelina M., and Rosso, Christopher. "The Index of Mis(Leading) Indicators." *Economic Issue Backgrounder*. Chicago: First National Bank of Chicago, August 1987.

Tainer, Evilina M. "A Trader's Guide to Economic Indicators." *Economic Issue Backgrounder*. Chicago: First National Bank of Chicago, March 1989.

Tainer, Evelina M. "A Trader's Guide to Economic Indicators: Inflation." *Economic Issue Backgrounder*. Chicago: First National Bank of Chicago, March 1991.

Trainer, Richard D.C. *Financial Market Commentary*. New York: Bank of Tokyo, February 19, 1992.

Trainer, Richard D.C. "Oui, Non ou Peut-être." *Financial Market Commentary*. New York: Bank of Tokyo, September 18, 1992.

U.S. Department of Commerce, Bureau of Economic Analysis. *Business Statistics, 1963–91*. Washington DC: GPO, June 1992.

U.S. Department of Commerce, Bureau of Economic Analysis. *An Introduction to National Economic Accounting* (Methodology Paper Series MP-1). Washington, DC: GPO, March 1985.

U.S. Department of Commerce, Bureau of Economic Analysis. *Corporate Profits: Profits before Tax, Profits Tax Liability, and Dividends* (Methodology Paper Series MP-2). Washington, DC: GPO, May 1985.

U.S. Department of Commerce, Bureau of Economic Analysis. *Foreign Transactions* (Methodology Paper Series MP-3). Washington, DC: GPO, May 1987.

U.S. Department of Commerce, Bureau of Economic Analysis. *GNP: An Overview of Source Data and Estimating Methods* (Methodology Paper Series MP-4). Washington, DC: GPO, September 1987.

U.S. Department of Commerce, Bureau of Economic Analysis. *Government Transactions* (Methodology Paper Series MP-5). Washington, DC: GPO, November 1988.

U.S. Department of Commerce, Bureau of Economic Analysis. *Personal Consumption Expenditures* (Methodology Paper Series MP-6). Washington, DC: GPO, June 1990.

U.S. Department of Commerce, the Council of Economic Advisors, and the Source Agencies. 1980 Supplement to *Economic Indicators*, Historical and Descriptive Background, Prepared for the Joint Economic Committee by the Office of Federal Statistical Policy and Standards. Washington, DC: GPO, 1980.

U.S. Department of Labor, Bureau of Labor Statistics. "The Consumer Price Index: 1987 Revision" Report 736, January 1987.

Wakefield, Joseph. "Federal Farm Programs for 1986–90." *Survey of Current Business*. Bureau of Economic Analysis, Department of Commerce, April 1986, pp. 31–35.

Weir, Dan. "Analysts Debate Accuracy, Uses of Johnson Redbook US Retail Data." *Knight Ridder News Services*, June 1, 1992.

White, Joseph B. "GM Plans to Sell Part of Its Stake in National Car." *The Wall Street Journal*, November 18, 1992.

Wilcox, David W. "The Construction of U.S. Consumption Data: Some Facts and Their Implications for Empirical Work." *American Economic Review*, September 1992, pp. 922–941.

Wilcox, David W. "Household Spending and Saving: Measurement, Trends, and Analysis." *Federal Reserve Bulletin*, January 1991, pp. 1–17.

Index